Begin Using the Programmer's Peg Board Immediately...

Order the *Dr. Dobb's Essential HyperTalk Handbook* Programs disk today!!

The Programmer's Peg Board is a stack that maintains a library of reusable software components including resources, scripts, and objects. It allows you to install components into any stack you select, it keeps track of what components are installed in what stack, and it facilitates removing components when you are done with them. It is written entirely in HyperTalk and does not require any other modifications to your stacks. All the source code, along with many components, is supplied on this disk. You will also find example code from the book and various reusable software components, such as author Michael Swaine's popular script analyzer, formatting scripts, and components for manipulating properties of objects.

To order, return this postage-paid self-mailer with your payment of $20, plus sales tax if you are a California resident, to: M&T Books, 501 Galveston Drive, Redwood City, CA 94063. Or, call toll-free 800-533-4372 (In CA 800-356-2002). Ask for Item #013-3.

YES! Please send me the *Dr. Dobb's Essential HyperTalk Handbook* programs disk for $20 _______

California residents add applicable sales tax _____% _______

TOTAL _______

_____ Check enclosed. Make payable to M&T Books.

Charge my ____ VISA ____ MasterCard ____ American Express

Card # ______________________________ Exp. date __________

Name ____

Address ____

City _______________________ State ________ Zip _________

7011

NO POSTAGE
NECESSARY
IF MAILED
IN THE
UNITED STATES

BUSINESS REPLY MAIL
FIRST CLASS PERMIT 871 REDWOOD CITY, CA

POSTAGE WILL BE PAID BY ADDRESSEE

M&T BOOKS
501 Galveston Drive
Redwood City, CA 94063

PLEASE FOLD ALONG LINE AND STAPLE OR TAPE CLOSED

Dr. Dobb's Essential
HyperTalk Handbook

Dr. Dobb's Essential
HyperTalk Handbook

Michael Swaine

M&T Publishing, Inc.
Redwood City, California

M&T Books
A Division of M&T Publishing, Inc.
501 Galveston Drive
Redwood City, CA 94063

M&T Books
General Manager, Ellen Ablow
Editorial Project Manager, Michelle Hudun
Editor, Dave Rosenthal
Cover Art Director, Michael Hollister
Cover Designer, Frank Pollifrone
Cover Photographer, Michael Carr

© 1988 by M&T Publishing, Inc.

Printed in the United States of America
First Edition published 1988

All rights reserved. No part of this book may be reproduced or transmitted in any form or by any means, electronic or mechanical, including photocopying, recording, or by any information storage and retrieval system, without prior written permission from the Publisher. Contact the Publisher for information on foreign rights.

Library of Congress Cataloging in Publication Data

Swaine, Michael, 1945–
Dr. Dobb's essential hyper talk.

Includes index.
1. HyperTalk (Computer program language)
I. Title. II. Title: Doctor Dobb's essential
hyper talk.
QA76.73.H96S83 1988 005.13'3 88-22981
ISBN 0-934375-98-4 (book)
ISBN 0-934375-99-2 (book/disk pachage)
ISBN 1-55851-013-3 (disk)

91 90 89 88 4 3 2 1

HyperTalk, HyperCard, and Macintosh are trademarks of Apple Computer, Inc.

Limits of Liability and Disclaimer of Warranty

The Author and Publisher of this book have used their best efforts in preparing the book and the programs contained in it. These efforts include the development, research, and testing of the theories and programs to determine their effectiveness.

The Author and Publisher make no warranty of any kind, expressed or implied, with regard to these programs or the documentation contained in this book. The Author and Publisher shall not be liable in any event for incidental or consequential damages in connection with, or arising out of, the furnishing, performance, or use of these programs.

How to Order the Accompanying Disk

The Programmer's Peg Board is a stack that maintains a library of reusable software components including resources, scripts, and objects. It allows you to install components into any stack you select, it keeps track of what components are installed in what stack, and it facilitates removing components when you are done with them. It is written entirely in HyperTalk and does not require any other modification to your stacks. All the source code, along with many components, is supplied on this disk. You will also find example code from the book and various reusable software components, such as author Michael Swaine's popular script analyzer, formatting scripts, and components for manipulating properties of objects.

The disk price is $20.00. California residents must add the appropriate sales tax. Order by sending a check, or credit card number and expiration date, to:

HyperTalk Disk
M&T Books
501 Galveston Drive
Redwood City, CA 94063

Or, you may order by calling our toll-free number between 8 A.M. and 5:00 P.M. Pacific Standard Time: 800/533-4372 (800/356-2002 in California). Ask for **Item #013-3.**

Contents

Introduction

"I've got a shelf of how-to-write books, and they all seem to me pretty much dreadful, especially the ones about the short story. They all seem to be written by old magazine hacks about a kind of "popular" formula fiction no one wants anymore anyway—Short Story Plotting Simplified, that kind of thing, complete with simple-minded examples from slick fiction.

"Then I've got another shelf of books, some of them seem to me great. These are college textbook anthologies of short stories, with analyses of the stories that sometimes get quite technical. Basically these are how-to-read books, like Mark Schorer's *The Story: A Critical Anthology*. But it seems to me that a beginning writer could learn more from any one of them—from, say, just the "Glossary of Technical Terms" at the back of Cleanth Brooks and Robert Penn Warren's *Understanding Fiction*—than he ever could from reading the whole damn shelf of the how-to-write ones.

"The difference of course is that the first shelf is trying to teach you how to write lousy stories, and the second shelf is trying to teach you how to read literature."

—Rust Hills, *Writing in General and the Short Story in Particular.*

I've got shelves of how-to-write-programs books, including a dozen books that touch on writing programs, or scripts, in HyperTalk, the programming language built into Apple Computer's HyperCard product. What I don't have is a book on HyperTalk that does what Rust Hills describes, that shows you how to read HyperTalk scripts by means of good examples and analyses and a really useful back-of-the-book reference section. It seems that the truism that we learn to read before we learn to write would carry over into books on writing programs, but I've never seen a book that was written on this principle.

So I tried my hand at writing one, and this is it.

About HyperCard and HyperTalk

HyperCard is a software product for the Apple Macintosh computer. Its creator, Bill Atkinson, calls it a "software erector set" because of the way it empowers users to develop their own software products. Most of the power for developing new applications from HyperCard comes from its built-in programming language, HyperTalk, envisioned by Atkinson and written by Dan Winkler. With HyperTalk, both experienced programmers and people who have never written a computer program before can write HyperTalk programs to create new applications.

HyperTalk is "English-like" in the words that it uses and in how it puts them together (its syntax), but make no mistake: it is a real programming language and has to be learned to be used. Fortunately, learning HyperTalk is nowhere near as difficult as learning a natural language like French, and can actually be fun.

About this Book

This book teaches how to read and write programs written in HyperTalk. It is intended to be useful both to the professional programmer and to the novice. The nine chapters are a tutorial exposition of the HyperTalk language, and the many appendixes are a language reference, the most thorough and extensive published to date on HyperTalk.

The tutorial begins by emphasizing getting the "feel" for HyperTalk, gaining an intuitive understanding of what a HyperTalk program, or script, is, and what it can do and what concepts it embodies. In fact, although the tutorial presents many examples of HyperTalk scripts, the reader is discouraged from going near a computer until the third chapter. This is unusual.

Books on technical subjects offer more opportunities to commit factual errors than do most books, and the errors tend to be more serious. In the course of writing this book, I checked every line of HyperTalk that I included, actually cutting and pasting running code from tested scripts directly into the book files. But many technical details, such as the precise performance of the **`date`** function and the use of equivalence operators for alphabetization, were not documented anywhere when I was writing this, and I had to work them out on my own. If I have corrected many errors of past books, I have undoubtedly discovered entirely new ways to be wrong. If you find any errors in this book, please let me know so that I can correct them in the next edition; you can reach me through M&T Books.

About the Author

I can't remember a time when I didn't think of myself as a writer, but programming is just a compulsion I fell into in my late teens, twenty-odd years ago. Programming turned out to be easier to get started with, harder to walk away from, and easier to make money by, but I never gave up writing. Eventually I started making a living as a writer and editor, and what I wrote about was programming, in over a thousand articles to date. I got sidetracked into running a programmer's magazine for a few years, but now I'm just writing again. This is my second book; the first, with Paul Freiberger, was a history of the making of the personal computer, called *Fire in the Valley*.

About the Reader

I wrote this book for a particular kind of reader. First, a *reader*, someone who enjoys the written word and who enjoys exploring new intellectual territory through reading. And second, one who uses or plans to use an Apple Macintosh computer and the HyperTalk programming language that comes with the machine. I tried to make it valuable to the reader who has never programmed, to the programming expert who is new to HyperTalk, and to the experienced HyperTalk programmer who has a shelf full of programming books and is still looking.

Part I
Preliminaries

1

Reading HyperTalk

About this Chapter

This first chapter attempts to give a feel for programming in HyperTalk. Its structure is a series of topics, each of which explains a concept, gives examples showing concretely what it means, and concludes with one or more puzzles to allow you to test your understanding of the concept and your feel for the language. None of the puzzles is "fair" in the sense that it can be solved by a rigid application of rules explicitly presented. Every puzzle is solvable if approached with the pragmatic intuition of a traveller in a foreign land trying to find a bathroom without a phrasebook.

The sequence of ideas in this and the subsequent chapters is more linear than in many programming texts. There are no "special notes," marginal annotations, boxed comments, "hints" set off from the running text, or other departures from normal linear exposition. This may be a confession of heresy in a book about HyperCard, which has been promoted as a nonlinear medium. But I believe that it is the author's responsibility to find the story and tell it. In the chapters of this book, I have tried to say everything that I thought needed to be said in what I thought was its natural place in the unfolding story.

In contrast, the appendixes in the back of this book make up, collectively, a dictionary of a foreign language, and have no story to tell. They provide the information and the indexing and cross-referencing tools to let the reader get at that information at need.

Experienced programmers may want to move through this chapter quickly, and those with some HyperTalk experience or experience with an object-oriented language may skip directly to Chapter 2 or even to Chapter 3. But if you are new to programming, a careful reading of this chapter is important.

About Reading HyperTalk

Shelves of books about computer programming have been written under the influence of the homily that you learn by doing. These books have dutifully attempted to teach programming languages by making their readers type in programs and run them. The emphasis is overwhelmingly on learning to write and run programs rather than on learning to read them.

I believe that this is a poor way to introduce anything as cerebral as a new language. It forces the beginner to focus on getting all the commas and periods in place at the expense of getting the ideas, and rewards accurate typing rather than clear understanding. Learning a new language should exercise your mind before it exercises your fingers.

The HyperTalk language embodies many new ways of thinking, both for the experienced programmer and for the novice. The language is also extremely Englishlike, so that an English reader's unprompted intuition about what a scrap of HyperTalk means will often be correct. As a consequence this book concentrates, in its first chapters, on learning to read HyperTalk programs for understanding. Chapters 1 and 2 present all the important concepts of the language, and show how the concepts are realized in actual HyperTalk programs, beginning a course in the reading of HyperTalk that culminates in the discussion of programming style in Chapter 9.

The conventional homily about learning by doing isn't wrong. Learning by doing is the only way to learn to type or to drive a car or to acquire any motor skill. It's also extremely useful in learning a programming language, and is employed heavily in this book. Starting in Chapter 3, you will have many opportunities to try things out using your Macintosh. But here at the start, you should turn off the machine. This chapter and the next are intended to be read at the beach, at the park, in bed, in your favorite chair—wherever you generally curl up with a good book.

Words and Sentences

In HyperTalk, words are combined to form meaningful utterances, much as words in a natural language like English are combined to form sentences.

The very words of HyperTalk are often borrowed English words, carrying some of the same meaning. HyperTalk utterances are filled with words like **if**, **then**, **the**, **this**, **is**, **add**, and **to**. In this book, to avoid confusion between HyperTalk words and the corresponding English words, I will always write HyperTalk words as I just did, in an alternate font.

To fully master HyperTalk programming, you must learn exactly what such words mean in the HyperTalk language, but when you are beginning, it is wise to assume that a word means exactly what you, as a reader of English, think it means. This is a good technique in learning French or Latin, and it is an even better technique in learning a programming language like HyperTalk. French and Latin words sometimes look like English words because of accidents of history and language development, but HyperTalk was created to look as much like English as possible. This means that, if you trust your intuitions, you already "know" a great deal of HyperTalk.

The individual lines of HyperTalk code that correspond to sentences tell HyperCard to do something, like imperative sentences in English. The normal syntax of a HyperTalk sentence is verb-object:

```
Show button "About"

Dial 555-1212

Print this card
```

The verbs, which will henceforth be called by their proper HyperTalk name of commands, are these words **show**, **dial**, and **print**. The back of this book contains many appendixes, and one of these, the HyperTalk Commands appendix, describes every command of the HyperTalk language and shows just how to use it, including the kinds of objects to which it can be applied. There are about 50 commands.

The "objects," the things that the commands act upon, are a different story. You will not find an appendix listing all the HyperTalk objects, because the list would be infinite. New objects can be created at will.

Most of these "objects," though, are truly objects in the official HyperCard sense: they are stacks, backgrounds, cards, fields, or buttons. You already know about them if you have used HyperCard. These five kinds of objects make up the HyperCard environment, and the whole point of HyperTalk is to manipulate that environment. The HyperTalk lines `Show button "About"` and `Print this card` both manipulate HyperCard objects, in one case a button and in the other case a card.

Knowing the names of some actions and some objects they can act upon is all that is required to begin making up HyperTalk utterances. The HyperTalk Vocabulary appendix contains the complete vocabulary of HyperTalk.

Puzzle 1

What do each of the following lines of HyperTalk accomplish? The lines contains elements of the language that have not yet been introduced, so there is no way, based on what has been covered so far, that you could *know*. But you can guess, and that's the point of this exercise, to discover how much of HyperTalk you can already read with comprehension.

Remember, too, that every HyperTalk utterance instructs HyperCard to do something, generally something involving the stacks, backgrounds, cards, fields, and buttons that make up the HyperCard environment. Comprehending a line of HyperTalk means realizing what it is instructing HyperCard to do with such objects.

Finally, when you've figured out what each line does, consider them as a sequence of instructions to HyperCard. If each of these instructions were carried out in order, what would be the result? Answering that question will tell you the meaning of the sequence of HyperTalk lines. Answering questions like that is how you understand what HyperTalk programs do.

The solution follows the puzzle, but you'll benefit most if you try to work it out before you look.

```
Go to stack "Magazines"
Go to card "Harper's"
Add 0.50 to field "Subscription Price"
Hide field "Subscription Price"
```

Solution to Puzzle 1

The first two lines cause a transfer to a stack named "Magazines" and to a card named "Harper's" within that stack. The third line causes the number 0.50 to be added to the value stored in a field on that card, and the last line makes the field turn invisible. Considering the lines as a sequence rather than as individual lines lets us make such default assumptions as the assumption that the field mentioned in lines three and four is on the card named in line two which is in the stack named in line one. In general, HyperTalk lets us make such assumptions when there is no ambiguity.

This puzzle also demonstrates that the verb-object characterization of HyperTalk instructions is something of an oversimplification.

Variables and Names

Lines of HyperTalk usually contain two kinds of words: words that are part of the language and that are defined in the appendixes in the back of the book, and words that you invent to identify objects that you create. If you name new stacks, backgrounds, cards, buttons, or fields, naming them gives you a way to refer to them later.

You can also create and give names to variables. A variable is a place to store information for later use, like a scratchpad for calculations. It doesn't correspond to any HyperCard object. The contents of a variable can be used to allow one line of HyperTalk access to information that another line has acquired.

Here is an example of the use of variables:

```
Put the time into myTime
Put myTime into yourTime
```

The preceding lines place the current time into a variable named **myTime** and then copy the value from that variable into another one named **yourTime**. There is no reason why a field could not have been used to store the time in this example. In fact, a variable contains information in much the same form that a field does. You could think of a variable as a kind of hidden field, except that it doesn't have very many other characteristics of a field. It doesn't belong to any particular card or stack and can never be seen. In fact, there is really nothing to a variable except its name and its contents. This turns out to make variables very flexible and useful.

In this book I follow Apple's convention of joining two or more English words to name one HyperTalk object or variable. It's a good convention, whether you are naming fields and buttons or variables.

```
thisIsALongVariableName
thisIsAnEvenLongerVariableName
```

Puzzle 2

What does the following sequence of HyperTalk lines accomplish?

```
Put the time into myTime
If myTime = field "Time"
Then beep
```

Solution to Puzzle 2

The three lines of the puzzle compare the current time with the time stored in a field named "Time." They use a variable named myTime for temporary storage and they use elements of the HyperTalk language not yet introduced, but whose meaning is discernible from context and cognates. If the current time matches what's in the field, the Mac will beep.

Containers and Chunks

At a first approximation, HyperTalk programs consist of sequences of lines, each containing a command and the stack, background, card, field, button, or variable on which the command is to act.

One refinement of this approximate description is the concept of a container. A container is not something new; it is just a term for referring to all those things that can contain values. So far, that means fields and variables. Having one word to refer to these things is handy, because there are some facts about the management of information in HyperTalk that apply to all things that can contain values.

The chief fact about containers is that they can contain different kinds of information.

```
Put the time into field "Time"
Put the date into todaysDate
Put 57 into varieties
Put 2 + 2 into theTotal
Add 1 to theTotal
Put "Mike" into field "Name"
```

Not only can containers contain different kinds of information, but they can contain structured information; not only items but lists of items: and not only individual words but sequences of words. Just as fields can contain many lines of information, any container can contain many lines or items of information. References to what a container contains can be detailed; you don't have to refer to the entire content. For example:

```
Put line 1 of field "NameAndAddress" into name
Put line 2 of field "NameAndAddress" into address
Put word 1 of name into firstName
```

These expressions are chunk expressions. Generically, any component of a container is called a chunk, and a reference to a specific component is called a chunk expression. The following puzzle shows more examples of the use of chunk expressions.

Puzzle 3

What do the following HyperTalk lines accomplish?

```
Put "Mike" into word 1 of field "Name"
Put "Swaine" into word 2 of field "Name"
Put "a,b,c,d,e,f" into theList
Put item 3 of theList into theThird
Put character 4 of word 1 of field "Name"
  into item 3 of theList
```

Solution to Puzzle 3

After the lines of the puzzle are carried out, field "Name" will contain "Mike Swaine," variable theThird will contain "c," and variable theList will contain "a,b,e,d,e,f." The main words that can be used in constructing chunk expressions are **`line`**, **`item`**, **`word`**, and **`character`**.

Events and Scripts

Programs in HyperTalk are not just sequences of HyperTalk instructions, but organized sequences called scripts. The simplest scripts consist of a sequence of HyperTalk instructions bracketed by two additional lines that indicate the circumstances under which the bracketed instructions should be carried out.

The word "script" is a good name for these programs if it is taken in the sense of the expression, "I do/don't have a script for this situation." The concept of specifying a situation or event and the actions to be taken in the situation or event is the most important concept in HyperTalk programming. All of Chapter 3 is dedicated to showing what it means in practice, but in theory it is easy to grasp. Here are two HyperTalk scripts:

```
On openCard
  Beep
End openCard

On mouseUp
  Beep
End mouseUp
```

The first and last lines of each of these scripts identifies the triggering event: the opening of a card (which just means that you've transferred to the card), the clicking on a button (which concludes with the mouse button going up). The first example causes a beep when you transfer to the card, and the other beeps when you click the button.

A HyperTalk script does not do its thing when a user invokes it, but when the specific event mentioned in the script occurs. This represents a different philosophy of programming from a language like C or Pascal or BASIC. While the BASIC programmer thinks simply in terms of instructing the computer what to do, the experienced HyperTalk programmer can think more in terms of defining the relationships that are to exist between events. The next chapter expands on these ideas.

2

Concepts

About this Chapter

HyperTalk embodies some concepts that may be as new to seasoned programmers as to novices. This chapter presents them in language that either group should be able to handle.

Nevertheless, some of this chapter may sound like obscure jargon to the novice. The word *paradigm* is used here not as programming jargon, but in the usual sense of a set of common values and a way of viewing problems and model solutions within a scientific community. But other terms and concerns may seem like conversation in a foreign language, overheard but not really understood. It is worthwhile at a certain point in learning Russian to tune in Russian broadcasts on the short-wave set. Even if you miss a lot of words, a sense should come through of the concepts regarded as important, the values held dear. Paradigms are acquired by cognitive osmosis.

To the more knowledgeable programmer, some of the contentions of this chapter may seem questionable. There is nothing like consensus on the definition of object-oriented programming, and the presentation here implies that the matter is simpler than it is. The aim is, though, to show the conceptual bases of HyperTalk, and to show how it is connected with an important new programming paradigm.

About Programming Concepts

Reading and writing computer programs is more than just examining or developing solutions to problems. Part of the process is defining the problem, and different programming languages lend themselves to different characterizations of problems. HyperTalk grew out of a relatively recent paradigm of programming that tends to characterize problems differently from the way conventional programming languages like C an Pascal and BASIC do. The differences run to what the goals of programming are and to what constitutes a program. The differences are significant enough that the author of HyperTalk doesn't even speak of writing programs, but of developing scripts.

It's important to know at the outset just what kind of language HyperTalk is, what its conceptual bases are, and what is meant by solving a problem using HyperTalk. Otherwise you may find yourself hiking over mountains that the HyperTalk paradigm has already built tunnels through.

Object-Oriented Programming

Half of the name "HyperTalk" comes from SmallTalk. The SmallTalk language and the object-oriented programming paradigm that it introduced form one of the conceptual roots of HyperTalk.

SmallTalk was developed at the Xerox Palo Alto Research Center, growing out of forward-looking research into personal computing environments that began in the early 1970s. The work done at Xerox PARC in the 1970s and '80s inspired many advances in computer technology, including the Macintosh computer. A half-dozen versions of SmallTalk have been developed over the past sixteen years, and the language has inspired object-oriented enhancements to many other languages, and to the development of entirely new languages, including HyperTalk.

The motive for adopting an object-oriented approach is usually the need to develop reusable software components. Programmers spend a lot of time re-solving old problems. On a Macintosh, most programs use movable, resizable windows, and the mechanisms for moving and resizing those windows require a lot of programming. It would be nice to be able to do all the window-oriented programming once and for all, and get on to other things, plugging in the windowing component wherever needed; and languages for the Macintosh provide abilities for doing just that.

All programming languages, for the Macintosh or any machine, provide some means of reusing code. (Programmers use the word "code" to speak of both programs and parts of programs without being specific about which they mean.) Old programs can be modified to new purposes, or subprograms or modules that solve general problems within larger programs can be reused to solve the same general problems in new programs. But the phrase "reusable software component" is usually applied to situations in which more than code reusability is needed; rather, some combination of code and data fits together and needs to be reused. That's what an object is: a data structure with a collection of its own programs, or methods, to use the name used in SmallTalk. Methods specific to a data structure are bound to it to form an entity that is neither data nor code but object.

An "object" in object-oriented programming may be little more than a collection of data and code, as just described, like a matrix of numbers and the matrix manipulation routines for operating on it. It can be, though, a more or less faithful simulation of some real-world object, like a desk calculator or an internal combustion engine or a brewery. Or it can be something in between, like an electronic spreadsheet.

Creating something as complex as a simulation of a brewery is no simple matter, but the object-oriented approach provides a paradigm for developing complicated objects by working from the general to the specific. Here's how it works. Any individual object is a member of a class, and its class is a subclass of another class, in a hierarchy of classes of objects that looks a lot like the Linnaean taxonomy of life forms. Programmers can spin off their own classes, and only have to specify those characteristics that make the new class different from its parent class. All the characteristics of the parent class, most interestingly the methods specific to the parent class, also belong to the new class and to any objects of that class, through a mechanism known as inheritance.

Inheritance makes it possible to develop powerful objects quickly in a true object-oriented language. For example, creating a spreadsheet involves all the complexity of displaying and maintaining a window on the Macintosh screen. But if you define a spreadsheet to be a subclass of the class Window, then all of the spreadsheet's fenestral behavior is handled automatically via inheritance. All you have to define are the aspects that distinguish a spreadsheet from any other window.

HyperTalk is not a true object-oriented programming language since it does not allow you to create new object classes, but it does let you create new instances of the classes that exist, and it does let you create objects that inherit methods from objects further up in the hierarchy. HyperTalk's five object classes are: stacks, backgrounds, cards, fields, and buttons. HyperCard itself can under certain circumstances be thought of as an object.

All programming that you do in HyperTalk involves creating methods for an instance of one of these object classes. The ways in which these methods are invoked add up to something called event-driven programming.

Event-Driven Programming

In the conventional paradigm of programming that has dominated software development since its beginning, a program is an inert bundle of bits until it is invoked, at which point it starts up, does its thing, and eventually terminates, falling back into its inert state. It is usually invoked by an explicit user action, such as typing the name of the program or double-clicking its icon. This is called the procedural paradigm.

HyperTalk follows the event-driven paradigm, which is an aspect of object-oriented programming and which differs most fundamentally from the procedural paradigm in the way in which programs are invoked. In the event-driven paradigm, programs can be invoked by a wide variety of events, and each program contains a specification of the kind of event that can invoke it. Clicking the mouse button while the pointer is over a button on the screen is a HyperCard event, moving from one card or stack to another is a HyperCard event.

You may see a disturbing circularity in this—the program isn't invoked until the specified event occurs, but it is the program that specifies the event to watch for. How can a program that isn't doing anything yet specify anything? It can't, and event-driven programming requires an operating environment that monitors events, sending messages to wake up the programs. Both the Macintosh operating system and HyperCard do this monitoring of events. The passing of messages is a key concept in object-oriented programming, in event-driven programming, and in HyperTalk.

There are infinitely many events, but only certain kinds of events are recognized by any event-driven language such as HyperTalk. When a HyperTalk event occurs, a message is generated. The message is sent not directly to a program, but to an object. If the object has a program for the message, it is invoked. These programs that are part of objects are called methods.

I have discussed how objects contain both data and code, and how the code comprises programs called methods. I did not explain that, in the object-oriented paradigm, all code is contained in methods.

In HyperTalk, the methods are called handlers, and they reside in the object's script. The short scripts introduced at the end of Chapter 1 were individual handlers. The first and last lines of a handler identify the event (and the message) that invokes it; the other lines are the program proper.

All programming in HyperTalk consists of writing such handlers and attaching them to HyperCard objects: stacks, backgrounds, cards, fields, and buttons. Here are some examples of HyperTalk handlers, indicating the objects to which they are attached and the messages they handle. Don't worry about what they do; but notice where the message name appears in each handler. The indentation pattern indicates the structure of the handler, and is done automatically by the HyperTalk script editor, which will be discussed in the next chapter. The capitalization scheme is unimportant: it's just a stylistic device I've used in this book.

Stack handlers for **openStack** and **idle** messages:

```
On openStack
  Show message box
End openStack

On idle
  Global autoCompact
  If the freesize of this stack > 100 ¬
  and autoCompact is true
```

```
    Then
      DoMenu "compact stack"
      DoMenu "compact stack"
      Put "FreeSize:" && the freesize of this stack
    End if
  End idle
```

Background handler for **openBackground** message:

```
On openBackground
  Go to card "Index"
End openBackground
```

Card handler for **arrowKey** message:

```
On arrowKey whatKey
  If whatKey is left then go to previous card
  If whatKey is right then go to next card
End arrowKey
```

Field handler for **mouseEnter** message:

```
On mouseEnter
  Click at 200,200
  Click at 200,200
End mouseEnter
```

Button handlers for **mouseUp** and **newButton** messages:

```
On mouseUp
  Beep
End mouseUp

On newButton
  Hide button "new Button"
End newButton
```

Layered Logic

The concept of a message is more far-reaching than I have indicated. Not only do external events like mouse clicks produce messages, but an object's handlers can produce messages and send them to other objects; and the commands of the HyperTalk language (**go**, **put**, **add**, etc.) can even be thought of as messages to HyperCard. (As mentioned, HyperCard itself can be thought of as a HyperCard object.) In fact, much of what is actually happening in any HyperTalk program is the passing of messages. So it's helpful to know how messages are passed.

Typically, a message will be dealt with by a handler in the script of the object to which it is initially sent, but if that doesn't happen, the message can trickle through the hierarchical structure of HyperCard objects. This possibility is very important; it is how HyperTalk implements the object-oriented concept of inheritance. It is basic to understanding how to program efficiently in HyperTalk, and we will see later in the book just how to use the HyperCard object hierarchy to increase the efficiency of your programming efforts.

Most messages are sent to the current card, or to a button or field if they pertain somehow to a button or field. From this entry point, they will, if not handled there, pass through the hierarchy. The hierarchy is discussed in the HyperTalk Object Hierarchy appendix, and are pictured in the Help stack supplied with HyperCard. The general picture is: a message moves from a button or field to the card or background to which it belongs, from card to background, from background to stack, from stack to Home stack, and from Home stack to HyperCard itself. Here is a picture of the message hierarchy, adapted from Apple's Help stack:

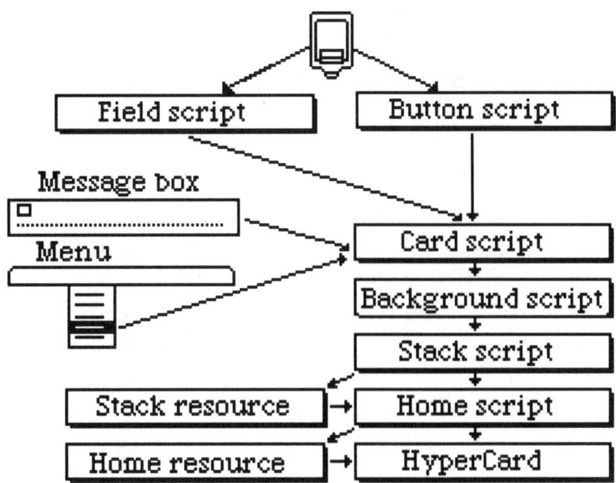

I mentioned that much of what is actually happening in a HyperTalk program is the passing of messages. Let me demonstrate. When the command **put** appears in a handler in a script of, say, a card, here's what happens: The message **put** is generated and HyperCard checks to see if there is a **put** handler in this card's script. If not, the message falls through to the current background, to the current stack, and to the Home stack, with HyperCard checking for a **put** handler at every stop. In the case of the current stack and the Home stack, it will also check the resource fork of the file to see if there is an external command of this name. You'll learn about resources and resource forks later in the book. If all else fails, the **put** message will finally reach HyperCard itself, and HyperCard will recognize it as a HyperTalk command and carry it out. This happens with every line of HyperTalk code executed.

To the experienced programmer, it may seem that the layers are inside-out: you expect the operating system to deal with thing first, then pass them back to you if it is unable to handle them. In HyperTalk, you get first crack at all messages and only if you can't deal with them do they get through to the operating system.

Data Design

All programming languages provide means for processing and organizing data. The data may consist of, among other things, numbers, strings of characters, the current date, or the time. Numbers can be added, letters can't; it is necessary that operations be applied to the right kinds of data. In some languages, it is the programmer's job to keep track of such data type information. HyperTalk works very hard to figure out what kind of data it is working with and how it should be interpreted, and often the HyperTalk programmer can forget about data types entirely.

The data-handling tools that HyperTalk provides to the programmer are simple and powerful. The key concepts are the container and chunking. A container is anything that can hold data, and this includes fields, variables, and the message box. HyperTalk has a set of data structuring tools that apply to all containers. It's called chunking, and the word chunk applies to any specifiable portion of a container.

The specifiable components of a container are: character, word, line, and item. A character is any single character, a word is any string of characters delimited by spaces, a line is any string of characters delimited by **return** characters, and an item is any string of characters delimited by commas. The components can be used in various ways to pick out parts of containers; the details of chunking syntax are spelled out in a subsequent chapter. Here are a few examples:

```
word 1 of line 1 of field "Clients"
item 2 of field "theList"
third character of last word of userName
char 3 to 5 of word 3 of line 9 of fld "Clients"
```

These are the tools for structuring data and accessing the structures of data within HyperCard. But through its object-oriented blending of data and program and its ability to link cards freely, HyperCard offers a higher level of structuring of information as well. A computer visionary named Ted Nelson, in books and articles and an ambitious endeavor called Project Xanadu, has articulated a vision of the successor to text. The vision is called HyperText, and that's where the other half of the name "HyperTalk" comes from.

Nelson's HyperText will, if and when it is realized, change the way we write, the way we think about writing, the way we think about thinking, and a couple of other permutations on thought and expression. HyperTalk is not HyperText, but it is a tool for exploring the ideas of HyperText. Another tool is *Computer Lib: Dream Machines, Revised Edition*, Microsoft Press, 1987, the most findable of Nelson's books and an amazing and delightful exploration of the meaning of machines and the augmentation of our abilities to communicate with one another and with ourselves.

Part II
Programming

3

Responding to Events

About this Chapter

You should turn on your Macintosh now. This and the following chapters cover the entire HyperTalk language on a topical basis. Each chapter will give you the means to become an expert in one aspect of HyperTalk programming, but you'll need to try out the things discussed in the chapters to earn the expertise.

This chapter shows how to write HyperTalk scripts that handle events and perform useful functions. Some of the examples will be familiar from Chapter 1, where they were presented as utterances in a foreign language, to be puzzled out via cognates and context. Similarly, some of the concepts from Chapter 2 will be re-introduced here. In this chapter, however, the examples will be used to give substance to the concepts, and both the examples and the concepts should take on new meaning.

Here are some HyperCard topics that you might want to review before you get too deep into this chapter:

- **Events, messages, and objects**. You should have read the preceding chapter and know the five kinds of HyperCard objects. You should know what the message box is. You should know that objects respond to messages, and that messages may signal events, and that programming in HyperTalk is a matter of telling objects how to respond to events. This chapter will give concrete meaning to these abstractions.

- **HyperCard basics**. You should know how to create a button.

- **Navigating and Macintosh basics**. You should know how to get to the last card of the Home stack, and you should know how to turn down the speaker volume.

About Responding to Events

HyperCard and the Macintosh operating system work by recognizing and responding to occurrences of certain events. Some of these events correspond to user actions: pressing a particular key, moving the mouse, clicking the mouse button. Some events, while they may be caused by user actions, involve objects on the screen: the cursor entering or leaving a window or text field, or an application program starting up or shutting down. The occurrence of an event is signaled by a message, and the various windows and fields and other objects of HyperCard and the Macintosh operating system receive and respond to such messages with appropriate actions.

HyperTalk provides control over this process. HyperTalk programming consists of specifying, for any given object, what messages it responds to and what action it takes in response to each message.

Immediate Programming

You begin programming in HyperTalk by telling HyperCard that you are a programmer. To do this, go to the last card of the Home stack and set the user level to 5 (scripting) by clicking on the appropriate radio button. You will have need of the message box, so if it is not visible, make it so by typing Command-M. Turn on blind typing (which will let you type into the message box even if it is not visible) by clicking on the appropriate check box, if it not already checked.

Each of the things you just did by clicking buttons or pressing keys was mediated by a HyperTalk command. Clicking the scripting button invoked the HyperTalk command **`Set userLevel to 5`**. You can issue these commands directly through the message box. Try the following. Click on the interior of the message box to get a text cursor in the box. Type this command:

```
Set the visible of message box to false
```

press the Return key, and the message box goes away. Now, since you have selected blind typing, you can type this:

```
Set the visible of message box to true
```

and press the Return key, and the message box returns.

This is programming in HyperTalk in its most direct and immediate form. You are actually entering and executing HyperTalk commands. Try another command:

```
Beep
```

You might want to turn your speaker volume down at this point; the Beep command is handy for learning about HyperTalk, but it can be annoying.

Typing directly into the message box may be direct and immediate, but it doesn't look much like my description of HyperTalk programming. This doesn't appear to be "specifying, for any given object, what messages it responds to and what action it takes in response to each message." In fact, this is not the usual way to program in HyperTalk.

Using the message box in this way is, nevertheless, one of the handiest tools a HyperTalk programmer has. There are many commands and other elements of the HyperTalk language to learn, and each has to be used properly. Usually, you can check your memory for the syntax of a command by trying it out in the message box. Can you tell the **beep** command how many times to beep? Try it; type:

```
Beep 9
```

into the message box. (I hope you turned the speaker volume down first.)

Writing Scripts

Most HyperTalk programming, though, is not done by typing commands into the message box. Rather, it's done by writing scripts.

A HyperTalk script specifies all the messages to which an object will respond, and the actions it will take in response to each message sent to the object. Every HyperCard object—every button, field, card, background, and stack—has a script, even if the script is empty.

Scripts are made up of handlers. For each message the object responds to, there is a handler, specifying the action it will perform. The name of the handler is the name of the message, and the lines of HyperTalk code making up the handler name actions to be performed. A script can contain many handlers, but often will contain a single handler, and we'll initially restrict ourselves to single-handler scripts. Most non-empty scripts are button scripts, so we'll start with button scripts.

The first thing you need to do to begin scripting is to create a new stack and card (never experiment on anything but a clean slate). Then create a button in this new stack, and name it "test." This is the button in whose script you will place various handlers, making it do various useful things.

The second thing you need to do is to invoke the script editor. The script editor is always used to create or modify a script. It works basically like any other Macintosh editor or word processor, with some qualifications. The menu bar is not accessible when you are in the script editor, so if you want to use the Cut, Copy, or Paste editing functions, you must do so via the Command-key equivalents (Command-X for Cut, Command-C for Copy, Command-V for Paste). To offset some of its deficiencies, the script editor has some added features, such as automatically indenting scripts for readability.

Invoking the editor is also different from invoking a word processor. You must first select the object whose script you want to edit; the editor won't give you a dialog box and allow you to select a script to edit. There are several ways to invoke the editor, and some techniques are unavailable in some versions of HyperCard. Since you will be invoking the editor a lot, you should have a comfortable and efficient way of doing it from the start, so I'll tell you now about all the ways to invoke the script editor, and you can select the technique that works best for you and forget the rest.

For HyperCard versions earlier than version 1.2, this is the standard technique for invoking the script editor on the script of an object:

- First, open the object's Info box. For cards, buttons, and stacks, this means selecting `Card Info...`, `Background Info...`, or `Stack Info...` from the `Objects` menu. For buttons and fields, this means choosing the button or field tool from the `Tools` menu, then selecting `Button Info...` or `Field Info...` from the `Objects` menu. You can also skip one menu step by double-clicking on the object after choosing the tool.

- Second, click on the Script button in the Info box.

- Third, to leave the editor, click on either the OK button (to save any changes you've made to the script) or the Cancel button (to abandon changes or if you have made none). You can also use the Enter key (not the Return key) to do the same thing as the OK button; this is a handy shortcut, but there is unfortunately no corresponding shortcut for the Cancel button.

- You can also Shift-double-click (hold down the Shift key while double-clicking) on an object (a button or a field) to more quickly open the editor on its script.

In version 1.2, Apple introduced several new techniques for getting into and out of the script editor. Most of them work with the browse tool. All of them require holding down the Command and Option keys, usually with another key or the mouse button to select the object. The techniques are:

- Command-Option-c to edit the script of the current card .

- Command-Option-b to edit the script of the current background.

- Command-Option-s to edit the script of the current stack.

- Command-Option-mouse click on a button to edit the script of that button.

- Command-Option-Shift-mouse click on a button or field to edit the script of that button or field.

- Command-Option to see where all buttons are.

- Command-Option-Shift to see where all buttons and fields are.

- Command-Option-mouse click or any key to leave the script editor. Leaving the editor in this way when changes have been made to the script brings up an alert box asking whether or not you want to save your changes.

You can also use Command-Option-mouse click with the button or field tool to edit the script of the clicked-on button or field, respectively.

Now invoke the script editor on the test button.

What you see when you do this is a skeleton handler that HyperCard supplies for every newly created button. Every message handler has the same basic structure: It begins with a line indicating the message it handles, ends with a line indicating the end of the handler, and between these two lines contains one or more lines indicating the action to be taken in response to the message. The name of the message must appear after the word **On** in the first line and after **End** in the last. The skeleton handler is a **mouseUp** handler; that is, it responds to the **mouseUp** message, sent to this test button when the mouse button has been pressed and released while the pointer is over the test button. Since the line between the first and last lines is empty, the handler performs no action in response to the **mouseUp** message, but we can change that.

Try one of the commands previously typed into message box: **Beep**. Type **Beep** into the middle line of the handler to create this script for your test button:

```
On mouseUp
  Beep
End mouseUp
```

and then exit the script editor, make sure the browse tool is selected, and click on the test button. You've created a beeper. The script that you wrote is invoked whenever you click on the button, and if you copy this button to another stack, the script will come along; the button will beep in the other stack, too.

You should stop for a moment to reflect on what you just did, and on what you have learned so far. You have written a complete HyperTalk script and have programmed an object to do what you want it to under the condition you specify. What this means is that you now know how to program in HyperTalk. Everything else in HyperTalk, everything else in this book, is just elaboration on the techniques you now understand.

You can skip the rest of the chapters if you want to explore on your own. You can look up other HyperTalk commands in the appendix and substitute them for the **beep** command, to make your button do different things. For example, you can substitute a visual annoyance for the auditory one:

```
On mouseUp
  Flash
End mouseUp
```

You can add commands, so that your handler does a number of things when the button is clicked, such as:

```
On mouseUp
  Beep
  Flash
  Beep
End mouseUp
```

You can substitute different messages for **mouseUp** in the script, making your button respond to different events. For example, if you substitute **mouseDown**, the command will be executed as soon as you press the mouse button down, without waiting for you to release the button. The new script looks like this:

```
On mouseDown
  Beep
End mouseDown
```

Note that you have to change the message name in both the first and last lines. If you substitute **mouseEnter**, the action won't even wait for the button to be pressed, but will take place as soon as you move the pointer over the button. That script looks—and I'm sure you're way ahead of me on this one—like this:

```
On mouseEnter
  Beep
End mouseEnter
```

You could attach this or any script you create to a different object. Some messages are not appropriate to some objects, but you could open the script of the card and enter one of these scripts. Then you could click somewhere on the card itself, rather than the button, and see what happens.

You could. But unless you are a reasonably sophisticated programmer, I recommend that you spend some more time on button scripts first.

Practical Button Scripts

Most HyperCard stacks should contain at least the three basic navigation buttons: Home, Next, and Prev. These buttons cause a transfer to the first card of the Home stack, to the next card of the current stack, and to the previous card of the current stack. The easiest way to add these buttons to a stack is to copy them from another stack, but you can also build them from scratch using HyperTalk. If you create three new buttons named Home, Next, and Prev, you can make them work by giving each the appropriate script:

```
On mouseUp
  Go home
End mouseUp

On mouseUp
  Go next
End mouseUp

On mouseUp
  Go prev
```

```
End mouseUp
```

To test the Next and Prev buttons, you'll need to add at least one card to your stack (that's just a matter of selecting **New Card** from the Edit menu). Testing the Home button will send you to the Home stack if it works; to get back, select **Back** from the Go menu. You can add First and Last buttons in this same way to jump to the first or last cards of your stack, or a Back button that will do what the **Go Back** menu selection does.

All of these scripts use the **Go** command, the main navigational command of the HyperTalk language. In the use of the **Go** command, the word **Go** is always followed by the destination, which must be a reference to a card or a stack. You can also supply the word **to** for clarity, but it's strictly optional. If the destination is a stack, the stack must be specified by name and the **Go** transfers to the first card of that stack. If the destination is a card, the card can be specified by its name:

```
Go card "Bobby Jo"
```

by its number:

```
Go to card 7
```

or by its ID number:

```
Go card id 7077
```

or by any of these sequencing words: **first, second, third, fourth, fifth, sixth, seventh, eighth, ninth, tenth, last, mid, this, prev, next,** and **any**. The last of these actually picks a card from the current stack at random.

If the card is specified by name, the word **card** is required to keep HyperCard from looking for a stack of that name. For a precise specification of the syntax of the **Go** command, see Appendix D: HyperTalk Commands.

You can also create a Help button with the following script, which causes a transfer to the stack named Help:

```
On mouseUp
  Go help
End mouseUp
```

I referred to the number and ID number of a button, and you may not be aware that buttons have these properties, or of what good they are, or of why a stack needs both. That will be discussed in a later chapter, but you can create a handler that forces a button to tell you its ID number or number. Try entering these two handlers as the script of your test button:

```
On mouseUp
  -- Clears message box
  Put empty into message box
End mouseUp

On mouseDown
  -- Displays button's id in message box
  Put the ID number of button "test" ¬
  into message box
End mouseDown
```

To test this script, click on the button, but wait before releasing the mouse button. The **mouseDown** event will cause the button's ID number to be displayed in the message box, and the **mouseUp** event will clear it.

This script introduces several new things. First, it's the first multi-handler script we've seen in this chapter, and you should notice that the order of handlers in the script doesn't matter; the **mouseDown** message gets to the button before the **mouseUp** message because the mouseDown event occurs before the mouseUp event. Second, there's the command **Put**, which is used here to display a value in the message box. Third, there are two special symbols used in scripts: The ¬ character is the HyperTalk continuation character and is used when you need to break a long line for readability; and the -- symbol is used to denote comments. Fourth, there is the constant **empty**, which is equivalent to an empty string of characters ("") and is useful in clearing the contents of containers.

Note that you can add more commands to the **mouseUp** handler to allow the button to do something useful besides introducing itself; for example, you could turn it into a Home button:

```
On mouseUp
  -- Clears message box and goes home
  Put empty into message box
  Go home
End mouseUp
On mouseDown
  -- Displays button's id in message box
  Put the ID number of me ¬
  into message box
End mouseDown
```

The word **me**, slipped into the **mouseDown** handler here, is very useful: it has as its value the name of the object in whose script it appears. It provides a more general way for an object to refer to itself, and we'll soon see how useful that can be when we discuss the object hierarchy.

The command **put**, used in these handlers to place a value into the message box and in one of them to remove it (by putting an empty string into the container), is one of the most useful HyperTalk commands.

Put, Get, and Containers

You can put a value into any container with a command of the form:

```
Put <value> into <container>
```

and you can retrieve a value from a container with a command of the form:

```
Get <container>
```

which leaves the value in the variable **it**. The variable **it** is like any other variable in that you can **put** values into **it** and **get** values from **it**. But **it** is automatically loaded with a value by **get** and by most commands that retrieve values: in general, if a command has retrieved a value from somewhere, that value will reside in the variable **it** until bumped out by another value deposited by another command. This makes **it** work very much like the English pronoun "it" and you will find that your intuitive sense of when **it** is appropriate to use in your code will generally be correct.

The syntax for the **put** and **get** commands differs because you must already have the value in order to put it somewhere, but to **get** a value only requires knowing where to look. The **<container>** can be any value-holder, as discussed in Chapter 2, and chunk expressions (introduced in Chapter 2) are allowed in **put** and **get** commands. So you can say, for example:

```
Put "Barks" into Variable2
Put "Ducks" into Variable4
Put "Carl" into Variable1
Put "Donald" into Variable4
Get Variable1
Put it && Variable2 into VariableA
Get Variable3
Put it && Variable4 into VariableB
Put VariableA && "and" && VariableB
```

This useless but instructive exercise includes the operator **&&**, which is used to combine two strings of characters into a new string. For example, **"Dave" && "Sim"** results in the string **Dave Sim**. The operation is called concatenation, and there are two concatenation operators: **&&** and **&**. The first of these puts a space between the concatenated strings, the second doesn't.

The actions of putting a value into a container and getting it back out are complementary, but the **put** command is more flexible in its use with containers than is the **get** command. In fact, **put** can do almost anything that **get** can do: You can use **put** instead of **get** to retrieve values from containers, and you may find it preferable to do so. You do this by supplying a container as the **<value>** in the **put** command, and the command uses whatever is in the container as the value to put into **<container>**. So if you had accidentally done this:

```
Put "The quality fo mercy, etc." ¬
into the message box
```

you could do this:

```
Put word 1 of the message box ¬
&& word 2 of the message box ¬
&& character 2 of word 3 of the message box ¬
& character 1 of word 3 of the message box ¬
&& word 4 of the message box ¬
into item 1 of the message box
```

to fix it. That would not be very efficient, but it does show how you can extract values and insert values even in the very same container. It also shows that "the message box" is a long name for such a handy container, and in fact there are some convenient abbreviations. The following forms are equivalent:

```
Put 57 into the message box
Put 57 into message box
Put 57 into the message window
Put 57 into message window
Put 57 into the message
Put 57 into message
Put 57 into the msg box
Put 57 into msg box
Put 57 into the msg window
Put 57 into msg window
Put 57 into the msg
Put 57 into msg
Put 57
```

The last one is exceptionally abbreviated. When using the **put** command, if you don't specify any <container>, the message box will be used. The next example uses the **put** command with numbers and variables, but more of its usefulness will be revealed in Chapter 5.

```
On mouseUp
  Put 3.1416 into x
  Put msg into y
  Put x * y into msg
End mouseUp
```

This example, which multiplies whatever you have put into the message box by 3.1416 and displays the result in the message box, hints at a limitation of using the message box for output. You can enter more than a number into the message box in this case; you can enter, say, an expression like **(18.5 + 17) * 52.8)**. If you enter a complicated expression, there is always the chance that you will make a typing error. But the result replaces the expression, so you can't see the input for the output. Later in this chapter we will see how to get around this problem by using fields for input and output.

Messages and the Object Hierarchy

Up to now, we have been dealing with messages generated in HyperCard in response to user actions: mouse moves and mouse clicks. But there are other kinds of messages that are generated by other kinds of events. Some, but no means all, of these messages are listed here and many of these will be exemplified in scripts in the rest of this chapter. All messages are defined and exemplified in the HyperTalk System Messages appendix.

There are messages that signal the current state of the mouse button or the position of the mouse with respect to a HyperCard object (button or field). These include: **mouseUp**, **mouseDown**, **mouseStillDown**, **mouseEnter**, **mouseWithin**, and **mouseLeave**.

There are messages that signal a change in the status of a HyperCard object. These include: **newButton**, **newField**, **newCard**, **newBackground**, **newStack**, **deleteButton**, **deleteField**, **deleteCard**, **deleteBackground**, **deleteStack**, **openField**, **openCard**, **openBackground**, **openStack**, **closeField**, **closeCard**, **closeBackground**, and **closeStack**.

There are messages that signal changes in the state of HyperCard itself. These include: **startUp**, **quit**, and **idle**.

Every message has an object to which it is directed. This object is called the message's entry point. The entry point for an **openCard** message, for example, is the current card. The entry point for a

mouseDown message will be a HyperCard button if the mouseDown event occurs while the pointer is over the button.

If the message's entry point script has a handler for the message, the receipt of the message by the object will trigger action. If not, that doesn't mean that the message will not result in action. As described in Chapter 2, HyperCard has a natural hierarchy of objects, and messages trickle through the hierarchy until they find a handler. A **mouseDown** message generated while the pointer is over a card button will be sent initially to the button's script, but if the script does not contain a handler for the message, the message will drop through to the next object in the hierarchy, in this case the card. If it has a **mouseDown** handler, that handler will be triggered by the message.

A message can fall all the way to HyperCard itself looking for its handler, or be caught along the way. The general idea is, messages that originally go to buttons or fields can fall through to the cards or backgrounds that these objects belong to if not handled by the original object; any message that gets to a card can similarly fall through to its background; and once a message gets to a background it can fall on through to the stack, and from there to the Home card and to the Home stack and finally to HyperCard.

One consequence of this hierarchical arrangement is that objects further along the hierarchy have a broader scope of influence than those that initially receive messages. Since all card buttons on a particular card will pass their unhandled messages to that same card, it is possible, for example, to put that **mouseDown** handler we wrote earlier into a card script, in which case the one handler will apply to all existing buttons on the card and even to fields and to future buttons and to the card itself. All these objects can be made to name themselves if we put the handler at the right level in the hierarchy (this requires using the version of the handler with the word **me**).

The full story on the hierarchy is contained in Appendix B: The HyperCard Object Hierarchy.

Fields and Field Scripts

You should now create a couple of card fields and at least two more card buttons. A card button and a card field both named "About" will come in handy for examples in this and the next chapter, and the first script below will require a card field name "IO" and a card button (name unimportant).

Up to this point I have been casual in referring to objects, suggesting that you "create a button" without indicating whether it is a card button or a background button. This should have caused no confusion because HyperCard creates buttons at the card level by default, and HyperTalk interprets script references to buttons as referring to card buttons by default. Unfortunately, while HyperCard also creates fields at the card level by default, HyperTalk assumes that any reference to a field in a script is referring to a *background* field. This can lead to confusions, but the confusions are easily avoided if you don't give HyperTalk the opportunity to assume anything. From this point on, I will be more explicit about creating card buttons or background buttons, card fields or background fields, and the scripts will be similarly explicit about the kinds of buttons and scripts they are referring to.

Although it is convenient to use the message box for output, we have seen that it can be annoying not to be able to see input and output simultaneously. We will now examine a button script that uses a field for input and output. Here is the script, which should be attached to a button:

```
On mouseUp
  Get line 1 of card field "IO"
  Put it into number1
  Get line 2 of card field "IO"
  Put it into number2
  Put number1 + number2 ¬
  into line 3 of card field "IO"
End mouseUp
```

You should have no trouble describing exactly what this script does. It's a **mouseUp** handler, so it is invoked when the mouse is clicked over its object, the button. It retrieves whatever values are in lines 1 and 2 of a card field named "IO" and puts these two values into two variables, **number1** and **number2**. One of the rules of good programming is that names should be descriptive, so you suspect that the handler is going to treat these values as numbers, and the next line confirms this, because **number1** and **number2** get added together. The result, the sum of the two numbers, is placed into the third line of the field. The script is a very simple one-function calculator, which reads its input values from a field and writes it output back to the same field, but on another line. To use it, you enter the values you want to add on lines 1 and 2 of the field and click the button. There are some other tricks to learn before this can be turned into something like Dan Winkler's clever HyperCalc mini-spreadsheet that is supplied with HyperCard, but before you reach the end of the book you'll have them.

For the next example, if you haven't already done so, you should now create that "About" button/field pair. (Giving the button and field the same name is strictly for human convenience; HyperCard will neither be confused by this name sharing nor will it connect the objects in any way as a result of it.) This example will give you a button that makes a field pop into view. The field itself will also contain a script, and that script will cause the field to disappear again when you pass the pointer across it. Such an "About" button is used in many commercial and public-domain stacks to provide pop-up notes, and has been implemented in a variety of ways. Here it is implemented as a pair of handlers, one for a button script and one for a field script. The first handler should be placed in the script of the card button named "About" and the second in the script of the card field also named "About."

```
On mouseUp
  -- Simple About button script.
  Show card field "About"
End mouseUp

On mouseLeave
  -- Simple About field script.
  Hide me
End mouseLeave
```

These handlers use the **hide** and **show** commands to turn the field invisible and visible (the word **me** was introduced earlier in the chapter). HyperTalk provides a lot of tools for hiding, displaying, and animating objects, nearly all of which are covered in the next chapter. If the **show** and **hide** commands are not available in your version of HyperCard (they were not introduced until version 1.2), you can peek ahead to Chapter 4 to see how to use the **set** command to do what they do.

To make this thing a useful tool rather than just an exercise, you can copy the field and button to another card that needs an explanatory note and enter that note into the field. (Copying a button or field, as you may know, is a matter of selecting the button or field tool from the object menu, clicking on the object, typing Command-C to copy the object, moving to the card where you want the object, typing Command-V to paste it, dragging it to the right spot, and finally selecting the browse tool.) It might be wise to set the lock text of the field (using its Field Info box) after you enter the text. Now whenever you need the reminder that you've hidden in the field, your About button will pop it up for you.

Earlier I said that you should do your experimenting on a clean slate, an empty stack. If you followed the suggestion of the last paragraph and pasted your functioning "About" button/field onto a card where it will do you some good and put useful text in the field, you were not working on a clean slate any longer. That's all right; you weren't experimenting, either. You were a stackware author installing a newly developed tool.

Card and Stack Scripts

One reason to leave the classroom of the test stack is, as just mentioned, to install a newly developed tool into an existing stack. Another reason is to go stack-snooping. HyperCard itself contains a wealth of good script examples. It's time to examine some of them.

Examining HyperCard's own scripts can be a dangerous business. There are several steps you can take to prevent your accidentally damaging HyperCard's scripts. I'll explain the risk and suggest the steps, but you'll have to assess for yourself the seriousness and likelihood of the risk, and the hassle level of the steps.

The only risk in examining the scripts is that you will accidentally make some change in the code and alter the working of HyperCard. This can only happen if you type something while the script is open and then save the change that results. The first step for avoiding this is, don't type anything while you are examining a HyperCard script, and this is sufficient if always followed. The second is, learn to leave the editor via the Cancel button, and learn it in the marrow of your bones, so that it is inconceivable that you will click the OK button by mistake. I confess that I rely on this one, but looking at it baldly stated, I don't trust it. Programmer's arrogance is going to get me one day. The third step you can take is the safest: Make a copy of your Home stack, and work on that. Of course, you should have the original Home stack filed away and be working on a copy anyway, but that's a different level of security, one you should forget about until you need it.

Go to the Home stack and open its script.

You should see several handlers, one of which looks like this:

```
On startUp
  GetHomeInfo
  Pass startUp -- to a startUp XCMD, if present
End startUp
```

(The capitalization will be different; I modified it to match a convention I am using in this book, but capitalization doesn't matter in HyperTalk.)

And you should see one that looks like this:

```
On resume
  GetHomeInfo
  Pass resume -- to a resume XCMD, if present
End resume
```

Neither of these may be particularly lucid, but what is worth noticing about these handlers at this point is what they handle. The messages **startUp** and **resume** are two that we have not dealt with yet, and that's because we have only dealt with button and field scripts. The **startUp** and **resume** messages are generated, respectively, when HyperCard is initially launched and when it is restarted after being suspended while another application is invoked. Buttons and fields have nothing to do with such events; buttons and fields don't respond to many messages beyond reports of mouse actions in their immediate vicinity and news of their own creation and demise. These events need to be handled at the card, background, or stack level, and probably just at the stack level, but we may not be prepared to conclude that just yet.

Now leave the Home stack script and open the Home card script. (Click on Cancel to leave the stack script.)

The script of the first card of the Home stack, as released by Apple, contains one handler. It looks like this:

```
On idle
  Put the time into card field "Time"
  Pass idle
End idle
```

This is an **idle** handler, and we will examine it more carefully (ignoring, for the time being, the third line). The **idle** message is being generated whenever nothing else is going on. An **idle** handler can be invoked several times a second, and that's exactly what we want if we are trying to keep the time displayed in a field accurate to the second.

This handler does that; it uses the function **time** to access the system clock and puts the value the function gives it into a card field named Time. It does this once and terminates. It is a very simple handler. But since it is invoked so often, the effect is that the Time field maintains a display of the time accurate to the second.

Could this be anything but a card script? As mentioned, buttons and fields don't respond to messages like **idle**. Could this be a stack or background script? What difference would there be in its action if it were either a stack or a background script?

Here is a script that would be useful at the card level or higher:

```
on mouseUp
  -- A card script.
  Put the clickLoc
end mouseUp
```

The function **clickLoc** returns a value that consists of two numbers corresponding to the horizontal and vertical coordinates of the point in the card window where the mouse was clicked. As a button script it would be pointless. Several related functions are: **clickH**, **clickV**, **mouseH**, and **mouseV**. Each of these returns a single number, reporting a horizontal or vertical coordinate of the point clicked on or of the current position of the mouse. There is also **mouseLoc**, which reports the current position of the mouse. If you replace the word **mouseClick** in this card script with each of these functions in turn, you will see exactly how they work.

Now go to the last card of the Home stack and open its card script.

There's an **openCard** handler here. You needn't puzzle over what it does (although you might notice the **Set userLevel** command that we started this chapter with). Again, the thing to consider is that there are such messages as **openCard** (and **openStack** and **openBackground**) and that any card, stack, or background can have a handler for its opening message. Such handlers are good for setting up things when something is getting started. In the next chapter we will see how to run a banner across the top of a card when it's opened.

The Conditional Structure

I'll end this chapter with another hands-on example. You should implement this script in a button of your own back in your test stack. In a return to the puzzle-solving style of Chapter 1, I'll let you figure out what this script does. You might think about the implications of those two lines beginning with **if** and **end if**.

```
On mouseUp
  If msg < 100
  Then put msg + 1 into msg
  Else put 0 into msg
End mouseUp
```

HyperTalk Language Elements Discussed in this Chapter

The elements of the HyperTalk language that were touched on in this chapter include: **any**, **back**, **background**, **beep**, **button**, card, clickH, clickV, closeBackground, closeCard, closeField, closeStack, deleteBackground, deleteButton, deleteCard, deleteField, deleteStack, else, end, field, get, go, help, Home, HyperCard, if, into, is, message box, mouseClick, mouseDown, mouseH, mouseLeave, mouseLoc, mouseUp, mouseV, name, newBackground, newButton, newCard, newField, newStack, on, openBackground, openCard, openField, openStack, prev, put, stack, the, and then.

4

Creating Visuals

About this Chapter

This chapter discusses the ways in which you can control the visual aspects of your stacks from within HyperTalk scripts. This includes control of the painting tools, making objects visible and invisible, moving and placing objects, and the use of visual effects and animation techniques. Along the way it introduces dozens of commands, functions, and properties, as well as the two control structures of HyperTalk, the `if` and `repeat` structures. You should not feel compelled to memorize all the language elements introduced here; the point of this chapter is to discover the techniques for controlling the visual presentation of your stacks.

About Visuals

I am using the term visuals in this chapter to cover all visual aspects of a stack's appearance and behavior. This includes cinematic visual effects like dissolves and wipes, but also covers the use of the paint tools and the display of objects.

HyperCard provides some remarkable tools for customizing the visual appearance of your work without doing any programming. What you gain from putting these visuals under the control of your scripts can be equally remarkable. You can make virtually all the static visual aspects of your stacks dynamic or contingent on particular events, you can combine visuals for meaningful effects that exploit the dimension of time, and you can create animations.

Objects, Properties, and Visuals

Here is a brief review of the HyperCard ideas that you should be noddingly familiar with as you read this chapter. If any of them remain truly obscure after the review, it might be a good idea to refer to the HyperCard help stacks or to a general HyperCard book.

There are basically five classes of objects that HyperCard recognizes: stacks, backgrounds, cards, fields, and buttons. HyperCard also recognizes four windows: the message box, the card window, the tool palette, and the pattern palette.

Every object of these five classes of objects and each of the four windows has certain properties associated with it. It is the properties of an object that you are setting when you click the check boxes and radio buttons in the information window for an object. To cite a few examples of properties, a stack has a name and a size; a field has a text font, text style, and the property of having wide or narrow margins; a button has a property that indicates whether or not is highlighted, a name, and a style; and any window has a location, a size and shape, and the property of being visible or invisible. Many of these properties affect the appearance of the object, and nearly all of them are controllable from HyperTalk scripts.

HyperCard provides a powerful set of painting tools that allow you to paint pictures on backgrounds and cards. The paint tools give access to a number of paint effects, like rotation, and a number of painting patterns. There are also properties specific to painting. Virtually all the paint tools, effects, properties, and patterns can also be controlled via scripts.

HyperCard's visual display consists of overlapping layers; the card layer is in front of the background layer, and a new layer is associated with each button or field object. Unless its **`style`** property has the value **`transparent`**, an object obscures objects and layers behind it. The layer of an object can also be changed in a script.

Finally, HyperTalk supports a number of special visual effects, such as dissolves and wipes, that can be invoked via scripts.

A Puzzle Solved

The last chapter ended with a puzzle involving the **if** structure. The first example of this chapter uses the **if** structure. Here between the two, you have the right to a solution to the puzzle and a discussion of the uses and syntax of this element of the HyperTalk language.

The purpose of the **if** structure is to permit conditional execution of HyperTalk commands; that is, it allows you to specify that an action be taken only under a certain condition, and to specify the condition.

There are several legal forms of the **if** structure. It always begins with the keyword **if** and the condition to be satisfied, followed by the keyword **then** and the action to be taken. These can appear on one line in a handler:

```
On mouseUp
  <possible lines of code>
  If X>7 then put X into card field "Answer"
  <possible lines of code>
End mouseUp
```

or the **then** part can appear on a separate line. (The following examples merely show the syntax of the **if** structure itself. An **if** structure must always appear in a handler, though.)

```
If X>7
Then put X into card field "Answer"
```

It is possible to specify several actions to be taken:

```
If X>7
Then
  Put X into card field "Answer"
  Beep
End if
```

in which case the above syntax, including the key phrase **End if**, on a line by itself, must be used. The reason for this should be clear: "Several" is indeterminate; some clue must indicate where the structure ends.

It is also possible to specify an action to be taken if the condition is not satisfied, and this action is signalled by the keyword **else**:

```
If X>7 then put X-7 else put 7-X
```

or:

```
If X>7
Then put X-7
Else put 7-X
```

As with the **then** part, the **else** can specify several actions:

```
If X>7
Then
  Put X into card field "Answer"
  Beep
Else
  Put 7-X into X
  Beep
End if
```

The indentation will be supplied for you by the script editor.

That should be more than sufficient to explain what the script from the last chapter does. It looked like this:

```
On mouseUp
  If msg < 100
  Then put msg + 1 into msg
  Else put 0 into msg
End mouseUp
```

It is a **mouseUp** handler for a button script, so it is invoked whenever the button is clicked. It examines the contents of the message box and takes one of two actions, depending on whether the message box contains a number less than 100. (We don't know from reading the handler what it will do if the message box is empty or if it contains something other than a number.)

If the value in question is less than 100, it adds 1 to the contents of the message box and puts the result back into the message box.

Otherwise, it puts 0 into the message box. Repeated clicks of the button will make the message box count to 100, then start over, looping forever or as long as your finger holds out.

So far these examples of the use of the **if** structure have been more pedagogical than practical, and there are a few more things to be learned from this one before we abandon it. These will be the first bits of advice on avoiding and tracking down bugs in your code—something that will become more important as your scripts get more complex.

First, what will happen if we put something other than a number into the message box before clicking the button? Or empty the box? Or enter a negative number? If you test these cases, you will find that negative numbers work as you might expect; that an empty message box seems to act like a message box with a zero in it, which might seem like an acceptable thing or it might not; but that almost any other value—well, you might try it and see if you can figure out why what happens happens.

More important than determining just what this particular handler does when confronted by inappropriate input is the realization that just about any HyperTalk scripts that gathers input from any source—a container, the user, a file—can sometimes be confronted with inappropriate input and act unpredictably. An important part of the programming process is thinking of all the wrong kinds of values that could somehow find their way to your script and making sure it can handle them—even if "handling them" just means displaying an error message to the user and quitting. We'll learn how to make a program throw up its hands and quit in the next chapter.

The second lesson of the script we've been examining is in the several mentions of the message box. It's a subtle point, but one that can lead to subtle errors if you don't understand it. In both line two and the beginning of line three of the script, commands are executed that cause HyperTalk to read the contents of the message box. First it must be read to evaluate the **if** condition: does it contain a number less than 100? Then there is a line that calls for adding 1 to the contents of the message box, and this command works by reading off the contents, adding, and writing the result back out. The fact that the two references to the message box both get their values by reading the message box implies that there is a chance, however slight, that they may not be referring to the same quantity. If something happens that alters the contents of the message box between the execution of these two lines, the script's behavior will become quite unpredictable. This is a bug, but not in this case a very serious one. In more complex scripts, you need to watch for this kind of problem.

The **if** structure is reminiscent in form of the message handler structure, and its function may seem similar, but the two are really quite different. In fact, the difference is the difference between event-driven and procedural programming. The message handler waits passively for the arrival of the message that triggers it; it does nothing until that message arrives. The **if** structure, which can only appear in a handler, begins to act when the **if** line is encountered in the interpretation of the handler, just as a command within a handler is executed. The **if** actively assesses the condition specified in its statement, and then takes action or does not. The condition it assesses is not a message, and the **if** does not respond to it, but rather polls it.

Even more important for present purposes is the fact that a message handler is a fundamental unit of HyperTalk programming, and the **if** structure is a useful tool that can be used in a handler.

The **if** structure will come in handy in creating visuals.

Controlling the Appearance of Objects

One of the most common visuals in HyperCard stacks is the About button/field. A pair of handlers to implement this visual in the last chapter included the first field script analyzed in the book, but there are other ways to implement the About concept. Here is one:

```
On mouseUp
  If the visible of field "About" is true
  Then set the visible of field "About" to false
  Else set the visible of field "About" to true
End mouseUp
```

This script uses the **set** command, which is used only and always to adjust the values of properties. We have already used the **set** command casually, but in this chapter we will do so with expertise. The syntax of the set command is:

```
Set <property> of <object> to <value>
Set the <property> of <object> to <value>
Set <property> to <value>
Set the <property> to <value>
```

When setting a property with the **set** command, the word **the** is strictly optional; in other uses of properties, it may be required. The rule is this: **the** is optional with all properties when used in **set** and **get** commands, optional in other commands when the property has parameters, and obligatory in commands other than **set** and **get** if the property has no parameters. Every window, stack, background, card, field, or button property has a parameter (the parameter specifies the object to which the property applies); global and painting properties have none.

That covered, we can see that what this script does is to set a particular property of a particular object to a particular value. In this case, the object is the card field About, the property is **visible**, and the values are **true** and **false**, but the technique works for all adjustable properties and their values and objects. The HyperTalk Properties appendix lists all the properties of all objects and all the values these properties can assume, and the following partial list should provide plenty of property-setting operations to try out. All of these properties can be controlled using a script like the About scripts.

Visual Properties of HyperCard Objects

Window Properties:

bottom	bottomRight	height
left	location	rectangle
right	top	topLeft
visible	width	

Background and Card Property:

showPict

Field Properties:

bottom	bottomRight	height
left	location	lockText
number	rectangle	right
scroll	showLines	style
textAlign	textFont	textHeight
textSize	textStyle	top
topLeft	visible	wideMargins
width		

Button Properties:

autoHilite	bottom	bottomRight
height	hilite	icon
left	location	number
rectangle	right	showName
style	textAlign	textFont
textHeight	textSize	textStyle
top	topLeft	visible
width		

Some of these properties have many possible values, which are listed for the property in the appendix. Many indicate the presence or absence of something, and these can take on only the value **true** or the value **false**. Others, such as the **width** of an object, take on numeric values, and some identify points with pairs of numbers. Of the properties listed above, all *except* the following are either true/false or numeric-valued properties: **style**, **textAlign**, **textFont**, and **textStyle**. These properties take on values that are words identifying the button or field's style (such as **scrolling** for a field), the alignment of text (**left**, **right**, or **center**), and so on. As properties are used in this book, their possible values will be mentioned, but you can always look in the appendix if you want to work with a property not yet discussed.

One property of fields, the **lockText** property, has an interesting side effect. Setting the **lockText** of a field to true makes it impossible to type into the field or to delete text from it; it protects the field's contents from the browsing or typing user. But it also allows mouse messages to reach the field; you can click on a locked field as you click on a button, and mouse handlers in the field's script can do all the things that such handlers in a button script would do. We didn't discuss **mouseUp** or **mouseDown** handlers for fields in the last chapter, and this is why. Using this knowledge, can you see how to modify the About button script and add a script to the field so that the field replaces the button when the button is clicked and the button replaces the field when you click in the field? In other words, exactly one of the two objects will be visible at any one time, and clicking on either object makes it disappear and the other appear.

Controlling the Size, Shape, and Location of Objects

It is also possible under script control to make an object appear at a particular location or to resize the object. There are two techniques for doing these things: setting the appropriate property, and using the **show** and **hide** commands, which were used in the About scripts of the last chapter.

The **show** and **hide** commands display or hide the menu bar, a window, or an object from view. Four syntax variations dealing with hiding background and card pictures were added in version 1.2. The full syntax specifications for these two commands are:

```
Hide menuBar
Hide <window>
Hide card window
Hide <object>
Hide card picture
Hide background picture
Hide picture <card>
Hide picture <background>
```

and:

```
Show cards
Show <count> cards
Show menubar
```

```
Show <window>
Show card window
Show <object>
Show card picture
Show background picture
Show picture <card>
Show picture <background>
Show <window> at <location>
Show card window at <location>
Show <object> at <location>
```

The <window> parameter must be one of the following window descriptors:

```
pattern window,
tool window,
message window,
```

or any other synonym for the message box.

The **show** and **hide** commands can do nifty things. Here are some examples:

```
On mouseDown
  Show pattern window
End mouseDown

On mouseUp
  Hide pattern window
End mouseUp
```

This pair of mouse handlers for a button script allow you to pop the pattern window up temporarily to see what painting pattern is currently selected. A click will then send it away.

And here's a shy button that sometimes jumps away from the pointer:

```
On mouseEnter
  If random(2) = 2
  Then show me at 250,300
  Else show me at 250,200
```

```
End mouseEnter
```

It is also possible to control the placement and size and shape of HyperCard objects by setting the appropriate properties. The **rectangle** and **location** properties position the corners and centerpoint, respectively, of an object, measured from the upper left corner of the card window. (Their descriptions in the HyperTalk Properties appendix list some exceptions, but the exceptions are not important for what we are doing here.)

A value for the **rectangle** property consists of four numbers separated by commas. These represent, in order, the pixel distance of the left edge of the object from the left edge of the card window (0 to 512), the pixel distance of the top of the object from the top of the card window (0 to 342), the pixel distance of the right edge of the object from the left edge of the card window (0 to 512), and the pixel distance of the bottom of the object from the top of the card window (0 to 342).

A value for the **location** property consists of two numbers separated by commas. These represent the horizontal and vertical pixel distances of the center of the object from the left and top edges of the card window, respectively.

It is even possible to hide an object by using negative coordinates.

```
Set the loc of card button "test" to -50,-50
```

Version 1.2 of HyperCard introduced several new properties for controlling the position and shape and size of an object. The **left**, **top**, **right**, and **bottom** of an object are identical to the first, second, third, and fourth items of the **rectangle** of the object. Adjusting the **rectangle** of an object can resize it, but these four properties can only be used to reposition an object. They are more efficient for this purpose than the **location** property. Each of the properties **topLeft** and **bottomRight** consists of a pair of numbers separated by a comma. **TopLeft** represents the top left corner of the object, and is identical to the first two numbers of the object's **rectangle**; **bottomRight** represents the bottom right corner and is identical to the other two **rectangle** numbers.

The following button script "tiles" one button with respect to another; that is, it sets the size and shape properties of the target button to those of the reference button, and places the target button next to the reference button. This is not terribly useful as it stands, but later in the book it will become part of a more complex script that tiles many buttons on a card.

It uses a new command, the **ask** command. **Ask** is documented fully in the HyperTalk Commands appendix and discussed in some detail in the next chapter, but here it is sufficient to see that **ask** prompts the user for input, which it stores in the handy variable **it**.

```
On mouseUp
  -- This handler prompts the user for
  -- the names of two buttons,
  -- then positions the second next to
  -- the first, adjusting the shape of
  -- the second to that of the first.
  Ask "What reference button?"
  Put it into a
  Ask "What target button?"
  Put it into b
  Set rect of card button b ¬
  to rect of card button a
  Set left of card button b ¬
  to 1+right of card button a
End mouseUp
```

One of the few properties of an object that is not directly settable is the **number** property. HyperCard sets and adjusts this property as you add and delete objects. For that reason, it is not wise to write scripts that depend on the value of this property; it can change unexpectedly. A technique for adjusting even this property is presented in Chapter 10. The technique also turns out to be useful in dealing with the problem of buttons and fields obscuring other buttons and fields.

Merely showing or hiding objects or setting properties in response to a mouse click is not very useful, of course. As important as knowing how to achieve these effects is knowing when to invoke them. A useful exercise is to look over the events and messages presented in the previous chapter and consider which of these could serve to trigger one of the effects discussed here. For example, many stacks hide the message box when they are opened. This requires a stack script like this:

```
On openStack
  Hide message box
End openStack
```

The last example of a script that manipulates a visual property of an object will operate on cards, and will be the first animation technique in this chapter. Later in this chapter I will discuss other animation techniques, but there is no simpler animation technique than the **show cards** form of the **show** command. You simply create a stack of cards with pictures on them and let **show cards** fan through the pictures. Since you want to focus all attention on the pictures, you might hide distractions like the menu bar and the message box. It's the technique used in a very nice animation stack from Acme Dot Co. called HyperMutoscopes. Here's a near-minimal implementation of the technique:

```
On openStack
  Hide menubar
  Hide message box
  Show all cards
End openStack
```

Dynamic Painting

Up to this point, this chapter has dealt with tools for controlling the visual aspects of HyperCard objects from within scripts. It now moves on to the script control of HyperCard's paint tools, paint properties, and paint patterns to affect pictures at the background and card levels.

Consider this card script:

```
On openCard
  Set the textAlign of card field "Title" to left
  Set textFont of card field "Title" to New York
  Set textStyle of card field "Title" to plain
  Set textSize of card field "Title" to 12
  Put "Welcome to..." into card field "Title"
  Set the textAlign of card field "Title" ¬
  to center
  Wait 50
```

```
    Set textFont of card field "Title" to New York
    Set textStyle of card field "Title" to bold
    Set textSize of card field "Title" to 24
    Put the name of me into card field "Title"
  End openCard
```

This script uses the techniques already introduced to type a title dramatically across the top of the screen when its card is opened. (It assumes a card field at the top of the screen with the name "Title," and it uses a new command, **wait**, which does nothing more than cause a delay in execution, here for dramatic effect.) Now consider the following one:

```
  On openCard
    -- Clear space for the title.
    Choose eraser tool
    Drag from 0,25 to 512,25
    -- Type the title directly onto the card.
    Choose text tool
    Set textAlign to center
    Set textFont to Boston
    Set textStyle to bold
    Set textSize to 12
    Click at 250,30
    Type the short name of this card
    -- Go back to the default tool.
    Choose browse tool
  End openCard
```

This script achieves a similar effect, but instead of typing into a field, it types its message onto the card itself, after erasing a suitable area. It uses the command **choose**, a powerful command that will see much use in this chapter. **Choose** does exactly what choosing a tool from the tool menu does. In this case, we choose first the **eraser** tool, then the **text** tool, and finally the **browse** tool.

We can in fact choose any tool in the tools menu. Consider this script:

```
  On mouseUp
    Set polySides to 6
    Set lineSize to 9
    Choose regular polygon tool
```

```
    Drag from 200,200 to 210,210
    Choose browse tool
  End mouseUp
```

Notice that using paint tools in a script requires thinking about the mouse clicks and moves necessary to achieve an effect, and specifying these actions; for example, the **drag** action in this script. This is a lot of effort for the minimal effects that these scripts display, but the **if** control structure introduced in the last chapter lets us decide between visual images:

```
  If showTheBkPic is true
  Then
    Show background picture
  Else
    Hide background picture
    Show card picture
  End if
```

The **if** structure allows this script to display either the background or the card picture. The word **showTheBkPict** is intended to be a variable into which some previous action has placed a value, either **true** or **false**. This script also shows the use of the **show** and **hide** commands with pictures, introduced in version 1.2.

The following script shows a variation on the **show cards** animation technique. This variation allows more control over the steps, and introduces the **repeat** control structure.

```
  On mouseUp
    Repeat with i=1 to the number of cards
      Go to card i
      Hide background picture
      Show card picture
    End repeat
  End mouseUp
```

The **repeat** and the **if** control structures, along with the handler structures, make up all the large-scale organizational tools of the language. Yes, "handler structures" with an "s"; there is one handler structure we have not discussed yet. After you have seen the second handler structure in the next chapter, you will know all the ways there are to structure HyperTalk code.

The Repeat Structure

The **`repeat`** control structure has the following syntax variations, which are explained fully in the HyperTalk Control Structures appendix:

```
Repeat for <count> times
  <commands>
End repeat

Repeat for <count>
  <commands>
End repeat

Repeat <count> times
  <commands>
End repeat

Repeat<count>
  <commands>
End repeat

Repeat forever
  <commands>
End repeat

Repeat until <logicalValue>
 <commands>
End repeat

Repeat while <logicalValue>
  <commands>
End repeat

Repeat with <count> = <lowCount> to <highCount>
  <commands>
End repeat
```

```
Repeat with <count> = <highCount> ¬
downTo <lowCount>
  <commands>
End repeat
```

Repeat causes the commands within its scope to be executed repeatedly. Like some variations of the **if** control structure and like the message handler structure, it consists of an opening line that begins with a keyword (**Repeat**) and closes with an **End** line, enclosing some number of lines of HyperTalk code between.

Knowing that, we can understand the script in which we introduced the **repeat** structure. It executes the sequence of commands between its first and last lines, then executes the whole sequence again, for as many times as are indicated in the first line—in this case, for as many times as there are cards in the stack. If each repetition were identical, this would be a pretty boring exercise. But the first line of the **repeat** structure indicates that the variable **i** is to get a new value on each repetition, the values running from 1 to the number of cards. Since the first line after the **repeat** line sends us to card **i**, we can see that this handler walks us through the cards of the stack, from card 1 to the end. The subsequent commands within the structure act on the *current* card, so they are operating on card **i** as well.

In general, the **repeat** structure only affects how often something is done. You may find it useful in developing scripts to get them working without **repeat**s first, then add the **repeat** structures after you know you're getting the right action performed.

The following script uses the **repeat** structure and the paint brush to draw a repetitive design dynamically. It changes the brush shape via the **brush** property, and switches patterns via the **pattern** property. It does several things not discussed yet, including placing **repeat** structures within **repeat** structures. Taking it apart with the aid of the appendices would be a good exercise.

```
On openCard
  -- This handler produces moiré patterns.
  -- It's halted by holding the mouse button
  -- down. A quick click of the mouse button will
  -- not stop it, but will force it to select a
```

```
    -- new pattern to use in its drawing.
    Put 256 into h
    Put 171 into v
    Choose brush tool
    Set brush to 32
    Put 3 into gap
    Put 0 into pat
    Repeat until the mouse is down
      Put pat into oldPat
      Repeat until pat is not oldPat
        Put random(31)+1 into pat
      End repeat
      Set pattern to pat
      Put 0 into i
      Repeat until i=87 or the mouse is down
        Put i*gap into j
        Drag from h,v to h+j,v-h+j
        Drag from h,v to h-j,v-h+j
        Drag from h,v to h+j,v+h-j
        Drag from h,v to h-j,v+h-j
        Add 1 to i
      End repeat
    End repeat
    Choose browse tool
  End openCard
```

The properties **`brush`** and **`pattern`** are not properties of objects, but painting properties. The full set of painting properties, along with possible values, is spelled out in the HyperTalk Properties appendix, but the following list covers the most interesting ones. You might want to write a simple button script to test the effect of setting some of these properties.

HyperTalk Global and Painting Properties

```
dragSpeed        editBkgnd        powerKeys
brush            centered         filled
grid             lineSize         multiple
multiSpace       pattern          polySides
textAlign        textFont         textHeight
textSize         textStyle
```

Controlling the paint tools and properties from scripts is a way of producing animation effects in your stacks. Here is a simple script that demonstrates a painting animation trick:

```
On mouseUp
  Choose brush tool
  Set brush to 1
  Put "8,8" into a
  Put "8,334" into b
  Put "504,334" into c
  Put "504,8" into d
  Repeat 10
    Set pattern to 16
    Drag from a to b
    Set pattern to 1
    Drag from d to a
    Set pattern to 16
    Drag from b to c
    Set pattern to 1
    Drag from a to b
    Set pattern to 16
    Drag from c to d
    Set pattern to 1
    Drag from b to c
    Set pattern to 16
    Drag from d to a
    Set pattern to 1
    Drag from c to d
  End repeat
  Drag from d to a
  Choose browse tool
End mouseUp
```

This script also demonstrates a phenomenon common in beginners' scripts: lack of sufficient generalization. There are a lot of lines of code here to do one very specific and simple thing. That's inefficient. How could the script be generalized? First, by removing the constants. If all those 1s and 16s and the like were replaced by variables, the variables could get their values from a field or the user, so that different kinds of boxes of different sizes and at different locations could be drawn with the same script. Second, in this script there is a sequence of almost identical pairs of lines; it is usually possible in such a case to find a way to turn the entire sequence into a couple of lines inside a **repeat** structure, and that is the case here. You might try your hand at it.

This discussion of dynamic painting tricks using global and painting properties and the **repeat** structure has only gestured in the direction of the tools and given some simple examples of their use. The ability to draw under script control is a very rich area for exploration. But the purpose of this book is not to examine HyperTalk as a language for graphics or visual design, but to show how to use the language. One important area in the control of painting will be discussed in Chapter 8: the control of painting effects like rotation.

This chapter will conclude with a look at the most dramatic and perhaps the simplest of visual tools that HyperTalk provides: special effects.

Special Effects

Thus far, this chapter has shown how to use the visual properties of objects to control the appearance, size, shape, and location of the objects from within scripts; and how to use the painting properties and tools to achieve painting effects from within scripts. HyperCard also supports certain visual special effects (not to be confused with the painting effects). These effects apply to the entire card window, and *only* take effect on leaving a card via the **go** command. The complete list of visual effects is: **plain, dissolve, checkerboard, venetian blinds, scroll up, scroll down, scroll right, scroll left, iris open, iris close, wipe up, wipe down, wipe right, wipe left, zoom open, zoom close, zoom out, zoom in, barn door open,** and **barn door close**.

The following scripts show the use of the **visual** command to specify visual effects:

```
On mouseUp
  Visual wipe left
   Go next
End mouseUp

On mouseUp
  Visual wipe right
   Go prev
End mouseUp
```

The complete list of syntax variations for the **visual** command is:

```
Visual <effect>
Visual <effect> <speed>
Visual <effect> to <image>
Visual <effect> <speed> to <image>
Visual effect <effect>
Visual effect <effect> <speed>
Visual effect <effect> to <image>
Visual effect <effect> <speed> to <image>
```

The <effect> must be one of the effects listed above; <speed> can be any of **very slow** or **very slowly**, **slow** or **slowly**, **fast**, or **very fast**; and <image> may be any of **white**, **gray**, **black**, or **card**. The only way to see what they do is literally to see them; you should try them out.

There is one other way to invoke these special effects: the **unlock** command, introduced in version 1.2. Its purpose will be covered later in the book, but its syntax is comparable to that of the **visual** command. Here is an example of its use:

```
UnLock screen with dissolve slowly to black
```

Visual effects do not take effect when the **visual** (or **unlock**) command is executed, but when you leave a card. For this reason, it is logical to place them near the **go** command that will cause them to take effect. In fact, Apple recommends strongly that you do place them so.

5

Mastering the Ins and Outs

About this Chapter

The subject matter of this chapter is not difficult. It's all about getting information into and out of your stacks: input and output, or I/O. What you need to know about input and output is simply what HyperTalk commands support I/O operations and how you use them, and that's what this chapter supplies. In passing, though, it also introduces some more difficult scripts and the topic of user-defined functions.

Occasionally, example code will include a detail that you haven't seen before. You should keep in mind that the point of any example is the point of that example; you don't have to understand every detail if you understand how the example exemplifies the point.

But you should also begin referring regularly to the appendixes to clarify or expand upon points discussed in the chapters. For most commands in this chapter, I give only an abbreviated description to get the idea across and to get on with the story. The full description is in the HyperTalk Commands appendix. There are individual appendixes on structures, the hierarchy, commands, functions, properties, messages, constants, operators, and other special words of the language. Each appendix begins with an explanation of its subject matter; the HyperTalk Operators appendix, for example, starts out with an explanation of what operators are. The HyperTalk Vocabulary appendix lists every word of importance in the HyperCard universe and indicates where you can find it described in the other appendixes.

About Input and Output

One of the simplest models of the generic computer program is the input-process-output model. Information comes in, is processed, and the result is sent back out. This chapter covers two-thirds of the model: input and output, particularly input from the user via the keyboard or input from disk files, and output through the speaker or modem or printer or to disk files.

Listening to the User

One of the keys to writing useful programs is responding to user input. A program that can stop and ask the user for information or present the user with a set of choices is a more useful tool than one that merely does its pre-programmed thing. HyperTalk has two commands for getting input from the user: **ask** and **answer**. Both these commands present the user with a dialog box and wait for the user to make a selection.

The basic syntax of the **answer** command is:

```
Answer <question>
Answer <question> with <reply>
```

The **answer** command displays a dialog box containing a question or prompt and from one to three labelled buttons. The last of the buttons will be displayed with a double border indicating that it is the default response.

At this point, the user must click on one of the buttons. Which button the user selects determines what value will be placed in the system variable **it**. If the user presses the Return key, the default response will be placed in the variable **it**.

Your script supplies the question or prompt and the reply alternatives. (If it supplies more than one reply, these must be separated by the word **or**. Three alternatives are the maximum.) These can be any expressions interpretable as text strings. Since HyperCard will interpret almost anything as a text string if possible, this is not very restricting. The parameters can be literal numbers, variables containing numeric values, logical values, and uninitialized variables.

The **answer** command is a convenient way to offer a restricted set of choices to the user; the **ask** command serves a somewhat different purpose.

You can use the **ask** command in these ways:

```
Ask <question>
Ask <question> with <reply>
```

The **ask** command displays a dialog box displaying the <question>, a text window that in turn contains the highlighted default <reply> if any, and two buttons, labelled "OK" and "Cancel."

At this point, the user must take some action. The user can click on Cancel or click on OK, and can modify the text in the text window or leave it alone. What the user does determines what value will be placed in the system variable **it**. If the user clicks on Cancel, with or without modifying the text in the text window, the special value **empty** will be placed in the variable **it**. If the user clicks on OK, the value in the text window will be placed in the variable **it**, either the default value supplied in the **ask** command or a value keyed in by the user.

The **ask** command is the primary means for getting arbitrary input from the user. Here are some examples of the **answer** and **ask** commands in use:

```
Answer "Sort cards by:" with "First name" ¬
or "Last name"
Put it into sortOrder

Ask "Who's buried in Grant's tomb?"

Ask "Edit the script of..." with "card button 1"
If it is not empty then Edit script of it

Ask "t/f" with true
If it then Put "Correct."
```

Talking to the User

In addition to its use in getting information out of the user, the **answer** command also sees service in delivering messages to the user. Without a <reply> parameter, it can be used as an Alert box to notify the user of a situation that requires attention, or as a debugging aid by supplying a value to be monitored in the <question>

```
Answer "Staff meeting in five minutes."

Answer "Current count value:" && countVal
```

A more involved message might deserve a field of its own, hidden when not in use. But HyperTalk also provides more sophisticated ways of communicating with the user, including communicating via sound. The Macintosh can output digitized sounds, including music and speech; HyperTalk puts control of these modalities in your hands.

It's all done with what are called sound resources. The system beep that annoys you when you make a mistake (and that is invoked by the HyperTalk command **beep**) is a sound resource, and you can substitute a different beep sound if you like. You do this is via the control panel desk accessory, by selecting the sound panel within it and picking a different beep sound. Later I'll describe how to extend your choices beyond those Apple gives you.

There two kinds of sound resources: beep sounds are one, and the sounds used by HyperCard to put out music and speech are the other. HyperCard comes with three of these sound resources: Harpsichord, Boing, and Silence. This list can also be extended.

All the music-producing capability of HyperTalk is invested in the **play** command, which plays back the digitized sound stored in a sound resource through the sound synthesizer built into the Macintosh. The syntax of the **play** command is complex:

```
Play <voice>
Play <voice> tempo <tempo>
Play <voice> <notes>
Play <voice> tempo <tempo> <notes>
Play stop
```

The <voice> parameter specifies the sound resource. The <tempo> parameter must be a positive number, high numbers representing faster tempos. The <tempo> parameter should not be used unless the <notes> parameter is used. The <notes> parameter consists of a sequence of notes, with the entire sequence surrounded by quotes and individual notes separated by spaces. Each note consists of from one to five components, as follows:

Note value: a, b, c, d, e, f, g, or silence (yields a rest). Required.

Accidental: # or b for sharp or flat, respectively. Optional.

Octave: a number. Use 4 for the octave based at Middle C. Optional.

Duration: w,h,q,e,s,t,x for whole note, half, quarter, eighth, sixteenth, thirty-second, and sixty-fourth, respectively. Optional.

Extension: either a dot (.) or a 3 for a dotted note or triple, respectively. Optional. If an extension is used, a duration is mandatory.

Note value and octave can also be specified by a single number. In this representation, 60 represents Middle C, and each half-step up or down is represented by a number one higher or lower, respectively. Some examples of legal <notes> parameter values are: `"c#"`, `"61"`, `"c e g"`, `"c3#e dq g gq."`. All parameters except for the accidentals stay in effect until changed.

The `Play` command allows you to write programs that play music. There are some eccentricities in the use of the `Play` command. Some sound resources are of long duration, and the `Play` command will continue to play them until they are finished unless cut off by the tempo setting or by the command `Play stop`. The `Play` command works in the background, so other commands can go on executing while the `Play` command is making sounds.

Here are some examples of the use of the play command:

```
Play harpsichord
Play silence
```

```
Play sitar tempo 400 "c3#e d3q g3q g3q. c3#e ¬
d3q g3h d3#e e3q a3q a3q. d3e e3q a3h"
```

But where are the sound resources? How do you add a sitar sound to your stack? Every Macintosh file, including HyperCard and all stacks, can have what is called a resource fork. A resource fork is a part of a file containing code or other special information. There are many kinds of resources; some of the most important for HyperCard use are fonts, icons, sounds, and external commands and functions. The ability to place resources in any file means, for example, that a document can use a peculiar font not used by any other document or application, and your stacks can have their own specialized fonts, icons, sounds, and the like.

Resources are created in various ways: an external command might be written in another language like Pascal, a sound resource might be a snippet of speech captured on tape and imported to the Mac using special equipment, an icon might be originally sketched in MacPaint. How you get your hands on the resource is another matter: resources live in files, so you might get resources in public domain or shareware or commercial stacks that come into your hands, or you might find useful resources in other kinds of files. Finally, getting the resource into your stack requires a program that operates on resources. Apple supplies you with ResEdit, which does the job, but there are some tools better adapted to HyperCard resource management.

An appendix in this book gives more information on the use of resources generally, and the code section of the book includes a stack that moves resources around for you, keeping track of where they are installed in your stacks.

HyperTalk provides a handy function for dealing with sounds, also.

A word or two about functions is in order here. A function is an element of the HyperTalk language that generates or computes a value. A variable or container is a slot that holds a value, but a function is code that produces a value on demand. Some functions require one or more parameters, which are values supplied to the function for its use in computing the value that it will return. For example, the square root function, discussed in the next chapter, needs to be given the number whose square root is desired; that's its parameter. You invoke a function (that is, cause it to produce its value) by placing its name (and any necessary parameters, in parentheses) where you want its value in your code. The concepts of returning a value, invoking a function, and working with function parameters will take on more meaning as we work with them in this and succeeding chapters.

The **sound** function requires no parameter, and returns the name of the currently active sound resource; i.e., the sound that is playing, or "done" if no sound is playing. The latter case is particularly useful, since you will frequently want to let the sound finish before proceeding. Here's how you use it:

```
If the sound is "done" then go Home
```

A sound resource is nothing more than digitized sound, so there is no reason why that sound can't be speech. There are many recorded speech segments available on electronic bulletin boards. However, you shouldn't assume that you will be able to download a digitized dictionary and begin constructing sentences from the words; combining words into spoken sentences requires the ability to modify the words themselves, and resources don't permit this. Combining words into sentences is a nontrivial task. Nevertheless, you can certainly use prerecorded speech segments in the place of or along with visual messages to the user via the **play** command.

Talking to the World

As the blue boxers of the 1970s learned to the telephone company's chagrin, the telephone system has a language of its own, composed of tones. Whistle the right notes and you dial the phone. That's what HyperCard's Phone stack does, via the **dial** command.

The **dial** command generally lets a modem produce the tones, being satisfied to send digits and modem control characters out over the modem port of the Macintosh. It can also produce the tones, sending them out through the speaker, and theoretically you could hold your telephone receiver up to the Mac and let the computer beep the number into the phone. You need to use a modem to transfer data, of course, and may need some sort of phone dialer hardware if you want to use your computer to dial the phone for you.

The syntax of the **dial** command is:

```
Dial <phonenumber>
Dial <phonenumber> with modem
Dial <phonenumber> with modem <modem string>
```

You'll find more on the syntax of the **dial** command in the HyperTalk Commands appendix, and you'll need to refer to a modem manual for specification of the modem control characters. You might find it enlightening to study the (rather involved) script in the HyperCard Phone stack, not just to see how it handles such telephonic issues as area codes and prefixes, but also as an example of some subtle programming techniques.

Printing

There are three broad categories of printing actions supported by HyperTalk, each taking a different syntax. These go beyond the options offered in the menu. You can: print an external document, print one card or all cards of a stack, and print selected cards.

The ability to print an external document is, for most HyperCard applications, a sort of auxiliary service; nice but not to the point. It becomes particularly relevant if you are developing a stack to help manage your desktop, which is an excellent application for HyperCard. You can print MacWrite or MacDraw documents, for example, using all the proper formatting. HyperCard will actually launch the required application and use it to print the chosen document. You do it like this:

```
Print chapter5 with MacWrite 4.6
```

If you want to print the current card or all cards of the current stack, all you have to say is something like:

```
Print card
Print card 3
Print 3 cards
Print all cards
```

What you can't do using this approach is to print several selected cards in a format placing more than one card on a page. The reason for this is clear on reflection: if you wanted to print 15 cards 8 to a page, HyperCard would do this by saving up cards until it had 8, then printing them, and it would not print the last 7 cards because it would be forever waiting for the card that completes the page.

For this situation, HyperTalk provides the **open printing** and **close printing** commands. These commands define a print job. **Close printing** terminates the job and flushes the buffer, causing all the remaining cards to be printed. It's important not to attempt to print an external file while in a print job.

Here's what print jobs look like:

```
Ask "How many cards?" with "one"
Put it into howMany
Ask "Starting with card number..." with "one"
Put it into startCard
Put howMany into field "count" of card "Title"
Open printing
Print card "Title"
Go to card startCard
Print howMany cards
Close printing
```

You can have more than one print job in a handler, and can have all three modes of printing in the same handler, as long as you don't attempt to print an external file while in a print job. Setting up a print job with **open printing** and **close printing** basically corresponds to using one of the menu commands Print stack... or Print report..., while printing with the **print** command alone is analogous to using the Print card menu selection.

HyperTalk also supplies a couple of constants that can have special significance in printing: **formFeed** and **lineFeed**. These special characters represent signals to the printer to move to the next page and next line, respectively. In ordinary uses of HyperTalk, you won't use these, since HyperTalk doesn't give line-by-line control of the printing process, but specialized applications could make use of them.

Reading and Writing Files

HyperTalk has several commands that support reading from and writing to text files on disk. These are read, write, open, and close.

The commands **`Open`**, **`Close`**, and either **`Write`** or **`Read`** are always used together when exporting text to or importing it from text-only external files. The **`Open`** command opens the text file (creating it if necessary), the **`Close`** command closes it to prevent inadvertent access to it, and between the **`Open`** and **`Close`** commands, any number of **`Read`** and/or **`Write`** commands can be executed to copy text from and to the file. It is not possible to use the **`Read`** and **`Write`** commands to access an external file without first using **`Open`** to open the file. It is not possible to close a file with the **`Close`** command unless it has been opened with the **`Open`** command.

The **`read`** command has the syntax variations:

```
Read from file <file> until <character>
Read from file for <number>
```

and the **`write`** command has only one syntactic form:

```
Write <text> to file <file>
```

Here are examples of their use:

```
Put "Major Major" into Major
Open file Major
Write "Major" to file Major
Close file Major

Open file Major
Read from file Major until "r"
Put it
Close file Major
```

Writing Functions to Filter Character Streams

Your scripts do not have to accept and transmit data uncritically. It is entirely possible to filter the data as it passes in or out. One set of tools for filtering data is the pair of functions **charToNum** and **numToChar**. The **charToNum** function returns the ASCII value corresponding to the first character of **<string>**. (The ASCII values are a standard ordering assigned to characters.) The **numToChar** function returns the ASCII character corresponding to **<number>**. If you know that the data you are receiving needs to be so converted, you can write an input handler that converts each character. Being able to convert characters to their ASCII values and back allows you to, for example, convert lowercase letters to their uppercase equivalents. Here's how you invoke **charToNum**:

```
Put charToNum("C") into the message box
```

HyperTalk also lets you create your own functions. Doing this is very much like writing message handlers. In fact, to create a new function, you write a function handler. A function handler differs from a message handler in these ways:

- a message handler starts with the line **On <messageName>** and a function handler starts with the line **Function <functionName>**;
- a message handler is invokes by using the message name as a message in a script and a function handler is invoked by using its function name as a function in a script;
- a function handler, like any function, returns a value; and
- a function handler contains a **return** command, which identifies the value the function will return on completion.

Here is a very simple function handler. All it does is give us an alias for the **charToNum** function. **CharToNum** is a long name for a function that you might use heavily in a script, and this function allows you to use the somewhat shorter but more cryptic **c2n**.

```
Function c2n theChar
  Return charToNum(theChar)
```

```
End c2n
```

You can now invoke this function just as you would **charToNum**:

```
Put charToNum("C") into the message box
```

There are two good reasons *not* to use this function handler: **C2n** *is* cryptic, and it will slow down any script in which it appears. This is because the interpretation of the **c2n** function has to be done on top of the interpretation of the **charToNum** function. But it does show how to write a function handler.

It is inefficient to examine input or output character by character in HyperTalk. If you really need to filter input or output in this way, you would be better off finding an external function to do the job—or writing such an external function. External commands, resources which are compiled code written in another language, are discussed further in Chapter 8. One reason to filter character streams in HyperTalk is to learn more about using the language. And if the external function you need is not available and you don't want to deal with writing external code, you will have to do the job in HyperTalk anyway. The rewards can be significant; for example, you might have a large name-and-address database, built up over a long time, that you want to import to HyperCard. Such a transfer is likely to require some filtering of special characters. Chapter 7 will show how to do some simple filtering operations by writing your own functions.

In introducing functions, we have touched on the last element of the structure of the language. You now know all there is to know about the large structure of HyperTalk, and everything else is mere details and applications.

HyperTalk Language Elements Discussed in this Chapter

This chapter dealt with these HyperTalk words: **answer**, **ask**, **beep**, **charToNum**, **close**, **dial**, **done**, **file**, **formFeed**, **function**, **lineFeed**, **modem**, **numToChar**, **open**, **play**, **print**, **printing**, **read**, **return**, **sound**, **tempo**, **write**. It also introduced the idea of writing your own functions.

6
Logic and Math

"What's one and one and one and one and one and one and one and one and one and one?"
"I don't know," said Alice. "I lost count."
"She can't do addition," said the Red Queen.

–Lewis Carroll

About Logic and Math

This chapter gets deeper as it goes along. Beginning programmers and those who want with all their hearts to avoid math whenever and to whatever extent possible may read the first half and hurry past the rest.

Serious programmers, those who will be developing stacks for others' use or who are just doing this for fun but take their fun seriously should know most of the material in the first two parts, but might skip the very last part.

The last part consists of specialized topics of even less general interest, and should probably only be read on first pass by the dedicated or compulsive.

Using Numbers

In Chapter 3 you began programming in HyperTalk by typing commands into the message box. That's how we will begin examining the tools HyperTalk provides for mathematical computations. We will start by using the message box as a simple calculator. Try each of the following expressions in the message box, pressing Return after each one to see the result of the calculation. (Like most programming languages, HyperTalk uses * for multiplication and ^ for exponentiation, raising a number to a power.)

```
2 + 2
2 * 2
2 - 2
2 / 2
2 ^ 2
2 + 3 * 4
```

That last example could have seemed ambiguous: do you add first, or multiply? It makes a difference; if you add first, you get 20, but if you multiply and then add, you get 14. In the first case it is as though the expression were written **(2 + 3) * 4**, and in the second case, as though written **2 + (3 * 4)**.

The rules regarding the evaluation of mathematical expressions in HyperTalk, as well as the use of parentheses, are essentially those of ordinary arithmetic, so the answer is that the multiplication is performed first, just as in ordinary arithmetic. These rules are referred to as operator precedence rules, but you don't need to take a refresher course in math to get the rules in mind. The best way to get comfortable with them is to try various complicated mathematical expressions in the message box and on paper. If you use small numbers, even complicated expressions are not hard to work out by hand, and you will become more comfortable with HyperTalk's calculations if you have some hands-on experience with the same calculations. The use of pencil-and-paper calculations is also an important technique often overlooked by programmers. And when you need to resolve any uncertainty about how expressions are evaluated, the HyperTalk Operators appendix explains the precedence of operators fully.

Here are some slightly more complex message-box expressions:

```
4 * 5 / 10
3.14 * 7 * 7
9 / 3 / 2
2 + 4 ^ 2
```

```
(2 + 4) ^ 2
-1 * 5
```

Using Number Words

The HyperTalk language includes an extensive mathematical vocabulary, most of it mercifully intuitive. It includes the following items:

- Cardinals: **zero, one, two, three, four, five, six, seven, eight, nine, ten**. These constants, described in the HyperTalk Constants appendix, can be used in place of the numerals they name.

- Ordinals: **first, second, third, fourth, fifth, sixth, seventh, eighth, ninth, tenth**. These words can be used in chunk expressions to identify objects or components of objects. They were introduced in Chapter 3.

- Operators: **(,), -, not, ^, *, /, div, mod, +, <, >, <=, >=, ≤, ≥, =, is, <>, ≠, is not, and, or**. These operators are used in forming mathematical and logical expressions. You have already seen many of them in this and earlier chapters. The ≤, ≥, and ≠ operators are produced by typing Option-<, Option->, and Option-=, respectively, and are synonyms for the **<=, >=,** and **<>** operators, and mean, reading from left to right: less than or equal to, greater than or equal to, and not equal to. The other two angle-bracket operators, **<** and **>**, represent less than and greater than. Those operators in this list that have not been discussed yet are all logical or integer arithmetic operators, and will be covered a little later in the chapter when those topics are addressed.

- Functions: **Abbreviated date, abbrev date, abbr date, abs, annuity, atan, average, charToNum, compound, cos, date, diskSpace, exp, exp1, exp2, heapSpace, ln, ln1, log2, long date, long time, max, min, numToChar, random, round, seconds, secs, short date, short time, sin, sqrt, stackSpace, tan,**

ticks, time, trunc, version. All of these functions are described in the HyperTalk Functions appendix, and the first example listed in that appendix for each function is intended to be typed into the message box for get-acquainted purposes.

Some of these functions perform pretty basic mathematical operations, like the square root and maximum and minimum and rounding functions. You should be aware that these functions exist and know where they are documented in the appendix so you can look them up when you need them. Others you may only look up *if* you need them. Some of these perform trigonometric functions (**atan, cos, sin, tan**), two of them perform financial calculations (**annuity, compound**), others do logarithmic calculations (**exp, exp1, exp2, ln, ln1, log2**), and most of the rest don't do math but just return values that are numbers. They're useful numbers, though, that can be examined or used in calculations.

- Commands: **add, subtract, multiply, divide, convert**. The last of these is used in working with date formats, and the first four implement the four basic arithmetic operations. Since HyperTalk includes operators for adding, subtracting, multiplying, and dividing numbers, these four commands are redundant. Their chief value is in adding readability to scripts. A common operation in scripts is incrementing a counter, and it is arguably more clear to do this with

  ```
  Add 1 to counter
  ```

  than with

  ```
  Put counter + 1 into counter
  ```

Here are some one-liners that you can type into the message box to try out a few of the numeric functions. You can come up with more of your own, or find a one-liner in the function's entry in the appendix.

```
abs(-10)
sqrt(16)
```

```
cos0.5)
log2(8)
round(4.6)
round(4.4)
```

Using Integer Arithmetic and Logic

Integers are whole numbers, as opposed to decimals (which are often called real numbers or floating-point numbers). Integer arithmetic is arithmetic in which operations are performed on integers and produce integer results.

If you know something about how integers are handled in other programming languages, you should note that HyperTalk does not have an integer data type: integers are not treated differently from floating-point numbers. HyperTalk does support integer arithmetic with two operators and two functions. The addition and subtraction and multiplication operators and commands already have the property of generating only integer results if given only integer values, but division is another matter. HyperTalk supports the integer arithmetic brand of division with the two operators **div** and **mod**. These return the integer portion and remainder of dividing one number by another, as the following script shows:

```
On mouseUp
  Ask "Dividend:"
  Put it into dividend
  Ask "Divisor:"
  Put it into divisor
  Put "Quotient:" && dividend div divisor ¬
  && dividend mod divisor & "/" & dividend
End mouseUp
```

HyperTalk also provides two functions for turning a decimal number into an integer. These are **round** and **trunc**, and they both round a number to an integer value. Essentially, **round** rounds to the nearest integer and **trunc** rounds downward, although you should check the HyperTalk Functions appendix for the full story. There is another subtlety in the **round** and **trunc** story that will be revealed later in this chapter.

You can test the effects of **round** and **trunc** by typing each directly into the message box. Here are some telling tests:

```
round(12.4)
trunc(12.4)
round(12.6)
trunc(12.6)
round(12.5)
round(13.5)
round(-12.4)
trunc(-12.4)
```

Titling this chapter "Logic and Math" was exaggerating the difficulty, if not the importance, of logical operations in HyperTalk. The fundamentals are simple:

- While there are many possible string values and arithmetic values, there are just two logical values: **true** and **false**.
- Just as string and arithmetic values can be assigned to containers and properties, so can logical values.
- Logical values can be examined and combined to form new logical values.

That doesn't explain what logical values are used for, but you have already seen that. One of the two most important uses of logical values is in the **if** control structure. The **if** structure, you will recall, has the general form:

```
If <logicalValue> then <action1> else <action2>.
```

Any container or expression that has a logical value can serve in the place of **<logicalValue>** in this structure.

The other important use is in properties, and this use is also familiar. Certain properties of objects and certain global and painting properties take logical values, as seen in Chapter 4.

It is possible to use logical property values in **if** structures; for example:

```
If (the visible of card field 1)
Then set the visible of card field 1 to false.
```

But the most common way of producing a logical value for an **`if`** structure is with logical operators. In fact, the example just given would be clearer if written with the logical operator **`is`**:

```
If the visible of card field 1 is true
Then set the visible of card field 1 to false.
```

It may seem odd that **`<`**, **`>`**, **`<=`**, **`>=`**, **`≤`**, **`≥`**, **`=`**, **`<>`**, and ≠ were included in the list of operators earlier in this chapter. They do not appear to "operate" on values in the way that, say, the addition and multiplication operators do. In fact, these operators, called "equivalence operators," do operate on values and produce results. The expression **`1 = 2`** produces a value, the logical value **`false`**. The operators **`is`** and **`is not`** are interchangeable with = and ≠, respectively.

There are also three explicitly logical operators: **`not`**, **`and`**, and **`or`**. The operator **`not`** reverses the truth value of the expression following it, the operator **`and`** produces the result **`true`** if and only if the expressions to its left and right both have the value **`true`**, and the operator **`or`** produces the value **`true`** if either of the expressions to its left and right has the value **`true`**. Along with the equivalence operators, they can be used to combine logical values into logical expressions.

Here are some examples of logical expressions, along with their values:

```
1=1                              value: true
1=2                              value: false
(1=1) and (2=2)                  value: true
(1=1) and (1=2)                  value: false
(1=1) or (1=2)                   value: true
(1=1) and not (1=2)              value: true
false=false                      value: true
(1=1) is true                    value: true
(1≠1) is false                   value: true
(1=1) and ((1=2) or (2=2))       value: true
not true                         value: false
not false                        value: true
```

```
1≤2                            value: true
1≥2 is not true                value: true
```

Mastering Space and Time

HyperTalk provides two functions that get rid of the digits after the decimal point of a number: **round** and **trunc**. Both of these actually change the value of the number, but what if you only want to get rid of the decimal digits on displaying the number, but want the precision retained for future computation? Here is how to deal with this situation:

```
Set numberFormat to 0
```

This line uses the **numberFormat** global property. We used global properties in Chapter 4 for visual effects, but here a global property is serving a mathematical purpose. The **numberFormat** property takes on values like:

```
0
0.00
00.00
0.##
0.######
```

The number of zeroes before or after the decimal point in the value of **numberFormat** indicates how many digits of the number, before or after the decimal point, will be displayed, even if they are zeroes. The # signs indicate the maximum number of digits to be displayed after the decimal point, but trailing zeroes will not be displayed. The first example value (**0**) drops the portion of the number after the decimal point, which is what we were looking for, and the last example value (**0.######**) displays at least one digit to the left of the decimal point and at most six digits to the right; it is HyperCard's default number format.

There are also global or stack properties and functions that concern such space issues as how much disk space is left. You can do more with these than just interrogate them; you can use them in calculations. This script performs a calculation on stack size and free space in the stack to determine the true size of the stack:

```
On openStack
  Global trueSize
  Put the size of me - the freeSize of me ¬
  into trueSize
End openStack
```

Some global properties and functions deal with time. We have seen (in Chapter 3) a script puts the time into a field, but it is also possible to do computations based on the time. The simplest is to compare the time with a constant time:

```
On mouseUp
  Ask "What time is your appointment?"
  Convert it to seconds
  Put it into appointment
  Put the time into now
  Convert now to seconds
  If now > appointment
  Then
    Put "You're late!"
  Else
    Put "Appointment in" ¬
    && (appointment-now) / 60 && "minutes."
  End if
End mouseUp
```

In order to compare two times, this script uses the **convert** command to convert them both to elapsed time. This command works with all time and date values. If we tried to compare two times directly, HyperTalk would do the comparison, but it would do it by treating the times as strings. Thus "10:00 PM" would come out as earlier than "2:00 AM" because that's the way they fall in strict alphabetical order.

Another way of working with elapsed time is to use the **seconds** or the **ticks** function. The **seconds** function returns the number of seconds since some past moment. One call to **seconds** is not very illuminating, but the difference between two calls gives you the number of seconds that elapsed between the two calls, or, in this case, two visits to a stack:

```
On openStack
  Global username,lastVisit
  Put "Welcome to" && ¬
  the short name of this stack & "," && ¬
  userName & "."
  If lastVisit is not empty
  Then
    Wait 50
    Put "I've been counting the seconds."
    Wait 50
    Get the long time
    Put it into t
    Convert t to seconds
    Put "There were" && t-lastVisit & "."
  End if
  Get the long time
  Convert it to seconds
  Put it into lastVisit
End openStack
```

This script is a phoney. It pretends to recognize you and remember how long it's been since you visited the stack, but in fact it just keeps track of the time since *anyone* opened the stack. And if you haven't told HyperCard your name, this script's attempt to read it from the global variable **userName** will fail. Notice that this script uses a different form of the **time** function than the last script did. You might consider what the consequences are.

The real message of that exercise was that you can use the **seconds** function to measure elapsed time, and you can do the same thing with the function **ticks**, which counts sixtieths of a second, for greater precision.

Measuring elapsed time in this way is the secret behind simple profiling tricks. Profiling is a programming method that helps to track down bugs in programs and helps locates inefficient techniques. In its simplest form, it consists of a few commands bracketing a section of code whose performance is suspect. The commands report how long the section of code took to execute, so you can make changes to the code to try to improve its performance. If its performance is far from your expectations, it may be doing something unexpected or not doing something expected, and discoveries like this can lead to finding bugs.

Here is a simple template for profiling a repeat structure:

```
On <whatever>
  <commands>
  Put the ticks into startTime
  <commands you want to time>
  Put the ticks - startTime into elapsedTime
  Put elapsedTime into the message box
  <commands>
End <whatever>
```

Mastering Logic and Math

The discussion of integer arithmetic earlier in this chapter needs some clarification for those who know something about data types. In his excellent book *Complete Turbo Pascal* [Scott, Foresman and Company, 1986, 1987], Jeff Duntemann says this regarding the Turbo Pascal integer arithmetic functions:

"**Round** and **trunc** are fence-sitters. They are both mathematical functions, in the sense that they provide a mathematical service, and they are also transfer functions, in that they provide a bridge between the incompatible types **Real** and **Integer**."

It is important to realize that this is *not* the case with the corresponding HyperTalk **round** and **trunc** functions. In HyperTalk there are no such incompatible data types, and these functions do no type conversion. They simply accept one number and return another that is a particular function of the first.

The remainder of this section will expand on the concept of operator precedence and expression evaluation. The evaluation of expressions according to rules of operator precedence is fundamental to the way in which a language handles numbers. The key elements of HyperTalk's rules are: parentheses, operator precedence classes, and left-to-right evaluation.

Parentheses are considered first in evaluating expressions. If a part of an expression is enclosed in parentheses, it is evaluated as a unit, and the value of that unit is combined with other parts of the overall expression.

Operator precedence classes come next. Operators are grouped into classes according to the order in which they should be evaluated. Multiplications, for example, are performed before additions. See the table below for the full story on mathematical and logical operator precedence classes.

Other things (i.e., parentheses and precedence class) being equal, operators are evaluated by HyperTalk as it encounters them in a left-to-right reading of the expression. Thus, **9 - 4 + 2** has the value **5 + 2**, or **7**, rather than the value **9 - 6**, or **3**. Exponentiation, the raising of a number to a power, is evaluated right-to-left, so **2^3^2** is **512**, not **64**. This should not be an issue unless you are in the habit of raising numbers to powers that are themselves powers.

Parentheses can *always* be used to control order of evaluation, or even simply to clarify it for a reader of the code.

The above discussion of expression evaluation appears in a somewhat different form in the HyperTalk Operators appendix, where the full version of the following table also appears. The shortened form of the table that appears here shows the precedence class for every mathematical and logical operator.

Mathematical and Logical Operator Precedence Classes

Precedence class	Operator	Function
1	( )	grouping
2	-	arithmetic negation
	not	logical negation
3	^	exponentiation
4	*	multiplication
	/	division
	div	integer division
	mod	modulo
5	+	addition
	-	subtraction
7	<	less than
	>	greater than
	<= ≤	less than or equal to
	>= ≥	greater than or equal to
8	=	equality
	is	equality
	<> ≠	inequality
	is not	inequality
9	and	logical and
10	or	logical or

Note that the same symbol, -, is used for two different operators of different precedence: the negation operator, which changes the sign of a number, and the subtraction operator.

Mastering User-Defined Math Functions

You have seen examples of user-defined functions and could generalize to writing math functions. But there are some advanced techniques in function creation that can be particularly powerful in mathematical operations. One of these is recursion.

Recursion is simply causing a function to invoke itself. Clearly, if a function is so written that every time it executes it invokes itself, it will never terminate (or anyway not without error), because each nth invocation will invoke an n+1st. Recursive functions are always written so that they don't always invoke themselves, so that there is one condition, at least, under which the function will not call itself. And they are also written so that each successive invocation of the function gets closer to the condition that causes the function not to call itself. So eventually the cycle ends.

For the function to behave differently on different invocations, something must change, and what changes is the parameter (or parameters) passed to the function. This implies that a parameterless function cannot be called recursively, and that is correct.

Here is a recursive function, along with a mouseUp handler to get a value and pass it to the function. It calculates the factorial of its parameter; that is, the product of all positive integers up to and including the parameter. The factorial of 3 is 1*2*3, or 6; the factorial of 6 is 1*2*3*4*5*6, or 720, and so on. This function considers two cases: the parameter is 1, and the parameter is > 1 (written properly, it should check for illegal parameter values like -1 and 3.14). If the parameter is 1, the function returns the parameter and quits. Otherwise, it returns the parameter times the factorial of the parameter-1. This second case is the recursive case, and it moves the parameter of the *next* call one step closer to 1 each time. Eventually, the call factorial(X-1) will be executed with X=2, so that the actual parameter of the call is 1, and the nonrecursive branch will be taken, and the recursion will end.

```
On mouseUp
  Ask "Compute the factorial of what number?"
  Put it into theNumber
  If theNumber ≥0 then put factorial(theNumber)
End mouseUp

Function factorial num
  If num=1
  Then return num
  Else return num*factorial(num-1)
End factorial
```

Recursive functions tend to run into memory limitations in HyperCard pretty quickly, which limits their usefulness. These handlers break down on factorial(14) on my machine. Nevertheless, recursion can be a good tool for developing complex collections of functions, even if the functions are later converted to iterative form for efficiency. (The alternative to recursion is iteration, which means repetition, which means, in HyperTalk, using the **repeat** structure.) It would be nice to be able to use recursion in HyperTalk for that purpose. The code section of this book contains a tool to make that a little more possible.

Specialized Math Functions

HyperTalk provides four trigonometric functions. These are: **atan**, **cos**, **sin**, and **tan**; and they compute the arc tangent, sine, cosine, and tangent functions, respectively.

Real trig is costly, but it can be the right tool to use when you need the precision and there is no obvious alternative. You can often save computation time, though, by using an approximation, and HyperTalk code will usually run considerably slower than optimized built-in functions that do the same thing. Here are three approaches to drawing a circle, with the execution time on a Macintosh II listed after each one.

```
On mouseUp
  -- Draws a circle using trig functions.
  -- Not an efficient method.
  Put the seconds into secStart
  Put 256 into H
  Put 171 into V
  Choose pencil tool
  Repeat with D=1 to 360
    Put D*2*pi/360 into R
    Put 100*cos(R) into Hdelta
    Put 100*sin(R) into Vdelta
    Click at round(H+Hdelta),round(V+Vdelta)
  End repeat
  Choose browse tool
  Put the seconds-secStart
End mouseUp

My time: 23 seconds
```

```
On mouseUp
  -- Draws a circle using Bresenham's algorithm.
  -- An efficient method.
  Put the seconds into secStart
  Put 256 into H
  Put 171 into V
  Choose pencil tool
  Put 0 into ix
  Put 100 into iy
  Put 0 into ie
  Repeat while ix ≤ iy
    If ie < 0
    Then
      Add iy+iy-1 to ie
      Subtract 1 from iy
    End if
    Subtract ix+ix+1 from ie
    Add 1 to ix
    Click at H+ix,V+iy
    Click at H-ix,V+iy
    Click at H+ix,V-iy
    Click at H-ix,V-iy
    Click at H+iy,V+ix
    Click at H-iy,V+ix
    Click at H+iy,V-ix
    Click at H-iy,V-ix
  End repeat
  Choose browse tool
  Put the seconds-secStart
End mouseUp

My time: 13 seconds

On mouseUp
  -- Draws a circle using the oval tool.
  -- When you have the tools,
  -- it's wise to use them.
  Put the seconds into secStart
  Put 256 into H
  Put 171 into V
  Set centered to true
  Choose oval tool
```

```
    Drag from H,V to H+100,V+100
    Choose browse tool
    Put the seconds-secStart
  End mouseUp

  My time: 1 second
```

HyperTalk provides six logarithmetic and exponential functions. These are: **exp**, **exp1**, **exp2**, **ln**, **ln1**, and **log2**. Each of the first three raises a constant to a power specified by its parameter and each of the last three calculates the logarithm of its parameter. The two with a 2 in their names use 2 as their base and the others use *e*, the base of the natural logarithms (2.71828...).

HyperTalk provides two financial functions. These functions, and formulas that they calculate, are:

```
annuity(interestRate,numOfPeriods)
```

is equivalent to:

```
(1-(1*interestRate)^-numOfPeriods)/interestRate
```

```
compound(interestRate,numOfPeriods)
```

is equivalent to:

```
(1+interestRate)^numOfPeriods
```

The **annuity** function is used to calculate the present value of a payment of an annuity. The value that it returns, however, must be multiplied by the size of the payment to get the actual present value. The **compound** function computes compound interest for a fixed rate over a number of periods. Neither of these functions is identical to the stated formula, which is only something you need to know if you use them for purposes for which they were not intended, giving them funny values for their parameters.

7

Designing the Data

About this Chapter

HyperCard is not a database program. Nevertheless, it is being used to manage data by many users, and indications are that it will see much more use in the future in applications where a database program would have been used before. It makes sense to know how to handle data efficiently and how to make it easy for whoever will enter the data. This chapter presents the fundamentals of data manipulation with HyperTalk.

Data in Containers

Whenever possible, HyperTalk treats data as strings of characters. The language contains many words for dealing with strings. There are string constants, including **space**, **quote**, **tab**, and **return**, each evaluating to the character of that name; and **empty**, which has the value of an empty string, a string of length zero. There are string operators: **&** and **&&**, each of which concatenates (combines) two strings into one (**&&** inserts a space between the component strings); and **contains**, **is in**, and **is not in**, each of which reports whether or not one string is contained in another. There are many string functions, two important ones being **offset**, which returns the ordinal character position of one string within another, and **length**, which returns the length of a string in characters.

Here are some examples you can type into the message box:

```
"12345" contains "23"
12345 contains 23
"23" is in "12345"
```

```
23 is in 12345
"23" is not in "12345"
23 is not in 12345
"abc" & "def"
1 & 2
"abc" && "def"
1 && 2
"John" && quote & "Shorty" & quote && "Powers"
length("thisString")
the length of "thisString"
offset("s","thisString")
```

HyperTalk's one major data structure is the container. Variables, the message box, and all fields are containers. What a container contains is a string, but HyperTalk provides several ways of referring to components of that string. These methods are collectively known as chunking, and the chunk-specifiable components of a container are called chunks.

There are four words, plus plurals and abbreviations for these words, used to identify chunks. These are: **character** (**characters**, **char**, **chars**), **word** (**words**), **item** (**items**), and **line** (**lines**). A **line** is a string of characters terminated by the Return character, an **item** is a string of characters delimited by commas, and a **word** is a string of characters delimited by Space characters.

You can **put** data **into** a container or **into** any chunk of a container or **get** data from it, and you can refer to chunks by number, by ordinal word (**first**, **second**,...), or by such selector words as **last**, **mid**, **middle**, or **any**:

```
Put middleName into word 2 of name
Put middleName into middle word of name
Put userName into line 1 of field userData
Put 27 into item 2 of line 7 of field "Nums"
Get first char of second word of third line ¬
of background field "Dictionary"
Get any character of "abcdefghijklmnopqrstuvwxyz"
```

You can **delete** a chunk or **put empty** into it; these are not the same thing, however. **Deleting** an **item**, for example, will also delete the comma; but **put**ting **empty** into an **item** leaves the comma, resulting in an empty **item**. You might try these:

```
Put "one two three" into count
Delete middle word of count
Put count

Put "one two three" into count
Put empty into middle word of count
Put count
```

You can **put** data **before** or **after** a chunk or container as well as **into** it.

```
Put middleName after word 1 of name
Put Return after msg -- executes command in msg
```

And you can refer to a range of chunk elements or use plurals to count chunks:

```
Put item 3 to 5 of itemList
Put the number of words of field "Dictionary"
If the number of lines of the script of me ≥ 3
Then edit the script of me
```

It's easy to remember that chunking applies to fields, since you can see the individual characters, words, items, and lines of a field. Variables are normally not visible, so it's possible to forget that they, too, can have the full structure that chunking provides. The message box, however, is not in this sense a full container, since it will hold only one line.

The Data in an Object

Objects contain data. All of the data is accessible by reference to the properties of the object: its name, for example. To demonstrate the manipulation of object properties, I present the next two scripts. Using the scripts may help you to get comfortable with manipulating properties of objects; studying the scripts may be enlightening, but one or two aspects of them may become more meaningful after you have read Chapter 8.

The first is a button script that "tiles" buttons on the screen, fitting them into a grid. It positions a target button with respect to a reference button, adjusting its dimensions to those of the reference button. It uses only "early" HyperTalk vocabulary; it could be simplified with new words introduced in version 1.2.

```
On mouseUp
  Ask "Target button:"
  If it is empty then exit to HyperCard
  Put it into target
  Answer "Target button type:" ¬
  with "Background" or "Card"
  Put it into targetType
  Ask "Reference button:" with "Help"
  If it is empty then exit to HyperCard
  Put it into ref
  Answer "Reference button type:" ¬
  with "Background" or "Card"
  Put it into refType
  Ask "Steps to the right:" with 0
  If it is empty then exit to HyperCard
  Put it into stepsRight
  Ask "Steps downward:" with 0
  If it is empty then exit to HyperCard
  Put it into stepsDown
  -- Find the location and dimensions
  -- of the reference button.
  Do "put the rect of " & refType & ¬
  " button ref into theRect"
  Put first item of theRect into l
  Put second item of theRect into u
  Put third item of theRect into r
  Put fourth item of theRect into d
  Put r-l+1 into width
  Put d-u+1 into height
  -- Calculate location for target button.
  Put l+stepsRight*width into l
  Put r+stepsRight*width into r
  Put u+stepsDown*height into u
  Put d+stepsDown*height into d
  Put l into first item of theRect
  Put u into second item of theRect
```

```
    Put r into third item of theRect
    Put d into fourth item of theRect
    Do "set the rect of " & targetType & ¬
    " button target to theRect"
  End mouseUp
```

The second script is also a button script. This one sets a specified property to a specified value for *all* card buttons of a card. It may be useful for playing with properties, but it doesn't prompt you with properties or values, so you have to know (perhaps by looking in the HyperTalk Properties appendix) what properties a button has, and what values are allowed. You could modify it to present you with lists of properties and values, by making fields visible and invisible. That in itself involves changing properties of objects, of course.

```
  On mouseUp
    Ask "Set what property?" with "Style"
    If it is empty then exit to HyperCard
    Put it into prop
    Do "put the " & prop & " of me into default"
    Do "ask " & quote & "What value for " & prop ¬
    & "?" & quote ¬
    & " with " & default
    If it is empty then exit to HyperCard
    Put it into propSetting
    Repeat with i=1 to the number of card buttons
      Do "set the " & prop & " of card button i ¬
    to " & propSetting
    End repeat
  End mouseUp
```

Data Entry and Fields

When a HyperCard stack is to be used for data entry, some consideration should be given to the sanity of the date enterer. It is common practice to build successive records—cards to us—by keying data into one field and jumping swiftly to the next field via the Tab or Return or Enter key. Certain actions may need to take place on the enterer's exiting a field, and the Enter or Return or Tab key press may be the appropriate trigger for such actions.

Does HyperCard support data entry practice and expectations? Well, all versions of HyperTalk support **enterKey** and **tabKey** and **returnKey** messages, but as these are messages sent to the current card, there is no way to customize response to them for individual fields. Version 1.2 introduced three tools for getting better control of the situation: the **returnInField** and **enterInField** messages, with field entry points, and the **autoTab** field property. These tools make it easier for the programmer to make it easier for the user to enter data.

The **autoTab** property, if set to true for a field, causes the following to be the case: a Return key press, while there is a selection or insertion point within the bounds of that field, and it is on the last line of the field, generates a **tabKey** message. If the insertion point or selection is elsewhere in the field, a **return** character will be inserted into the field. This process is mediated by the **returnInField** message. The reason for doing this is chiefly to allow the Return key to double for the Tab key in moving the insertion point to the next field.

Under version 1.2, an **enterInField** message is sent to a field if the Enter key is pressed while there is a selection or insertion point within the bounds of the field. If the **enterInField** message is not intercepted and the contents of the field have been changed, HyperCard will send a **closeField** message.

The described effects are the default effects of these new messages, but a handler placed in a field can customize response to the Return or Enter key for that individual field. If the customization only involves an additional action, the message should be passed, via the **pass** command, documented in the HyperTalk Commands appendix.

Merely being able to jump from field to field via the Tab (or Return or Enter) key is less than ergonomic excellence if you can't dictate the order in which the fields will be jumped to. You can, but the technique involved could be more straightforward. It is the **number** property of the field that determines its order in various HyperCard operations, from searching to tab jumping.

Unfortunately, you can't change the **number** property directly via the **set** command, as you can most properties, but you can adjust it by using the **Bring Closer** and **Send Farther** menu selections. The **doMenu** command, discussed in detail in Chapter 8 and in the HyperTalk Commands appendix, is necessary if you want to change it in a script. But you shouldn't have to do it under script control: HyperCard adjusts the **number** property of fields at will, but it doesn't will to do so unless you add or delete fields. Once you have built your stack, your field tab order should not change. If you add a field, that field will initially sit at the end of the tab order. Locked fields are skipped over in the tab order, and the tab order jumps from card to background fields; that is, when it has left the last (highest numbered unlocked) card field it jumps to the first (lowest numbered unlocked) background field, and vice-versa.

HyperCard imposes some limitations on sizes of things. Fields, in particular, can only contain about 32,000 characters. One way around field size limitations is to use more fields. You can create an invisible backup field to handle overflow from a field, create a script that checks the size of the main field and offloads some text if it's getting too full, and modify all handlers that access the field to also check the backup field. But that's a lot of work. You might consider storing the data in a text file.

Selecting, Searching, and Sorting Data

HyperTalk provides several ways to search for data in fields and several ways to sort cards on the basis of data in fields.

You can sort cards via the **sort** command, with a choice of sort orders and sort types. The syntax is:

```
Sort by <value>
Sort <sort order> by <value>
Sort <sort direction> by <value>
Sort <sort direction> <sort order> by <value>
```

The parameter <value> must be a designator of a field or part of a field. The parameter <sort direction> must be one of the following keywords: **ascending** or **descending**. It determines whether the cards are ordered lowest to highest or the reverse with respect to the selected ordering. The default is **ascending**. The parameter <sort order> must be one of the following: **dateTime**,

numeric, or **text**. It determines which of the four orderings of characters is used. The default is **text**. If you put dates or time values into a field and sort cards on their values, you need to make sure you are using the **dateTime** sort order. For number taken as numbers, be sure to use the **numeric** order.

Although you can only specify one value on which to sort, you can effectively sort on multiple keys—more than one value—by invoking the **sort** command more than once in succession, ending with the major key—the value on which you want the full stack to be ordered when you're finished. In other words, to sort by last name and by first name within cards holding the same last name, you should sort first by first name, then by last name.

Here are some examples of the uses of the **sort** command:

```
Sort by field address
Sort dateTime by field dateEntered
Sort descending numeric by field score
Sort by lastName & firstName
```

Note that this last example involves only *one* key. The **find** command has abilities not apparent in its menu selection equivalent. When you choose **Find...** from the menu, it merely puts the **find** command into the message box to be executed. It doesn't suggest that there are several different search techniques, or algorithms, hidden in the **find** command. The basic syntax of the **find** command is:

```
Find <target>
Find chars <target>
Find characters <target>
Find word <target>
Find whole <target>
Find string <target>
```

The **find** command searches all fields of all cards of the stack for the string <target>. The **find** form matches its target if it appears at the beginning of a word, the **find chars** (or **characters**) form matches the string anywhere, the **find word** form matches only complete words, and the **find whole** and **find string** forms are analogous to the **find word** and **find chars** forms. **Find whole** permits spaces in the target string, so it will find not just words but phrases; **find string** acts just like **find chars** unless target contains one or more spaces followed by three or more non-space characters, in which case a fast search algorithm is employed.

You can also restrict the search to a particular field. This must be a background field, but you do not have to be in that background when you invoke the command.

For example:

```
Find Apple
-- Above will also find also Appleton,
-- but not crabApple.
Find chars yper
-- Above finds HyperTalk, HyperCard, etc.
Find word mac -- Ignores smack, mace, Macintosh.
Find chars (415) in field phoneNumber
-- Quotes not needed in above.
Find whole "ball of wax"
-- But not "snowball of wax" or "balloon of wax."
Find string "ple Comp"
-- Use this form, in this case, for speed.
```

When you've completed a search using the **find** command, you may want to do something with the element found. Four functions for manipulating the result of a **find** command were added in version 1.2. The **foundChunk** function returns a chunk expression for the location where the most recently executed **find** command found its target string. The **foundField** function returns the name of the field where the **find** succeeded. The **foundLine** function returns a chunk expression like foundChunk, but for the entire line, not just for the found chunk. The **foundText** function returns the text actually found, which, if the **find** command succeeded, should be the target given to the command.

For example:

```
Put the foundText into what
Put the foundChunk into where
Put the foundField into whatField
Put the foundLine into whatLine
```

What holds for **finding** text also holds for selecting it. We saw in Chapter 4 that it is possible to select text under script control by double-clicking on a word or by dragging through a field. You can also use the **select** command.

The **select** command, added in version 1.2, (1) chooses the appropriate tool (button or field) and selects the specified object as though it had been clicked on with the mouse, (2) selects text in a field or in the message box as though clicked on or dragged over, or (3) deselects the selected object or text. It is documented fully in the HyperTalk Commands appendix; here are its syntax variations:

```
Select <button>
Select <field>
Select target
Select me

Select <chunk> of <target>
Select before <chunk> of <target>
Select after <chunk> of <target>
Select text of <target>
Select before text of <target>
Select after text of <target>
Select text of target
Select text of me

Select empty
```

The most important variations for present purposes are those that make selections in containers. The **before** and **after** variations place the cursor before or after the specified chunk expression. **Select empty** deselects whatever was selected.

Once text is selected, it can be pasted elsewhere, for example. Several functions exist for manipulating the result of a selection operation, most added in version 1.2. These are very much like the find-related functions. The **selectedChunk** function returns a chunk expression for the location where the most recently executed selection was done. The **selectedField** function returns the name of the field. The **selectedLine** function returns a chunk expression for the line. The **selectedText** function returns the text selected.

There is also the **selection** function, which returns the text selected. The **selection** is not a true function, because you can put values into it as well as get them out.

For example:

```
Put the selectedLine into prevLine
Put the selectedText after field "Selections"
Put "*(found)" after the selection
```

HyperTalk Language Elements Discussed in this Chapter

The following HyperTalk words were used in this chapter: **&**, **&&**, **after**, **ascending**, **autoTab**, **before**, **blindTyping**, **by**, **char**, **character**, **characters**, **chars**, **contains**, **dateTime**, **delete**, **descending**, **empty**, **enterInField**, **enterKey**, **find**, **foundChunk**, **foundField**, **foundLine**, **foundText**, **in**, **it**, **item**, **items**, **length**, **lines**, **me**, **of**, **offset**, **powerKeys**, **quote**, **returnInField**, **returnKey**, **select**, **selectedChunk**, **selectedField**, **selectedLine**, **selectedText**, **selection**, **sort**, **space**, **string**, **tab**, **tabKey**, **text**, **whole**, **word**, **words**.

8
Owning the Interface

Intelligence is the faculty of making artificial objects, especially tools to make tools.

—Henri Bergson

About this Chapter

This is the final chapter on the HyperTalk language. It deals with more advanced topics and introduces some commands and features of HyperTalk not dealt with before. Even if you don't intend to do any "advanced" programming, you might want to read through this chapter to see what it covers.

You can think of HyperCard as the virtual computer for which HyperTalk is the language. This chapter tells you how to manipulate aspects of HyperCard, and of HyperTalk itself, that are not obviously accessible to scripts. The image of event-driven programming is that of blocks of code, sitting quietly until external events stir them to action. You've written such blocks of code, and, as user of your stacks, supplied the external events. In this chapter you will learn how to write scripts that don't wait for the user to act, but simulate user actions, and you will learn how to write code that changes: code that writes code, code that edits code, code that rewrites itself, and code that extends the HyperTalk language. By the end, you will know how to use HyperTalk to make HyperCard do exactly what you want it to do. By this point in the book you should be referring to the appendixes regularly. In this chapter I will mention several new HyperTalk language features with no or little definition. Each of these, including the *pass, send,* and *global* commands and the target function, are defined in the appendixes.

DimSum

Here is a trick that I probably should have shared with you earlier: my DimSum Home stack handlers. These two handlers address the very first topic presented in these language chapters. Back at the beginning of Chapter 3, I introduced the idea of testing your understanding of the syntax of a command by typing it into the message box. This is a subject near and dear to my heart, since I tested every line of code in this book, and tried nearly every syntax variation I could think of for every command. There were long stretches of keying in a string, hitting Return, noting the result, wondering if I had typed it right, retyping it and checking the result again, then typing in another string that differed from this one in some small but important way, and on and on. DimSum kept me sane.

If you're old enough to remember calculators (that's a joke, I think), you know the fundamental problem with using a simple four-function calculator (one with no printing tape) for any important calculation. You key in the calculation, and when you see the result, you can no longer see what you keyed in. If the result isn't what you expected, you suspect that you hit the wrong key, but you don't really know, and the only way to find out is to redo the entire calculation. If you get the same answer, you know you were probably correct—assuming you remember the first answer.

Using the message box to check your understanding of the syntax of a command presents the same problem. And of course the message box can itself be used as a calculator, as we saw at the beginning of Chapter 6. DimSum implements a simple one-element memory for the contents of the message box. It saves the contents in a global variable called dimSum, and when the user touches Function key 12, dimSum's contents get put back into the message box. I can toggle between expression and value by resting my thumb on the Return key and my middle finger on Function key 12. It's very handy.

DimSum consists of the following two handlers, to be placed in the Home Stack script:

```
On functionKey k
  -- DimSum functionKey handler added by MS 6/88.
  -- Puts the contents of the global variable
  -- dimSum into the message box. One of a pair
```

```
    -- of handlers for short-term msg memory.
    Global dimSum
    If k=12 then put dimSum into msg
  End functionKey

  On returnKey
    -- DimSum returnKey handler added by MS 6/88.
    -- Puts the contents of the message box into
    -- global variable dimSum. One of a pair of
    -- handlers implementing short-term msg memory.
    Global dimSum
    Put msg into dimSum
    Pass returnKey
  End returnKey
```

I guess I have to explain the name. It's a joke about Chinese food: one puts msg into dimSum. That's not a very big joke, but it crouches on the shoulders of a giant body of legend regarding programmers and Chinese food, which is unfortunately beyond the scope of the present work.

And I should say a word about global variables. A global variable retains its value even when the script is done, even if you were to move to another stack. You declare a variable to be global with the **`global`** command. Any handler that so declares a global variable can use its global value, and no other one.

DimSum could be implemented as one handler rather than two. You might enjoy the exercise of figuring out how to do this, and then figuring out how to do it so that the required keystrokes seem natural to you. It's a good exercise in taking control of the keyboard with your scripts. There are many other ways of implementing the simple idea embodied in DimSum, and by this point in your knowledge of HyperTalk programming you will immediately see one or two ways in which the script cries out for generalization.

I present DimSum here exactly as I have implemented it in my own Home stack for a reason. I wrote most of the scripts in this book for specific pedagogical purposes, and even the more useful of them may as a result need to be tweaked to serve your (or even my own) day-to-day needs. On the other hand, I have abundant empirical evidence that DimSum satisfies a real need for at least one user, and I thought that the book should contain some field-tested scripts to balance the academic exercises.

Simulating Key Presses

DimSum introduces no new ideas. You already knew how to deal with keypresses as events to respond to, and in Chapter 7 you learned the subtleties of dealing with messages generated by keypresses. In this chapter, you will look at keypresses from a different perspective, seeing how to write scripts that simulate keypresses at two different levels of reality. These are: (1) producing the message, and (2) producing the event.

The idea of a script producing a message is also not new. As already mentioned, commands can be thought of as messages. If you've looked through the HyperTalk Messages appendix, you may have noticed that there are HyperTalk messages corresponding to certain keypresses, specifically **returnInField**, **enterInField**, **returnKey**, **enterKey**, **tabKey**, **arrowKey**, **functionKey**, and **controlKey**. The first two were added in version 1.2, and have fields as their entry point; the others all have the current card as entry point. You can use these messages in your scripts, either directly:

```
On mouseUp
  Click at the location of the message box
  ReturnKey
End mouseUp
```

or via the **send** command:

```
Send functionKey 12 to card 2
```

In the first case, the message goes to its entry point in the normal flow through the hierarchy.

The second case, which uses the send command to **send** the message explicitly to an object, is interesting. Since we don't actually go to card 2, whatever happens will happen in the context in which the command was executed; if we execute this from card 1, the context will be card 1. But a functionKey handler defined only for card 2 (in that card's card script) can in this way be applied to card 1. This is tricky business, and you shouldn't do this sort of thing unless you really need to.

As an example of the potential for confusion, consider four apparently equivalent ways in which the **functionKey** handler in card 2's card script might refer to card 2 itself. If it makes no explicit card reference, the current card is assumed. The script can also specify **this card**; in either case, the current card is understood. When this handler is triggered from another card, *that* card will be the current card. On the other hand, if the handler refers to card 2 using **me** or **the target**, the reference will continue to mean Card 2, even when the handler is invoked from another card. Following the object hierarchy is usually the best policy.

It is worth pointing out that, while it is always possible to **send** a message explicitly to its entry point, it is not generally efficient to do so. The reason is that the **send** command itself must then traverse the hierarchy before the message can start its trip.

The parameters used with certain messages are explained in the HyperTalk Messages appendix.

In these examples, the script is not producing a keypress, but sending the message normally produced by a keypress. For the keys under consideration, the distinction is moot; the event of an Option keypress has no consequences not mediated by the message. In the case of most keys, this is not true. When you type on the keyboard, you place characters somewhere on the screen as a result—and this is a result of the event, not of the message that the event produces.

A script can also produce a keypress event. It does so via the **type** command, which produces an effect identical (from HyperCard's point of view) to typing characters on the keyboard. So the script can actually place text in a field, the message box, or on a card or background picture in paint text, just as though the user were exercising the keyboard.

Compared with generating keypress messages in a script, this is a different level of reality—or virtuality. It's still not real: no fingers touch the keys, the keys do not move up and down, no electrical signal flows from the keyboard to the computer. But an event enters the HyperCard system and producing its effects, only one of which is a message. Exactly what these effects are depends on where the text cursor is when the **type** command is executed. Consequently, you will generally use the **type** command after a command that places the cursor:

```
On mouseUp
  Click at the location of the message box
  Type "beep" & return
End mouseUp
```

This will achieve the same effect:

```
On mouseUp
  Click at the location of the message box
  Type "beep"
  ReturnKey
End mouseUp
```

The point of these keyboard exercises is that scripts need not merely await these events and messages, but can control all aspects of the user interaction,to the point of simulating the user. (Well, that's a little extreme. Simulating the actions the user can perform in interacting with HyperCard, I should have said.)

Simulating Menu Selections

At this point, we have seen how to do, under script control, much of what the user can do—typing into the message box or into a field, clicking on buttons or fields. A moment's reflection will show that we can also invoke certain menu selections by sending a command-Key message while typing a character.

In fact, we can invoke any menu selection, and generally we can do so more directly than by using Command key equivalents. This rounds out the simulation of the user interaction, which is really what we're up to here. Pulling down menus and making selections is the other thing the user can do. Your scripts can, too.

Well, scripts don't actually pull down the menu. There is a special command for making menu selections from within a HyperTalk script: **doMenu**. The **doMenu** command will select any active selection on any of the menus available when it is executed. The syntax is simply:

```
doMenu <menu selection>.
```

There are two things to remember about **doMenu**: the menu selection has to be available at the time the command is executed, and you must supply the selection in the exact form in which it appears in the menu, including the three dots. (That's three periods, not an ellipsis character, which looks the same but isn't.)

```
On idle
  -- AutoCompact handler added by MS 6/88.
  Global autoCompact
  If the freeSize of this stack > 100 ¬
  and autoCompact is true
  Then
    DoMenu "compact stack"
    DoMenu "compact stack"
    Put "FreeSize:" && the freesize of this stack
  End if
End idle
```

When an invoked selection ends with three dots, generally you can't do anything further until the user responds to some dialog. Here is an exception:

```
On mouseUp
  DoMenu "Find..."
  Type toBeFound & return
End mouseUp
```

The **doMenu** command doesn't work when there's no selection name to supply. Two of the HyperCard menus, Tools and Patterns, offer pictures as selections. To make those selections, you need to **choose** the tool and **set** the pattern.

There is no rule that you have to select HyperCard menu selections. There are always other menu selections available, and **doMenu** knows about them. You can use **doMenu** to select desk accessories, MultiFinder applications, or MacroMaker menu selections, all within scripts.

And you can write a handler to deal with doMenu messages. This allows you to turn off certain menu options. Be sure to **pass** the doMenu command, or you will be turning off all menu control, for yourself as well as your user. This script disables one menu selection:

```
On doMenu menuItem
  If menuItem is not "Delete stack..."
  Then pass doMenu
End doMenu
```

With these tools, you can make your scripts do anything the user can do. The next step is to learn how to make them do anything the programmer can do.

Writing Code that Writes Code

Analogous to the **doMenu** command for menu selections is the **do** command for commands. Just what, you ask, does **do** do? It interprets a string of characters as a HyperTalk command.

```
Do "put 7 into line 1 of field 3"
```

And why would we want to do that? Isn't **put 7 into line 1 of field 3** by itself sufficient? Yes, but if we go beyond literal strings of characters, things start to get interesting:

```
Do "put" && line 1 of field 3 && "into ¬
line 1 of field 3
```

In this example, we are building a command from pieces. We could also select from a collection of handy commands:

```
Do line i of card field "Commands"
```

The **do** command lets you write commands that write commands. This is very powerful. And just as the **do** command forces an extra level of interpretation of a string of characters, the **value** function forces an extra level of evaluation of an expression.

The following invocation of the **value** function is from the HyperCalc stack background script. HyperCalc was written by HyperTalk author Dan Winkler and is distributed with HyperCard. This script, invoked when a value in a field is changed, reads a string from one field, uses the **value** function to interpret it as an arithmetic expression and to evaluate the expression, and places the value into another field.

```
On closeField
  Repeat with i = 1 to the number of fields
    Get line 3 of field i
    If it is not empty then put the value of it ¬
    into line 2 of field i
  End repeat
End closeField
```

I'll mention in passing that another way to force evaluation of a string of characters is to **type** it into the message box. The example used earlier to demonstrate the **type** command produces an effect equivalent to supplying the string to the **do** command.

Writing Code that Understands Code

With the **do** command, you can make your script produce and execute a line of code that you never wrote. You can do more, you can write scripts that operate on entire scripts, but that takes more than the **do** command. There are two ways to work on a script from within a script: you can invoke the editor, or you can place the script in a container and operate on it like any string of characters.

Invoking the editor doesn't really bring the editing under script control, but it does have some interesting wrinkles. You can throw the user into the editor when certain kinds of errors occur, for example. For the most part these will be errors that you define, but it is possible to react to what HyperTalk regards as errors, too.

There are a couple of indications of errors, indications that you can make your scripts look for. One way to spot errors is by monitoring the function **result**. The **result** function returns the status of the last command. If the command was successful, it will return the value **empty**; otherwise, it will return a string identifying the nature of the failure. In the case of the **open** command, for example, it might return "no such application."

The way to modify a script on the fly, though, is by putting it into a container and operating on it like any string. When you're through, you then need to **set** the script to the container's value—scripts are properties and must be **set**. The next time the script is invoked, the updated value will be used. This card script turns all of the card's button scripts' **mouseUp** handlers into **mouseDown** handlers:

```
Repeat with i=1 to the number of card buttons
  Put the script of card button i into bScript
  If line 1 of bScript is "on mouseup"
  Then
    Put "on mouseDown" into line 1 of bScript
    Put "end mouseDown" into last line of bScript
    Set script of card button i to bScript
  End if
End repeat
```

There are three functions that give inside information about handlers. These are **param**, which returns one of the actual parameters passed to a handler; **paramCount**, which returns the number of parameters passed; and **params**, which returns the entire parameter list, including parameter 0, which is the message or function name.

Scripts can construct commands on the fly via the **do** command. They can modify other scripts. And they can also modify themselves. Here's how:

```
-- This handler invokes the script editor
-- on the script of a user-specified object.
-- It uses self-modifying code.
-- This handler works with any version of
-- HyperCard, but is really useful with versions
-- before 1.2, which has better editing tools.
On mouseUp
  -- This line's part of the self-modifying code.
  Put the script of me into thisScript
  Ask "Edit the script of " with "card button 1"
  If it is not empty then
```

```
    Put it into targetObject
    -- The main self-modifying block begins here.
    -- It searches for the line to modify,
    -- Then modifies it or signals an error.
    Put false into foundLine
    Put 0 into lineNo
    Repeat until foundLine
      Put lineNo+1 into lineNo
      If lineNo>the number of lines of thisScript
      Then
        Beep 1
        Put "Error in edit script."
        Wait 100
        Edit thisScript
      Else
        If word 1 of line lineNo of ¬
        thisScript="ask" then
          Put "ask " & quote & ¬
          "Edit the script of..." & ¬
          quote && "with" && quote ¬
          & targetObject & quote ¬
          into line lineNo of thisScript
          Put true into foundLine
        End if
      End if
    End repeat
    Set the script of me to thisScript
    -- The main self-modifying block ends here.
    Edit script of targetObject
  End if
End mouseUp
```

Writing Code that Reads Foreign Code

This section introduces a somewhat different topic. It is possible to write code in languages other than HyperTalk and to integrate that code into HyperCard. The purpose in doing so is to extend the language beyond its limits. As powerful as HyperTalk is, (1) it produces code that is not generally as fast as, say, compiled C code, and (2) it only manipulates its virtual machine, the HyperCard environment. To speed up HyperTalk or to allow it to do other things that the Macintosh is capable of, you need to resort to a compiled Macintosh programming language. HyperTalk was designed to make it relatively easy to add commands and functions to the language via foreign code.

The portion of HyperCard that integrates foreign code is called the external interface. The foreign code is either an external command (XCMD) or an external function (XFCN), and once integrated, acts just like an internal HyperTalk command (or function). For example, the **Flash** command is an XCMD.

Further information on XCMDs and XFCNs is contained in the Writing for XCMDs and XFCNs appendix. You will need other resources as well if you are going to develop XCMDs and XFCNs: Gary Bond's book *XCMD's for HyperCard* [1988, MIS Press, Portland, Oregon] covers just about everything you need to know and has many useful XCMDs and XFCNs written in *both* C and Pascal. But you should also get the *HyperCard Developer's Workshop* from The Apple Programmer's and Developer's Association (APDA), 290 SW 43rd Street, Renton, Washington, the distributor for Apple developer tools. This package contains routines you'll need to allow your external routines to get at HyperCard's internals.

The basic advice on writing external routines is: keep them small and follow Macintosh and HyperCard user interface guidelines.

HyperTalk Language Elements Discussed in this Chapter

This chapter has attempted to show you how to gain tight control of the HyperCard interface by writing scripts that simulate user actions, write and edit code, and otherwise extend the HyperTalk language. It has touched on writing external commands and functions to extend the language further.

There are other ways to gain more control of the interface, including reading and using the version number, and exploring the uses of the **pass**, **quit**, **resume**, **send**, and **suspend** commands. The more you explore the advanced features of HyperTalk, the more you will make the HyperCard interface your own. This chapter used or discussed the following elements of the HyperTalk language:

ArrowKey, click, clickLoc, commandKey, controlKey, debug, do, doMenu, edit, functionKey, id, idle, message box, number, open, optionKey, param, paramCount, params, pass, quit, result, resume, script, send, shiftKey, suspend, target, type, userLevel, version.

9

The Programmer Over Your Shoulder

About this Chapter

This chapter attempts to communicate some principles of good programming. Most of the advice here is borrowed from other programmers and writers whom I respect. I say "programmers and writers" because I think the two activities of writing programs and writing prose are subject to many of the same deep principles of good composition and effective communication.

In discussing good programming, this chapter addresses Macintosh-specific concerns, HyperCard-specific concerns, concerns in writing for others, and concerns when you are the only audience for your work. It also discusses the market for stackware, and suggests some specific opportunities for stackware developers.

While the preceding chapters dealt with (relatively) uncontentious facts and techniques, this chapter is mainly about values. Other writers may disagree with me about the relative importance of some of the values I discuss here; you may also disagree with me. I believe, though, that the issues brought forward in this chapter are all worth thinking about, and if this chapter inspires you to think about some of them that you might otherwise have ignored, it will have done its job.

The chapter's title derives from an excellent book on writing, *The Reader over your Shoulder*, by Robert Graves and Alan Hodges, in which the authors submit the writing of well-known people to detailed scrutiny. HyperTalk more than any other programming language encourages programmers to scrutinize each others' work in the same way. My advice: do so.

About Good Programming

Good programming means writing programs—or stacks—that satisfy. The satisfaction can be momentary, as when you write a quick handler to calculate a value for you. The satisfaction can be subtle, as when you write a program that does its job so quietly in the background that you forget it's there. The satisfaction can come from seeing a user smile or from knowing that there is no faster way to sort that field of numbers than the way you developed or from standing back ten feet from the listing of your code and admiring its form (well-written code is actually better looking than poorly-written code).

As good programmers know, the satisfaction can be great.

A First Principle

I'll start with what I consider to be the first principle of stackware development: Do No Harm. Doctors learn this principle early in their professional education, and so should the creators of stackware. Stackware developers are in the value-adding business. Each new stack adds to the value of HyperCard and to the value of the Macintosh. They should—*you* should—make sure that the value you add is not negative.

There are commercial products and strategies that violate this principle and take away capabilities of the machine; for example, products that employ copy protection.

The best that can be said for copy protection, a scheme that makes it difficult to make a copy of a program, is that it's a necessary evil. Most people involved with personal computers today would argue with the "necessary." The point here is that copy protection takes away a normal capability of the computer's operating system, something that the user has already paid for: the ability to make a copy of any disk or file. Copy protection subtracts value.

There are HyperCard products that subtract value. A script I examined in researching the stackware market violated the principle. It brought to HyperCard buttons the technique used in menus of graying options to show that they are inactive. The author had created buttons that became gray when in some sense "deactivated." A background button might be appropriate on most cards but not on one; you could gray it to show that it was inactive on that card. Unfortunately, the button thus created, while it looked like a HyperCard button, could not be moved or copied or renamed without considerable work. It was something less than a real button. The point here is not that this particular button was crippled, but that a stack distributed with such a button on it takes something away from the user. It takes away the general principle that buttons have certain predictable properties and characteristics. As I will argue later in this chapter, such expectations are part of the product that the user bought. To make them false is to take something away from the user.

Exceptions in which you might want to remove or mask some of HyperCard's abilities spring immediately to mind: turnkey systems, data entry by temporary workers, cases where the security of data and even the code mitigates for locking some users out. But even here, the principle should apply—after all, somebody besides a data-entry temp is going to need access to the stack; software needs to be maintained. Even turnkey systems should provide full HyperCard power to the system administrator at least, and allow that person to lock naive users into something less.

This particular issue, discussed here at some length, shows at once the subjective nature and the importance of being concerned with the quality of the stacks you create. It's a model for all the other topics that will be presented here more briefly.

In applying value judgements to stacks, one must ask *cui bono*: of value to whom, and for what? I suggest that when you write stacks you are usually writing simultaneously for several targets.

Writing for the Macintosh

"Writing for the Macintosh" doesn't mean writing to please the Mac, but writing with an understanding of what a Macintosh application is, and what users can reasonably expect of one. The ultimate beneficiary is the user, but the issue is more specific, and comes down to honoring the Macintosh user interface.

The arguments for honoring the Macintosh interface are much the same as the arguments for using a single copyediting style on all articles in a magazine. Consistency in presentation leads to a better match with user (reader) expectations and avoids ambiguity. And, less often noted, it empowers the writer: If a magazine has no consistent policy on the use of *that* and *which*, then a writer cannot make a point that depends on the distinction between the uses of *that* and of *which*. And a software product can't use the standard interface or play off the standard interface, if there is no standard interface.

The source on the Macintosh user interface is a book from Addison-Wesley titled *Human Interface Guidelines: The Apple Desktop Interface*. If you do serious stackware development, you should get the book. Here are some of its general principles that pertain to stack development:

- Design by drawing your metaphors from the real world, giving the user as much control as possible, and making that control work via direct manipulation of objects in the real-world metaphor. The supplied HyperCard metaphor is bizarre, but does conjure up an image: a stack of cards containing textual information and wired with little buttons that do things when pressed. If you depart from that metaphor, do so consciously and for a purpose, and make the resulting metaphor at least as real. You do that in part by letting the user manipulate the components of the metaphor. And keep the metaphor in mind. Ted Nelson: "If the button is not shaped like the thought, the thought will end up shaped like the button."

- Make actions reversible. Users make mistakes and change their minds; let them. Some actions are hard to reverse, and it is wise to warn the user before carrying them out. For other actions, consider implementing a handler for the `Undo` menu selection.

- Avoid modes whenever possible. A mode is a context in which a user action is interpreted ideosyncratically. The same actions should generally produce the same effects. One obvious exception is a button that turns a field invisible if it is already visible, and turns it invisible otherwise. In such a case, the function of the button is contextual but clear, and should not confuse the user.

The book contains detailed specifications of the functions of components of the desktop interface, including the various kinds of windows, menus, and controls like buttons.

Does HyperCard comply with the guidelines in detail? No. Then why should you? You shouldn't, blindly; but you also shouldn't violate them without knowing why you're doing so, what the costs and benefits are. You can't know that without knowing what the guidelines are. You might also reflect on the fact that you're not Bill Atkinson. Hardly anybody is Bill Atkinson; he is a remarkably good programmer, and his work embodies most of the traits I identify as desirable in this chapter. When he breaks the rules it is usually for a good reason. And his is one of the names on the inside of the original Macintosh case; he has such credentials that his violations of the interface can be viewed as incremental refinements to its definition. That credit given, I can curse him for ignoring the Mac II user of HyperCard.

The other reason that HyperCard's noncompliance is at least tolerable and in some ways commendable is that HyperCard is a new kind of software product, with good reasons for extending the Apple interface. In fact, HyperCard has software development guidelines of its own.

Writing for HyperCard

Apple is developing stack design guidelines and will eventually put them into a book. In the meantime, the Apple Programmers' and Developers' Association (APDA) publishes a short document that gives some advice.

The first serious questions are always the design questions: should you put your brainchild into one stack or several, and do you need more than one background?

The chief reason for using more than one stack is to reduce individual stack size and complexity at the expense of disk space and inconvenience in moving across the stack boundaries. Stacks are separate disk files, so you generally should implement one product as several stacks only if the user might actually want to use only one portion of the product in a given session. The Apple stacks Datebook, Months, and Daily are examples of a single product implemented as related stacks.

If you decide on implementing your idea as several interrelated stacks, you should remember that any common functionality will either have to be duplicated in the individual stacks' scripts or placed in the Home stack, and modifying the user's Home stack is somewhat questionable. There is a debate among HyperTalk programmers as to whether a new HyperCard facility is needed that would allow developers to apply functionality to a set of stacks. Some argue for a superstack or stack background (analogous to a card's background) that would lie between a stack and the Home stack in the hierarchy. This could be used to tie related stacks together as a background ties cards together. Others argue for a way of indicating that certain capabilities of one stack apply to another, a sort of lateral pass of message handling. My own leaning would be toward extending the hierarchy if necessary rather than diverting it, but it is not clear that any such step is really necessary.

Within a stack, however, backgrounds let you apply common functionality to a group of cards. This is a powerful organizational tool, and you should not think of backgrounds just as the place to put fields and pictures.

Apple champions the principle of one idea per card. Certainly you should think of the card as a single, coherent visual image presented to the user. Step back from it and see what it looks like as a whole.

You should give users at least the sense that they know what kind of information is on all the cards and how to get to any card. That might require an index. It certainly requires support for the basic navigation tools. If possible, put Next and Prev arrow buttons on all cards. (I violate Apple's advice in putting Prev buttons on the first cards of some of my own stacks and Next buttons on the last cards. This certainly violates the stack metaphor, but it reflects the true circularity of HyperCard stacks, and I frequently do want to wrap around from the last card to the first.)

Writing efficient code in any language depends on knowing where the language is and isn't efficient. Jumping from stack to stack, for example, takes a lot of time. So does updating the screen. You can save time in the first case by batching the trips to another stack, rather that jumping there every time you need an item of information. In the other case, you can lock the screen before doing things that affect the screen if there is no need for the user to see them happening, then unlock the screen afterward.

But even if you do write for HyperCard, which HyperTalk are you writing for?

HyperCard and HyperTalk are not static entities. We're up to the third significant version now, version 1.2, with version 2.0 in the works. The product is evolving over time, a fact that is both blessing and curse to the author of books purporting to explain the product, and a fact that has some implications for the stackware developer, too.

Bill Atkinson has proclaimed his commitment to keeping HyperCard upwardly compatible forever. This means that any stack ever created ought to work without modification under any future version of HyperCard. (You may need to recompact it.) It doesn't work the other way, though; stacks developed under new versions of HyperCard will not work under older versions if those stacks take advantage of the new capabilities of HyperCard, such as new HyperTalk commands or properties. What does this mean to you as a stack developer? Atkinson offers this advice: If your stack requires features that do not exist in all versions, use an **on openStack** handler to check the version of HyperCard running. This is an instance of the principle of engineering user expectations, discussed later in this chapter. If the stack isn't going to work for a user, let the user know that immediately, so that expectations are not set up only to be frustrated.

This advice of Atkinson's is so sound that it really ought to be taken as law. But I believe that in many cases you should be able to do even better by the user. Thus far, with the exception of dealing with read-only media, most enhancements to the product do not provide fundamental new capabilities. They just make things easier or more efficient or more intuitive or more reliable. If so, there is no reason why you can't do what you want to do both ways. A handler that uses a capability only present in, say, version 1.2, simply checks the HyperCard version number just before using that capability, and if the version is prior to 1.2, invokes a special handler that does the job the hard way, without the 1.2 capability. You would, of course, have to do this every time a version 1.2 capability was used. Theoretically, you could have several alternative handlers to support various versions, but given the cost of an upgrade, support for the present and immediately preceding versions is probably all any user can expect of you. A warning to the user in an **on openStack** handler would still be thoughtful.

Writing for Others

Good HyperTalk programming is good programming. But what constitutes good programming depends on the intended use. AT&T's Bell Labs programmers developed an entire language, with the euphonious name of AWK, just to write extremely short programs that you use once and throw away. In a sense, there is no such thing as a good or bad AWK program, only one that solves your problem in the time you can afford to allocate to writing and running it. When you write throw-away programs in HyperTalk, the same standards (or lack of same) apply. But if you plan to use the code again, you will begin to care about its quality. If you are developing reusable software components, you will want to make them sparkle.

When you write code for others to use, you take on a responsibility. This is no less true if you give the code away than if you sell it. The user of your code is going to trust it to do what you say it will do, and you have no way of knowing how great an inconvenience or catastrophe it will be if your code proves unreliable. Reliability is the most important quality issue in code written for others. There are three keys to making code reliable: design clarity, alpha testing, and field testing.

Design clarity means knowing what each component does; writing so clearly that you can pick up the code weeks after you've written it and identify immediately the major divisions, the tricky spots, the ways in which one handler depends on another. Design clarity both cuts down on errors and makes it easier to find them when they occur.

Alpha testing means trying to "break" the program; giving it the worst cases to work on; looking for errors, and, when you find and fix them, re-examining the clarity of the design and fixing *that* if necessary to eliminate ugly special-case patches. One place to look for bugs is in boundary cases. If you do something that depends on the cursor being within a region you have defined, examine what your code does when the cursor is on the boundary. Many software bugs live on such boundaries, either literal boundaries like this one, or more abstract boundaries.

Field testing means finding out what the program does in the real-world situation for which it was designed and in the hands of its intended users. The hardest part of field testing is accepting the criticism of users who obviously don't know how to use your wonderful tool properly. Understanding why it is true that the customer is always right is the satori of capitalism.

If the users of your stack don't use it as you intended, it may be that the stack ought to do what the users expects, rather than what it does. It may be that the stack does the right things, but that these things do not fit together into one thing: do all the nifty functions really belong, do they add up to one product whose purpose you can summarize in twenty-five words or less? If not, maybe you have more than one product in your hands. But it's also possible that there is nothing at all wrong with your stack, and you just haven't told your users what it's for.

The most powerful tool you have for getting across to the users of your stack what it does, how it does it, and why they should care is a wonderful invention that didn't come from Apple Computer: the English language. Most stackware developers, and in fact most software developers, abuse it shamefully. Few pieces of software are decently documented.

There are many ways to document HyperCard stacks. Commercial products can be sold with printed manuals, but shareware and free stacks usually contain all their own documentation. Some stackware developers clearly enjoy the experiment of finding ways to use HyperTextual links to put the explanation just where the user will need it. You can explain a stack in a visible field on the first card of the stack; or on a "help" card invoked by a button on the first card; or in a hidden field on the first card, made visible by a button; or you can invent your own methods. Whatever you do, you'd better give the user some indication, on the first card shown, of where to find information on how to use the stack and what it's for.

Beyond that introduction, you can make documentation highly contextual by putting spot explanations in pop-up fields made visible by invisible buttons placed over asterisks in text; you can make individual words of a field "hot" with clever field scripts; you can even construct help messages on the fly, building them from standard components and the knowledge of exactly where the user is at the moment.

If you really want to let the user explore your stack and learn about it, you could implement a Help tool that turns the cursor into a question mark and allows the user to click on any object in the stack and get an explanation of what it's for. Just as you read code for scripting ideas, you should examine others' documentation. Pull apart Carol Kaehler's Help stack, distributed with HyperCard. I think that documenting a stack can be as rewarding as developing it in the first place, but then I'm by profession a writer.

If you are developing a stack for commercial distribution, you owe it to your users to produce a professional-quality product. An amazing number of software developers and publishers don't seem to realize that this principle applies to the documentation as much as to the code. Consider hiring a professional wordsmith to turn your words into something that honors your work rather than making you look like a boob. Consider doing this even if you are working with a publisher who offers this service. What kind of wordsmith? There are several kinds of editing skills that should be applied to any published work.

First, there's the specialized skill of human interface analysis and design. There are already a number of HyperTalk design consulting firms that will give you a critique of the effectiveness of your documentation in getting across your stack's purpose and function, but you can also get enormously useful feedback at considerably less cost by presenting your stack to novices and watching where they get confused or annoyed.

Second, there is copyediting, which is always a bargain. Copyediting is a skill requiring broad knowledge, specialized training, and an ability to read on more than one level simultaneously. A good copy editor will clean up your grammar, eliminate inconsistencies, and make your own style show through. Believe me, you need copyediting. Even most professional writers would look like illiterate bozos without copyediting. Most stackware authors are not professional writers and do not get copyedited.

Finally, there is proofreading. This is also a specialized skill and not the same thing as copyediting. If you produce typeset documentation you will have to read the galleys to make sure that what you sent to typesetting is what came back, but generally the author of a work is the worst proofreader for it. Proofreading requires reading below the level of meaning, and the author can't often get away from the meaning of the words.

The goal of documentation is to make the user's expectations match the product's capabilities. But there are other means for engineering the user's expectations. Remember the opening lines from the old television series, "The Outer Limits"? "We control the video, we control the audio...."?

Well, you do. When you develop a stack, you do control the video and the audio, and other aspects and features of the user interface. You also control something less obvious: you control the potential users' expectations. This can lead to problems. Here's Michael Bywater, assistant editor of *Punch* magazine, writing in the British *MacUser* about the raising and dashing of hopes:

"It's like cellular telephones...your ordinary telephone can only stay in one place, so you accept that, and, while away, make the best of things. But your cellphone is mobile; hence colossal rage and tantrums when you find that its mobility is not universal—you can't use it in darkest Cornwall, and it won't work in railway tunnels, and when you ring someone up in London you can't get a line, and when you want to ring someone up on his cellphone and the little voice says, '...please try later...' you just want to scream. The promise is Be In Touch At All Times, and as soon as that promise is unfulfilled, total fury sets in."

Microsoft, for example, engineered trouble for itself when it released a powerful spreadsheet program that encourages you to design spreadsheets with lots and lots of cells and then didn't fix the memory problem in the program that keeps you from filling the cells with data.

One of the most subtle design problems in software development is making the product look just like what it is, no more and no less, and certainly not like something entirely different. Most of the aspects of this problem are situation-specific and require placing yourself in the user's place, even trying the stack out on a naive volunteer. But one aspect is easy to state and easy to solve.

Give your product a meaningful name. Maybe you're not planning to ask money for your stacks, but if you distribute your work at all, it will someday present itself to a potential user in Macon, Georgia, as a name and size of stack on some electronic bulletin board somewhere. That potential user will have to decide whether or not the stack is worth downloading on the basis of available information. If he or she decides to do so and discovers afterward that it was a mistake, your name will be mud in Macon. A good stack name can save your own.

Writing for Yourself

When you write for yourself, you don't have to worry about engineering the user's expectations, just living up to them. Part of that is writing your code as tightly and efficiently as you know how.

Writing for efficiency might seem like it belongs under the heading of Writing for Others, but in fact it is first of all an internal discipline. Often an improvement in the efficiency of a program will be unnoticed by every user. You have to believe that by making your programs better you make yourself a better programmer.

I touched on some of HyperTalk's efficiencies and inefficiencies earlier. Here I'd just like to mention two very general approaches to improving the efficiency of your code. One of these is profiling, and the other is the paper run.

Profiling means producing a report on the performance of a program or a part of a program. In HyperTalk, it means putting commands into your code that will report, probably in a handy field, how long key portions of the code took to execute, how many times repeat loops executed, and similar information. Profiling is easy to do and can give you clues to improving your code's performance, especially if you use it to compare alternative ways to solve a problem.

By a "paper run" I mean putting yourself in the place of the HyperTalk interpreter and stepping through the code a line at a time, performing calculations on sample data, writing down the intermediate results and the contents of all significant containers. You have to be selective in doing this; the purpose of writing programs is to avoid doing the work ourselves. But there is no more powerful technique for understanding what a program is actually doing than putting yourself in the place of the interpreter.

Another thing you need to do for yourself is to document your code. Documenting code is the most important step in creating reusable software components, the most important step in producing maintainable programs. Code that is not in some way elucidated is extremely hard to fix when it breaks. There are several tools for documenting the code itself.

Comments, either on separate lines or at the ends of lines of code, can serve several purposes. Comments at the top of a script can indicate revision information, as for example, a comment in the Home stack script indicating that it is a standard release Home stack script with the addition of an **idle** handler and a one-line modification to the **startUp** handler. Comments at the beginning of a handler can identify what function the handler serves, point out how it is invoked, and summarize its actions. Comments within a handler can introduce major components like **repeat** loops and describe them much as the handler itself is described, and can explain tricky lines of code.

Comments should be put into the code as you develop it, not added after you've written 100 or so undocumented lines. One way to encourage yourself to put meaningful comments in right at the start is to combine top-down programming with place-holder comments. Top-down programming refers to developing the program in broad outline first, filling in details later, working downward to the smallest details. In this approach, it is necessary to put dummy lines in in place of code not yet written, in order to test the top-level logic. If the dummy lines are comments explaining what the code to come will be required to do, then the comments can be left in as documentation when the real code is supplied. The techniques ensure that the tough components will get documented, since those are the ones you're sure to defer writing.

As important as comments are, they are no more important than the techniques for making the code explain itself. The most important point here is to choose names that are meaningful, but it is also useful to read over code carefully, looking for ways to recast the code to make it clearer. Are you using one variable to stand for two different things, because you know that the two things must always have the same value? Your code may be clearer if you "waste" a variable by allowing different things to have different names. (It may also be less clear; it depends on what is obvious from context.)

But finally, writing HyperTalk code, like any form of creative writing, is enjoyable. It has to be. We wouldn't subject ourselves to all this pain if it weren't a lot of fun, would we? Amuse yourself, break the rules to see what happens, push back the boundaries, play god.

Writing for Posterity

In preparing the Charles Eliot Norton Lectures that he was to have delivered in 1985-86, author Italo Calvino listed six values to strive for in writing and to carry forward into the next millennium. These are:

- Lightness
- Quickness
- Exactitude
- Visibility
- Multiplicity
- Consistency

I believe that these are important values and that they apply to the writing of software as much as to the writing of literature. Perhaps Calvino would have agreed, as my glosses on these excerpts from his lectures are intended to suggest:

Lightness. "[T]here is such a thing as a lightness of thoughtfulness, just as we all know there is a lightness of frivolity." And there is the lightness of software: "The second industrial revolution, unlike the first, does not present us with such crushing images as rolling mills and molten steel, but with 'bits' in a flow of information traveling along circuits in the form of electronic impulses. The iron machines still exist, but they obey the orders of weightless bits." But software can be more or less soft, more light or more ponderous. Ted Nelson, one of the conceptual progenitors of HyperTalk, writes of what he calls virtualities. The term "virtuality," as Nelson uses it, contrasts with the tangible. It fits Calvino's notion of lightness. Virtualities are not simply metaphors, but the microworlds you construct when you write software. They are alternate realities that you construct in the user's mind. Write lightly, and send virtualities aloft.

Quickness. "I dream of immense cosmologies, sagas, and epics, all reduced to the dimensions of an epigram. In the even more congested times that await us, literature must aim at the maximum concentration of poetry and thought." It is the nature of problems to be knotty and of the best solutions to be direct; be like the batter who, when told that the pitcher he would be facing threw a mean curve ball, said, "Don't worry, I'll straighten it out."

Exactitude. "To my mind exactitude means three things above all: (1) a well-defined and well-calculated plan for the work in question; (2) an evocation of clear, incisive, memorable visual images; and (3) a language as precise as possible both in choice of words and in expression of the subtleties of thought and imagination."

Visibility. "If I have included visibility in my list of values to be saved, it is to give warning of the danger we run in losing a basic human faculty: the power of bringing visions into focus with our eyes shut, of bringing forth forms and colors from the lines of black letters on a white page, and in fact *thinking* in terms of images." The best programs spring from a single sharp image in the programmer's mind and construct a clear and pleasing image in the user's.

Multiplicity. Here Calvino was thinking of "the contemporary novel as an encyclopedia, as a method of knowledge, and above all as a network of connections between the events, the people, and the things of the world...a 'system of systems,' in which each system conditions the others and is conditioned by them." Independent objects, responding to events, sending messages to one another in a system of systems that lets you study the lives of your creations.

Calvino did not live to finish the lecture on consistency, and when his wife released the lectures in book form she left this topic to the contemplation of the reader.

Writing for Money

So how is all this going to make you rich? Beats me. The stackware market is problematic. Lots of stacks are being created, but many of them are being given away, which makes it a little harder than it would otherwise be to distinguish your stack as being worth paying for. There are many thousands of stacks out there. On the other hand, stackware fits the shareware channels of distribution nicely; you can upload your stack to an electronic bulletin board or information service with a shareware notice and with all the documentation nicely incorporated into the stack, and you have manual, product, order blank, and advertisement all wrapped up in one file for downloading. Other people will upload your stack to other electronic media for you.

Product ideas have to be evaluated in the light of the market realities. To take a case closer to my heart than to yours, perhaps, but one that puts HyperCard in a broader perspective, should I publish my first novel as a HyperCard stack? In considering it, I must keep in mind that: few first novels sell enough copies to be profitable, only a fraction of the potential readers have computers, only a fraction of those have Macintosh computers, and not all Macintosh computers support HyperCard. When developing a software product, you can assume that all your potential customers have computers, but all the other concerns apply.

Let's assume, though, that you have decided that you are comfortable restricting yourself to the Macintosh market, and within that, to the stackware market. Assessing the market for your stack requires considering what kind of stackware product it is. True to their object-oriented heritage, stacks are both code and data, and stackware products can be more data than code or more code than data.

The former are information stacks, and there are many people doing interesting things in information publishing using HyperCard. This market seems very open, and you ought to be able to price an information stack on the basis of the value of the information (as well as the value you have added in collecting and packaging and providing access to it).

The latter are more like conventional programs, and most stackware that falls into this category would be classified as utility software. There are a few larger applications, and some programs that supply capabilities that HyperCard is lacking, such as the Reports program from Ten Point ø that gives HyperCard report-generation capability. These products that fill an obvious gap are likely to do well, but if the gap is obvious, then the competition to fill it is likely to be great, too.

Here are some still-open opportunities to fill HyperCard gaps. These are some of the things that everyone knows belong in HyperCard but that are missing. They are items that I know are not on page one of Bill Atkinson's to-do list, and they are all hard.

- Color. At least one stack exists that gives color to HyperCard, but it has its limitations. So would anyone else's, probably, since there seems to be no really satisfactory way to solve the color problem until Atkinson modifies HyperCard. Nevertheless, I have found Color for HC from Imaginetics Neovision useful and have done some satisfying things with color using it. Another implementation that took a different approach could be equally useful.

- Stack merging. You give someone a copy of your address stack and she adds some names of her own. Meanwhile you add names to your original version. Now you want to merge the stacks together into one big stack. What does a merge program do when you and she have both added George, but with different addresses? Or when you've added Bob and she's added Robert (she's always been a little more formal than you)? This is the easy case, two stacks with exactly the same structure. How about a somewhat more general merge program? How general? What do you generalize? This is not a simple problem.

- Typed links. You can link cards, link a word in a field to another word elsewhere, but all the links are, well, just links. You can specify that a relationship exists between two entities, but you can't name the relationship. That doesn't prevent your having links that quite effectively serve different purposes, but it does preclude writing handlers that act differently depending on the type of link that they encounter.

But the biggest opportunity in stackware is surely in information publishing. One well-executed example of an information stack that could make a lot of money for its creator and that depends on specialized but easily obtainable knowledge beautifully packaged is a stack of skiing information I came across. It contains maps of ski areas around Lake Tahoe and maps showing individual slopes, plus much information on resorts. But I don't know who created it. If the author can find a forward looking travel agency in the San Francisco area, she may have a buyer for this excellent product.

In writing this book I feel as though I've gone back to college. I've become a student of HyperCard, HyperTalk, and the stackware market. My studies convince me that HyperCard offers an unprecedented opportunity for lots of people to create lots of useful or interesting or beautiful new artifacts. I'm curious about what these artifacts will be. I'm interested in what *you* will make out of HyperCard. If you do create something useful or interesting or beautiful, I'd like to hear about it. Feel free to drop me a line via M&T Books.

Part III
Reference

Appendix A

The HyperTalk Vocabulary

About this Appendix

This word list at the end of this appendix contains every word of the HyperTalk language—that is, every distinct lexical unit recognized by HyperTalk—and points to the main source(s) of information about that word in the following appendixes. It does not tell how the individual word is used; the other appendixes provide that information. The text in this appendix does provide a brief *general* discussion of the ways in which HyperTalk words can be put together to form meaningful HyperTalk utterances.

In the listing, a version number in brackets following the word indicates that it was first introduced, or its use was significantly altered, in that version of HyperCard.

The information in all these appendixes is as timely, complete, and accurate as I could make it. All facts were checked and rechecked, and should be consistent with the state of HyperTalk at the time of final board check in August 1988. This covers the final release form of version 1.2. Most of the examples, however, will work with earlier versions as well.

This book contains many appendixes, and in order to make the data as accessible as possible, I have had to repeat information occasionally. Pardon the redundancy. This reference section should, of course, be a HyperCard stack.

About the Words of the HyperTalk Language

Although programming languages, such as HyperTalk, don't have the expressive power of true natural languages, it does make sense to call them languages. Elements that look a lot like words are put together in structures that look something like sentences, and the relationship between word and sentence in a programming language is roughly the same as the corresponding relationship in a natural language like English: the words usually refer to things or actions, and the sentences they form are meaningful utterances, declarations, or commands.

In fact, HyperTalk reads more like English than does just about any other programming language. But HyperTalk is not English, and it is important to understand its rules for combining words into sentences, rules that do not always live up to an English speaker's intuitions. Some words, for example, can appear only in certain constructions, like the adverb **slowly**, which can appear only in the context of the command **visual**. Collectively, these rules are called the syntax of the language, and you will find the syntax for each significant language element carefully spelled out in the appropriate appendix. But there are also some general principles that it is appropriate to itemize here.

A few such principles are involved in the naming of things. HyperCard ignores case, so it doesn't matter if you use uppercase and lowercase consistently in naming and referring to variables, functions, and objects. Variable names and names of user-defined functions and handlers can be up to 31 characters long, and can't contain any special characters (i.e., they are restricted to letters, digits, and the underline character). This means that you can't create a function named **cube root**, although you can delete the space and have the legitimate name **cubeRoot**.

Names of objects can contain spaces, and, while there are many "reserved" words in HyperTalk, these are not really reserved at all. So you can name a stack "this card" and a card "stack Home" if you want. You will find, though, that such names will need to be disambiguated for HyperCard, usually by putting them in quotes whenever you use them. The same is true of names that begin with a digit (not a wise practice).

An excellent convention regarding capitalization and naming is this: when you create a portmanteau name like **cubeRoot** or **myFirstStack**, capitalize the first letter of each component English word as shown here. This makes the English words distinguishable for the human reader, but keeps the whole as one word for HyperCard's purposes.

Use of the word **the** is a little confusing: sometimes it's required, sometimes forbidden, sometimes optional. It's only used before a function or property name. See the HyperTalk Functions and HyperTalk Properties appendixes for guidance in its use in each of these contexts.

Many of the most common words in HyperTalk have aliases, or alternate forms. In general, these aliases are interchangeable: anywhere you can use one form, you can use the other, as long as the word is being used as a HyperTalk word. Note, however, that you can't invoke the **find** command with the string "bkgnd" and expect it to find the string "background." This is not an instance of the use of the HyperTalk word **bkgnd**, but just a reference to a particular string of characters. Also, some words have more than one meaning: you can't use **sec** for **second** when the meaning is "the one after the first," but only when it is referring to time. Furthermore, singulars and plurals are, in general, not interchangeable. The Special Words appendix has a discussion of the use of plurals in HyperTalk. The following is a list of some of the aliases for HyperTalk words. A version number after a word means that it was introduced, or its use was significantly altered, in that version.

```
abbreviated, abbrev, abbr
background, bkgnd, bg[1.2]
backgrounds, bkgnds, bgs[1.2]
bottomRight[1.2], botRight[1.2]
button, btn
buttons, btns[1.2]
card, cd[1.2]
cards, cds[1.2]
character, char
characters, chars
field, fld[1.2]
fields, flds[1.2]
gray, grey[1.2]
highlight, highlite, hilight, hilite
loc, location
message window, msg window, message box, msg box, message, msg
middle, mid
```

```
picture[1.2], pict[1.2]
polygon, poly
previous, prev
rectangle, rect
regular, reg
second[1.2], sec[1.2]
seconds, secs
slowly, slow
```

Also, any month or day of the week can be abbreviated to its first three letters, and the words **in** and **of** are interchangeable. This latter fact is useful in some contexts, though you wouldn't want to say **the sqrt in 7** for the **sqrt of 7**. But you can.

HyperTalk user-defined variables, system variables such as **`it`** and **`me`**, the message box, and fields are collectively referred to as containers. Not only does HyperTalk not make distinctions among containers on the basis of data type, it also does not make distinctions on the basis of data structure. Any HyperTalk container can have the full complexity of data structuring permitted by the language. This data structuring is called chunking. The words used to form chunk expressions are word, item, character, and line.

About the Other Appendixes

The elements of the HyperTalk language can be classified into the following categories: control structures, commands, functions, properties, system messages, operators, constants, and special words. Most of these elements are individual words, but some are made up of several words, like the **`if...then...else...end if`** control structure, or permit additional modifying words, like **`visual effect dissolve slowly to black`**. The capabilities of HyperTalk can also be extended by the use of external commands and functions written in other languages; these are called XCMDs and XFCNs, respectively. Each of these categories of language elements, as well as the category of external commands and functions, is dealt with in one of the other appendixes of this book.

Here are brief descriptions of the contents of the other appendixes:

In the object-oriented paradigm of programming, objects (that are neither code nor data but some hybrid entity) send messages to other objects. These messages move through hierarchical channels like orders through a military chain of command. The HyperCard Object Hierarchy appendix describes the kinds of objects recognized by HyperCard, and the channels through which they send their messages.

Programming in HyperTalk consists of writing scripts. The large-scale structure of a HyperTalk script is dictated by the control structures used. HyperTalk recognizes exactly four control structures, and they are explained in the HyperTalk Control Structures appendix.

Most lines of HyperTalk scripts invoke a command. HyperTalk commands are the verbs of the language; they name actions that you can direct HyperCard to perform. All the HyperTalk commands are listed, discussed, and exemplified in the HyperTalk Commands appendix.

One of the most powerful tools available to the command or control structure is the function. Functions operate on values to produce other values; for example, when given a number, the absolute value function **abs** returns the absolute value of the number. Functions are documented in the HyperTalk Functions appendix.

HyperTalk objects are imbued with changeable properties, such as **style**, **size**, and **location**. There are also properties global to HyperCard itself. HyperTalk commands and functions can test and change these properties. These are all discussed in the HyperTalk Properties appendix.

Much of what a HyperTalk script does is, in fact, done by sending a message to some object. Each message has a class of object to which it is normally directed, called the entry point for the message. The pre-defined messages of HyperCard, along with their entry points, are documented in the HyperTalk System Messages appendix.

Perhaps the humblest words and symbols of the HyperTalk language are the operators and constants. HyperTalk operators are symbols, like those used in elementary arithmetic, and they perform the same kinds of functions, such as adding two numbers together. HyperTalk constants are words of the HyperTalk language that refer to fixed, unalterable values as proper nouns in a natural language like English refer to specific individuals. HyperTalk operators and constants are discussed in the HyperTalk Operators and HyperTalk Constants appendixes, respectively.

In addition to the above categories of words, HyperTalk uses a number of words and symbols in special ways, such as to name visual effects or tools, or as adverbs or other modifiers. These uses are spelled out in the HyperTalk Special Words appendix.

The remaining appendixes deal with special uses of HyperTalk.

The HyperTalk Vocabulary

Term	Appendix
"	Special
&	Operators
&&	Operators
()	Operators
*	Operators
+	Operators
-	Operators
--	Special
/	Operators
<	Operators
<=	Operators
<>	Operators
=	Operators
>	Operators
>=	Operators
^	Operators
≠	Operators
≤	Operators
≥	Operators
¬	Special
Abbr	Functions
Abbrev	Functions
Abbreviated	Functions
Abs	Functions
Add	Commands
After	Special
All	Special
AM	Special
And	Operators
Annuity	Functions
Answer	Commands
Any	Special
Apr	Special
April	Special
Arrow [1.2]	Properties, Special
ArrowKey	Commands, Messages
Ascending	Special
Ask	Commands
At	Special
Atan	Functions
Aug	Special
August	Special
AutoHilite	Properties
AutoTab [1.2]	Properties
Average	Functions
Back	Special
Background	Hierarchy
Backgrounds	Hierarchy, Special
Bar	Hierarchy
Barn	Special
Beep	Commands
Before	Special
Bg [1.2]	Hierarchy
Bgs [1.2]	Hierarchy, Special
Bkgnd	Hierarchy
Bkgnds	Hierarchy, Special
Black	Special
Blinds	Properties, Special
BlindTyping	Properties
Bold	Properties
BotRight [1.2]	Properties
Bottom [1.2]	Properties
BottomRight [1.2]	Properties
Box	Hierarchy
Browse	Special
Brush	Properties
Btn	Hierarchy
Btns [1.2]	Hierarchy, Special
Bucket	Special
Busy [1.2]	Properties, Special
Button	Hierarchy
Buttons	Hierarchy, Special

Feb------------------------------------Special
February----------------------------Special
Field--------------------------- Hierarchy
Fields ------------ Hierarchy, Special
Fifth---------------------------------Special
File ----------------------------Command
Filled-------------------------- Properties
Find ------------------------- Commands
First---------------------------------Special
Five-----------------------------Constants
Flash------------------------------XCMDs
Fld [1.2]----------------------- Hierarchy
Flds [1.2]--------- Hierarchy, Special
For----------------------------Structures
Forever-----------------------Structures
FormFeed ------------------- Constants
Forth ------------- Command, Special
FoundChunk [1.2]--------- Functions
FoundField [1.2]------------Functions
FoundLine [1.2]-------------Functions
FoundText [1.2]-------------Functions
Four----------------------------Constants
Fourth-----------------------------Special
FreeSize----------------------- Properties
Fri ------------------------------------Special
Friday ------------------------------Special
From--------------------------------Special
Function----------------------Structures
FunctionKey Commands, Messages
Get--------------------------- Commands
Global-------------------------Structures
Go---------------------------- Commands
Gray---------------------------------Special
Grey [1.2] ------------------------Special
Grid---------------------------- Properties
Hand [1.2] -------- Properties, Special
HeapSpace ------------------- Functions
Height [1.2]------------------ Properties
Help----------Commands, Messages
Hide [1.2]------------------- Commands
Highlight-------------------- Properties
Highlite ---------------------- Properties
Hilight ------------------------Properties
Hilite --------------------------Properties
Home ------------------------ Hierarchy
HyperCard -------------------Hierarchy
IBeam [1.2] -------Properties, Special
Icon --------------------------- Properties
Id -------------------------------Properties
Idle----------------------------- Messages
If ------------------------------Structures
In ------------------------------ Operators
International -------------------Special
Into --------------------------------Special
Inverse ----------------------------Special
Iris ---------------------------------Special
Is ------------------------------- Operators
It ------------------ Vocabulary, Special
Italic----------------------------Properties
Item ------------------------Vocabulary
Items ----------- Vocabulary, Special
Jan ---------------------------------Special
January ------------------------- Special
Jul-----------------------------------Special
July ------------------------------- Special
Jun----------------------------------Special
June ------------------------------ Special
Language ------------------- Properties
Lasso ----------------------------- Special
Last ------------------------------- Special
Left [1.2] ----------------------Properties
Length -----------------------Functions
Line --------------- Vocabulary, Special
LineFeed ---------------------Constants
Lines ------------Vocabulary, Special
LineSize ----------------------Properties
Ln ------------------------------Functions
Ln1 ----------------------------Functions
Loc -----------------------------Properties
Location ----------------------Properties
Lock [1.2] ------------------- Command
LockMessages---------------Properties
LockRecent ---------------- Properties
LockScreen ---------------- Properties

Word	Category
Pop	Commands
PowerKeys	Properties
Prev	Special
Previous	Special
Print	Commands
Printing	Commands
Push	Commands
Put	Commands
Quit	Messages
Quote	Constants
RadioButton	Properties
Random	Functions
Read	Commands
Recent	Special
Rect	Properties
Rectangle	Properties
Reg	Special
Regular	Special
Repeat	Structures
Reset	Commands
Result	Functions
Resume	Messages
Return	Structures, Commands, Constants
ReturnInField [1.2]	Messages
ReturnKey	Commands, Messages
Right [1.2]	Properties
Round	Functions
RoundRect	Properties
Sat	Special
Saturday	Special
ScreenRect [1.2]	Functions
Script	Properties
Scroll	Properties
Scrolling	Properties
Sec [1.2]	Special
Second [1.2]	Special
Second	Special
Seconds	Functions, Special
Secs	Functions, Special
Select [1.2]	Commands
SelectedChunk [1.2]	Functions
SelectedField [1.2]	Functions
SelectedLine [1.2]	Functions
SelectedText [1.2]	Functions
Selection	Functions
Send	Structures, Commands
Sept	Special
September	Special
Set	Commands
Seven	Constants
Seventh	Special
Shadow	Properties
ShiftKey	Functions
Short [1.1]	Functions
Show [1.2]	Commands
ShowLines	Properties
ShowName	Properties
ShowPict [1.2]	Properties
Sin	Functions
Six	Constants
Sixth	Special
Size	Properties
Slow	Special
Slowly	Special
Sort	Commands
Sound	Functions
Space	Constants
Spray	Special
Sqrt	Functions
Stack	Hierarchy
StackSpace	Functions
StartUp	Messages
String [1.2]	Special
Style	Properties
Subtract	Commands
Sun	Special
Sunday	Special
Suspend	Messages
Tab	Constants
TabKey	Commands, Messages
Tan	Functions
Target [1.2]	Functions, Special
Tempo	Commands
Ten	Constants

Appendix B

The HyperTalk Object Hierarchy

About this Appendix

The following pages describe all the classes of objects recognized by the HyperTalk language, and detail the way in which messages move through the objects: the object hierarchy. Like the other technical appendixes, this one is intended for reference purposes. For a more tutorial presentation of the material covered here, you should read the rest of the book.

It's probably impossible to write accurately about technical topics without using a lot of technical terms; at least I haven't been able to do it. This appendix does not attempt to define or exemplify some basic terms that are dealt with elsewhere. For more on messages, you should see the HyperTalk System Messages appendix. If you are having trouble with the concepts of objects and messages and object hierarchies, you might take another look at the Concepts section. For terms that completely mystify, see the HyperTalk Vocabulary appendix.

About Objects, Messages, and Inheritance

HyperTalk contains aspects of what is known as object-oriented programming. In this paradigm of programming, objects (which are neither code nor data but some hybrid entity) send messages to other objects, and the message-receiving objects respond to those messages, if they have message handlers for the messages, exactly as their message handlers dictate. If an object does not have a handler for the message, it may be forwarded to another object that has a handler for the message. There is a natural hierarchy of the HyperCard object classes that controls the default way in which messages move through the system, and every HyperTalk programmer must know it. The classes and the hierarchy are defined in this appendix.

HyperCard Object Classes

There are five classes of HyperCard objects: stacks, backgrounds, cards, fields, and buttons. You can create, modify and destroy instances of these classes, but the classes themselves are part of the definition of the language. HyperTalk does not provide any capability for creating new classes. In addition, there are some other objects important in generating messages: the menu bar with its menu choices produces messages, and the message box allows you to type in commands directly (and commands are messages). The message box is an instance of a class of object called windows, which is a Macintosh system class rather than a HyperCard class; HyperTalk provides limited tools for manipulating objects like windows. Other windows that HyperTalk knows about are the card window, the tool window, and the pattern window, the last two of which are the relocatable windows shown by pulling off the tool and pattern menus from the menu bar.

Origins of Messages

HyperCard in action is a flurry of messages being generated and handled. There are two general ways in which messages can originate: they can be generated by the system or they can be generated by the programmer.

The system generates messages in response to events. These include user actions, such as selecting a menu item or clicking the mouse or pressing the Tab key; as well as context-aware events like clicking the mouse while the pointer is within the boundary rectangle of a particular button, or closing or opening a particular field or card or stack.

It is important to distinguish the message from the event that prompted it. When a user takes some action that results in a stack being closed, for example, the stack-closing event is already in motion when the `closeStack` message is generated. The message does not cause the stack closing; it reports on it. So a script can intercept and respond to this **closeStack** message, causing certain things to happen as the stack is closed. But such a script can't keep the stack from actually closing; no script can, because by the time the message has been generated, it's too late.

There are two ways in which the programmer can generate a message. The first is to type the message into the message box and press return. The second is to use the message in any syntactically correct form in a script.

An obscure point not for the beginning HyperTalk programmer is this: a message can be used in a syntactically correct way in a script and yet not be directly interpreted as a message. Here's how: it is possible, within a line of HyperTalk code, to construct and cause to be executed a different line of HyperTalk code, the latter line never explicitly appearing in that script or in any script. You can use the **do** command to accomplish this. It is even possible to construct lines of code that construct other lines of code that construct yet other lines of code that.... In any such complex and confusing script, a message name can be supplied, not as a syntactic element of the HyperTalk language (which a message normally is), but as a character string. In terms of identifying the origin of the message, though, this possibility does not alter cases: the origin is still the script in which the message name appears.

The event or events that can prompt any particular message are specified in the description of the message in the HyperTalk System Messages appendix.

Entry Points of Messages

Every messages has at least one entry point class, the class of objects that normally handle the message. There are three possibilities: button, field, and card.

Whenever a message is generated, it also has an actual entry point, the particular object to whose script the message will be directed for handling unless somehow diverted.

If the entry point class is card, the actual entry point is the current card. If the entry point class is button or field, the actual object that serves as the entry point depends on the current location of the pointer (or cursor).

If the pointer is within the rectangle of a button (or field) when a message is generated and if that message has a button (or field) entry point, the frontmost button (or field) enclosing the pointer is the actual entry point. The term "frontmost" is defined by these rules: all card buttons and fields are in front of all background buttons and fields, a card button (field) is in front of another card button (field) if the first has a higher **number** property than the second, and a background button (field) is in front of another background button (field) if the first has a higher **number** property than the second. If the pointer is not within the rectangle of any button or field when the message is generated, the current card is the actual entry point.

Sometimes a message is not directed to its entry point on generation. Here is what happens in the case of each kind of message origin:

- A message generated by the system is always directed to its entry point.

- A message appearing in a script is directed to a handler for that message in the same script, if there is one. If there is none, or if the handler contains a **pass** command, the message is directed to its entry point; in the first case immediately and in the second case when the **pass** command is executed. When a message name appears in a **send** command in a script, the message is directed to the object mentioned in the **send** command.

- A message typed into the message box is directed to its entry point, which is the current card.

The entry point classes of messages are defined under the entry point heading in the HyperTalk System Messages appendix.

Paths Followed by Messages

Once a message reaches an object, it may continue on to other objects. The path a message follows through object space is dictated by what the object does with the message and by that object's position in the object hierarchy.

If an object to which a message has been directed has no handler for the message, the message drops through to the next object in the object hierarchy.

If the object has a handler for the message, that handler is invoked and the message goes no further, unless there is a **pass** command in the handler.

If the object has a handler for the message and that handler contains a **pass** command, the message drops through to the next object in the object hierarchy when the **pass** is executed.

If the object in whose script a message appears is not in the current card or stack, there are two possible hierarchies to follow. This situation can arise when a script executes a **go** command, and when it occurs, both object hierarchies are followed: first the hierarchy of the object in whose script the message appears, and then the hierarchy of the current card. If the two hierarchies contain common elements (the Home stack and HyperCard are likely to be common to the two hierarchies, for example), the common elements are visited only once and only after the divergent paths are traced.

The basic paths of the natural object hierarchy are:

- card button -> card -> background -> stack -> stack resource fork -> Home stack -> Home stack resource fork -> HyperCard,
- card field -> card -> background -> stack -> stack resource fork -> Home stack -> Home stack resource fork -> HyperCard,
- background button -> background -> stack -> stack resource fork -> Home stack -> Home stack resource fork -> HyperCard,
- background field -> background -> stack -> stack resource fork -> Home stack -> Home stack resource fork -> HyperCard,
- card -> background -> stack -> stack resource fork -> Home stack -> Home stack resource fork -> HyperCard.

Appendix C

HyperTalk Control Structures

About this Appendix

The following pages detail the salient facts about each HyperTalk control structure: its syntax, a prose description of what it does, and one or more concrete examples of its use. It also provides information for each syntactic component of each structure. Like the other technical appendixes, this one is intended for reference purposes. For a more tutorial presentation of the use of HyperTalk control structures, you should read the earlier portions of the book.

This information on control structures is as timely and as accurate as I could make it. All facts were checked at final board stage, and should be consistent with the state of HyperTalk at that time. I checked structure syntax and example code with HyperCard, then pasted the properly running code directly into the text, minimizing the opportunities for errors to creep in.

It's probably impossible to write accurately about technical topics without using a lot of technical terms; at least I haven't been able to do it. If you get tripped up by any technical term or topic in this appendix, you may find clarification in one of the other technical appendixes. For more on commands, functions, or system messages, you should see the corresponding appendix. The HyperTalk Object Hierarchy appendix covers how messages trickle through the objects of a HyperCard stack. If you are having trouble with the concepts of objects and messages and object hierarchies, you might take another look at the Concepts section. For terms that completely mystify, see the HyperTalk Vocabulary appendix.

About HyperTalk Control Structures

HyperTalk control structures are the large-scale grouping tools of the language. They organize individual commands into logical groupings that perform coherent actions. There are only four control structures in HyperTalk: the message handler, the function handler, the **If** structure, and the **Repeat** structure.

The general form that every structure takes is:

```
<structureStart>
   <any number of commands,
   possibly including more structures>
<structureEnd>.
```

Usually a structure is spread over several lines, as shown here, with the first line being the <structureStart>, and the last line the <structureEnd>, although the **If** structure accepts variant forms that collapse the elements into fewer lines. What I have identified as the <structureStart> is always a unique word identifying the structure plus other structure-specific words. What I have identified as the <structureEnd> is almost invariably the keyword **end** followed by the unique word used in the <structureStart>; the exception is in the case of a collapsed **If** structure. Structures may also contain other keywords, such as the keyword **else** used in the **If** structure and discussed in this appendix.

Structures define when and how often the statements they enclose are to be executed.

It's worth pointing out that two of the structures can be considered informally as commands, and can be used in many places where a command is appropriate. This includes using structures in other structures. In fact, the **If** and **Repeat** structure must appear in at least one other structure, since the message handler and function handler are the top-level structures of the language, and all other structures must reside within them. But **If** and **Repeat** structures can also be "nested" within other **If** and **Repeat** structures quite freely. Message and function handlers cannot be nested within other structures.

It's also worth emphasizing that these four structures are the only large-scale grouping tools of the language. If you have other programming experience you know that in other programming languages the program itself is normally the largest-scale grouping tool. People write programs to perform particular coherent actions. If the script in HyperTalk seems in some ways to correspond to the program in other languages, it is not comparable in this sense. HyperTalk scripts consist of message handlers and function handlers, and although there are important consequences of those handlers residing in the same script, it is a mistake to think of them as subroutines and of the script as a program. The end result of HyperTalk programming is sometimes called stackware, but that's just a reference to the medium of distribution. The somewhat disorienting fact is that when you've finished the job the result is likely to be not a single magnum opus to which you can point with pride, but instead several interrelated entities in a complex cybernetic ecology.

The conventional programmer builds a tree; the HyperTalk programmer engineers a forest.

The Message Handler Structure

Syntax:

```
On <messageName>
  <commands>
End <messageName>

On <messageName> <parameters>
  <commands>
End <messageName>
```

Description:

The **Message Handler** structure is invoked when its message is received by the object in whose script the handler resides. Once invoked, it executes its list of commands and terminates.

A handler can be defined to accept one or more parameters. On invocation, these must follow the message name, and if there are two or more parameters, they must be separated by commas. The names used for the parameters in the definition of the handler are called the formal parameters; any parameters supplied when the handler is invoked are called the actual parameters. If the handler is invoked with parameters, it uses the actual values passed to it in the place of the corresponding formal parameters. If more actual parameters are used than there are formal parameters, the excess parameter values are ignored. If fewer actual parameters are supplied than there are formal parameters, the remaining formal parameters are assigned the value **empty**. If the handler looks like this:

```
On moosh leftOne rightOne
  Put leftOne && rightOne
End moosh
```

and if it was invoked by this message:

```
Moosh "Harry", "James"
```

then it will do the same as this command:

```
Put "Harry" && "James".
```

The structure elements **`Exit`** and **`Pass`** can alter control flow in any structure. Each can terminate a structure and divert control elsewhere. Each is documented further in the next section.

Examples from a Home stack:

```
On record
  -- MacroMaker handler added by MS 6/88.
  Global recording
  If recording
    Then doMenu "stop recording"
    Else doMenu "start recording"
  Put not recording into recording
End record

On functionKey k
  -- DimSum functionKey handler added by MS 6/88.
  -- Puts the contents of the global variable
  -- dimSum into the message box. One of a pair
  -- of handlers for short-term msg memory.
  Global dimSum
  If k=12 then put dimSum into msg
End functionKey

On returnKey
  -- DimSum returnKey handler added by MS 6/88.
  -- Puts the contents of the message box in the
  -- global variable dimSum. One of a pair of
  -- handlers implementing short-term msg memory.
  Global dimSum
  Put msg into dimSum
  Pass returnKey
End returnKey
```

The Function Handler Structure

Syntax:

```
Function <functionName>
  <commands>
  Return <returnValue>
  <commands>
End <functionName>

Function <functionName> <parameters>
  <commands>
  Return <returnValue>
  <commands>
End <functionName>
```

Description:

The **Function Handler** structure is invoked when its message is received by the object in whose script the handler resides. Once invoked, it executes its list of commands and terminates. A function returns a value, which takes the place occupied by the function and its parameters in the invoking handler. The value returned by a user-defined function is the value specified in the **return** statement.

A function handler can be defined to accept one or more parameters. On invocation, these must be enclosed in parentheses after the function name. The names used for the parameters in the definition of the function handler are called the formal parameters; any parameters supplied when the function handler is invoked are called the actual parameters. If the function handler is invoked with parameters, it uses the actual values passed to it in the place of the corresponding formal parameters. If more actual parameters are used than there are formal parameters, the excess parameter values are ignored. If fewer actual parameters are supplied than there are formal parameters, the remaining formal parameters are assigned the value **empty**. If the function handler looks like this:

```
Function moosh leftOne rightOne
  Return leftOne && rightOne
End moosh
```

and if it was invoked by this message:

```
Put moosh("Harry", "James")
```

then it will do the same as this command:

```
Put "Harry" && "James".
```

The structure elements `Exit` and `Pass` can alter control flow in any structure. Each can terminate a structure and divert control elsewhere. Each is documented further in the next section.

Example from Apple's stacks:

```
Function thisHalfYear myDate
  Convert myDate to dateItems
  If item 2 of myDate > 6
  Then put 7 into myMonth
  Else put 1 into myMonth
  Put item 1 of myDate & "," & myMonth ¬
  & ",1,0,0,0,0" into myDate
  Convert myDate to seconds
  Return myDate
End thisHalfYear
```

The If Structure

Syntax:

```
If <Boolean> then <command>

If <Boolean>
Then <command>

If <Boolean> then
```

```
  <commands>
End if

If <Boolean>
Then
  <commands>
End if

If <Boolean> then <command> else <command>

If <Boolean>
Then <command>
Else <command>

If <Boolean> then
  <commands>
Else
  <commands>
End if

If <Boolean>
Then
  <commands>
Else
  <commands>
End if

If <Boolean> then
  <commands>
Else <commands>

If <Boolean>
Then
  <commands>
Else <commands>
```

Description:

The **If** structure permits conditional execution. It evaluates the Boolean expression **<Boolean>**; if this evaluates to true, the commands following the **then** are executed; if **<Boolean>** is false, the commands following the **else** are executed if an **else** is present; if **<Boolean>** is false and no **else** is present, nothing happens.

There are ten basic variations on the syntax of the **If** structure. These are distinguished by the presence or absence of the **else** element, by the presence or absence of the **end if** element, and by the **then** element's being on the same line as the **if** or on the following line. Those with an **end if** permit more than one statement to follow the **then** and the **else**.

The structure elements **Exit** and **Pass** can alter control flow in any structure. Each can terminate a structure and divert control elsewhere. Each is documented further in the next section.

Example of a handler showing nested **If** and **Repeat** structures, from a Home stack User Preferences card:

```
On mouseUp
  -- Handler added by Mike Swaine, 5/88.
  Global fgColor,bgColor,fgPrefColor,bgPrefColor
  If short name of the target contains "color"
  Then
    Put the short name of the target ¬
    into theButton
    Set the hilite of button theButton to true
    If word 1 of theButton is "fg"
    Then
      Put word 3 of theButton into fgPrefColor
      Put fgPrefColor into item 1 ¬
      of card field colors
    End if
    If word 1 of theButton is "bg"
    Then
      Put word 3 of theButton into bgPrefColor
      Put space & bgPrefColor into item 2 ¬
      of card field colors
    End if
    Repeat with i=1 to the number of buttons
      If word 1 of the short name of button i ¬
      = word 1 of theButton ¬
      and word 2 of the short name of button i ¬
      = word 2 of theButton ¬
```

```
      and word 3 of the short name of button i ¬
      ≠ word 3 of theButton
      Then set the hilite of button i to false
    End repeat
  End if
End mouseUp
```

The Repeat Structure

Syntax:

```
Repeat for <count> times
  <commands>
End repeat

Repeat for <count>
  <commands>
End repeat

Repeat <count> times
  <commands>
End repeat

Repeat<count>
  <commands>
End repeat

Repeat forever
  <commands>
End repeat

Repeat until <BoleanValue>
  <commands>
End repeat

Repeat while <BooleanValue>
  <commands>
End repeat
```

```
Repeat with <count> = <lowCount> to <highCount>
  <commands>
End repeat

Repeat with <count> = <highCount> down to <lowCount>
  <commands>
End repeat
```

Description:

The **Repeat** structure causes the sequence of statements within its first and last lines to be executed repeatedly. The first line of the structure specifies the number of repetitions or the conditions under which repetition should continue.

Any of the syntactic variants of the **Repeat** structure can also contain one or more instances of the structure elements **Exit repeat** and **Next repeat**. These elements both alter the flow of control in the **Repeat** structure. **Exit repeat** causes immediate termination of the repeat structure and **Next repeat** causes termination of the current loop of the structure.

The structure elements **Exit** and **Pass** can alter control flow in any structure. Each can terminate a structure and divert control elsewhere. Each is documented further in the next section.

Examples:

```
-- Nested Repeats, modified from something in
-- Apple's Home stack script.
Repeat with i = 1 to the number of cards
  Go card i
  If the script of this card contains pattern
  Then edit script of this card
  Repeat with j = 1 to the number of card buttons
    If the script of card button j ¬
    contains pattern
    Then edit script of card button j
  End repeat
  Repeat with j = 1 to the number of card fields
    If the script of card field j ¬
    contains pattern
```

```
    Then edit script of card field j
  End repeat
End repeat

On mouseUp
  -- Same example as used for If structure.
  -- Shows If and Repeat nesting.
  Global fgColor,bgColor,fgPrefColor,bgPrefColor
  If short name of the target contains "color"
  Then
    Put the short name of the target ¬
    into theButton
    Set the hilite of button theButton to true
    If word 1 of theButton is "fg"
    Then
      Put word 3 of theButton into fgPrefColor
      Put fgPrefColor into item 1 ¬
      of card field colors
    End if
    If word 1 of theButton is "bg"
    Then
      Put word 3 of theButton into bgPrefColor
      Put space & bgPrefColor into item 2 ¬
      of card field colors
    End if
    Repeat with i=1 to the number of buttons
      If word 1 of the short name of button i ¬
      = word 1 of theButton ¬
      and word 2 of the short name of button i ¬
      = word 2 of theButton ¬
      and word 3 of the short name of button i ¬
      ≠ word 3 of theButton
      Then set the hilite of button i to false
    End repeat
  End if
End mouseUp
```

Elements of Command Structures

The remainder of this appendix describes each of the elements of the structures—each word that can form a part of a structure.

Else

Syntax:

```
Else
If <Boolean> then <commands> else <commands>
```

Description:

The element **else** is used to introduce the command or commands to be carried out if the condition of an **if** structure is not satisfied. See the **If** structure.

End

Syntax:

```
End <messageName>
End <functionName>
End if
End repeat
```

Description:

The element **end** is used to signal the end of a structure. It must introduce the last line of any instance of any of the four structures, except in the case of an **if** structure not requiring it. See descriptions of the message handler, function, **If,** and **Repeat** structures.

Exit

Syntax:

```
Exit <messageName>
Exit repeat
Exit to HyperCard
```

Description:

The element **exit** effects an immediate departure from a structure. When an **exit** is encountered, no further commands within the structure are executed. See descriptions of the message handler, function, **If**, and **Repeat** structures.

For

Syntax:

```
Repeat for <count> times
Repeat for <count>
```

Description:

The element **for** is used to introduce the count value controlling the number of repetitions in one form of the **repeat** structure. It is optional in all uses. See the **Repeat** structure.

Forever

Syntax:

```
Repeat forever
```

Description:

The element **forever** signals that the **repeat** structure in which it occurs should repeat without termination. See the **Repeat** structure.

Function

Syntax:

```
Function <functionName>
Function <functionName> <parameters>
```

Description:

The element **function** introduces a function handler. It is followed by the name of the function and any parameters. See the description of the function handler structure.

If

Syntax:

```
If <Boolean>
If <Boolean> then
If <Boolean> then <command>
If <Boolean> then <command> else <command>

End if
```

Description:

The element **if** introduces the **if** structure. It is followed by an expression that must evaluate to true or false. See the **If** structure.

Next

Syntax:

```
Next repeat
```

Description:

The element **next**, always used with **repeat**, causes any other lines following it within the **repeat** structure immediately enclosing it to be skipped, and execution to pick up with the next iteration of that **repeat** structure. See the **Repeat** structure.

On

Syntax:

```
On <messageName>
  <commands>
End <messageName>

On <messageName> <parameters>
  <commands>
End <messageName>
```

Description:

The element **on** introduces a message handler. It is followed by the name of the message and any parameters. See the description of the message handler structure.

Pass

Syntax:

```
Pass <message>
```

Description:

Pass causes program flow to jump to the next handler for the message <message>. "Next" in this context means the next such handler encountered in the HyperCard hierarchy.

The parameter <message> must be a single word, and that word must be the name of the handler in which **Pass** appears. Quotes around the word are acceptable, but not necessary. No parameters to <message> are allowed; whatever parameters (if any) that were given to the handler in which **Pass** appears will be passed along with the message to the next handler. This necessitates that the parameters to the former handler be appropriate to the latter.

Pass allows you to "trap" a message that would normally be handled lower in the HyperCard hierarchy, perform some action in response to the message, and then **Pass** the message on through the hierarchy to be handled as it normally would be. It wasn't designed to send out arbitrary messages; only to pass along a message so that it can provoke more than one handler. There are two methods for sending out other messages: To generate a particular message (other than the message currently being handled) for processing by the next handler for that message, you simply use the message as you would any command. To send a particular message to a handler in the script of a particular object, you use the **Send** command. See descriptions of the message handler, function, **If**, and **Repeat** structures.

Examples:

```
-- The following pair of handlers show how you can
-- use a specialized Beep handler to beep in various
-- voices and tempi.  Note that the second call to
-- Beep is syntactically illegal; the specialized
-- Beep handler must not pass it.
On mouseUp
  beep 1
```

```
  beep 1,1
End mouseUp
-- The specialized Beep handler:
on beep arg,tempo
  put the params
  if the paramCount < 2
  then
    pass beep
  else
    play line arg of field "voices",tempo
  end if
end beep

-- This handler intercepts the Help message and
-- uses it to call up a specialized Help stack.
-- The user can still get to the HyperCard Help stack
-- by holding down the cmd key while invoking Help.
-- By, for example, holding down the command key
-- while pressing the Help key on a Mac II keyboard.
on help
  if the commandKey is down
  then
    pass help
  else
    go AddressHelp
  end if
end help
```

Repeat

Syntax:

```
Repeat for <count> times
Repeat for <count>
Repeat <count> times
Repeat<count>
Repeat forever

Repeat until <BoleanValue>
```

```
Repeat while <BooleanValue>

Repeat with <count> = <lowCount> to <highCount>
Repeat with <count> = <highCount> downTo <lowCount>

Next repeat
End repeat
```

Description:

The element **repeat** introduces the **Repeat** structure. The line on which this element occurs also contains a specification of the number of repetitions or the conditions under which repetitions will continue or cease. See the **Repeat** structure.

Return

Syntax:

```
Return <expression>
```

Description:

As an element in a user-defined function or message handler, **Return** evaluates <expression> and causes the function or handler to terminate, returning the value of <expression> as the value of the function or, in the case of a handler, making it accessible via the function **Result**. See the description of the function handler structure.

The parameter <expression> can be any expression. If <expression> evaluates to **empty** or if no **Return** is supplied in the handler, the value **empty** will be returned. If a **Return** is present but no <expression> is supplied, it is an error.

Examples:

```
-- Using Return in a message handler:
On mouseUp
  CheckLoc
  Put the result
End mouseUp
On checkLoc
  Return the loc of me
End checkLoc

-- Creating Basic-style aliases for two
-- cumbersome HyperTalk functions:
Function Chr theNum
  Return numToChar(theNum)
End Chr
Function Asc theString
  Return charToNum(character 1 of theString)
End Asc
```

Then

Syntax:

```
Then
If <BooleanExpression> then <commands>
```

Description:

The element **then** is used to introduce the command or commands to be carried out if the condition of an **if** structure is satisfied. See the **If** structure.

Until

Syntax:

```
Repeat until <BooleanExpression>
```

Description:

The element **until** is used to specify a termination condition for the **repeat** structure in whose first line it appears. As long as the expression following the **until** is false, the structure will repeat. See the **Repeat** structure.

While

Syntax:

```
Repeat while <BooleanExpression>
```

Description:

The element **while** is used to specify a continuation condition for the **repeat** structure in whose first line it appears. As long as the expression following the **while** is true, the structure will repeat. See the **Repeat** structure.

With

Syntax:

```
Repeat with <count> = <lowCount> to <highCount>
Repeat with <count> = <highCount> down to <lowCount>
```

Description:

The element **with** is used to supply a count variable that indicates the current number of repetition of a **repeat** structure while it is executing. See the **Repeat** structure.

Appendix D

HyperTalk Commands

About this Appendix

The following pages detail the salient facts about every HyperTalk command: its syntax, a prose description of what it does, and one or more concrete examples of its use. The syntax description is in template form, which I think is clearer for beginning and intermediate programmers than some of the more concise ways of specifying syntax. It should be fairly easy to match any correct use of a command to one of its syntax templates. Like the other technical appendixes, this one is intended for reference purposes. For a more tutorial presentation of the use of HyperTalk commands, you should read earlier portions of the book.

Some things that have been called commands are not documented in this appendix. Just what is and what is not a command should be unambiguous, but unfortunately the object-oriented nature and the extensibility of HyperTalk cloud the issue. I have had to make decisions about where to document elements of the language, and some of those decisions may not be in line with your intuition. If you think it's a command and don't find it here, the index will tell you in which appendix I've documented it.

Some things that act like commands are not documented in the appendixes because they are not in fact part of the language. It is possible to, in effect, add commands to the language by writing programs in another programming language and incorporating them into HyperTalk via what are called XCMDs, or external commands. The potential number of such external commands is infinite, and would exceed the page budget for this book. Some XCMDs, however, such as Bill Atkinson's **`Flash`** XCMD, are so familiar that they are often thought to be HyperTalk commands. I have tried to say what needed to be said about them on their first mention in the book. Consult the index.

Some authors use different names than I do for some of the commands. The difference should not be confusing, since in every case my name is just a shorter version of theirs. I have adopted the convention that the name of a command is one word; that there are no multi-word commands. I treat the other words that accompany some commands as parameters and keywords. This seems to me simpler than the alternative, reduces the number of commands to remember, and is consistent with the uncontentious observation that HyperCard messages are never longer than one word. (Messages are documented in the HyperTalk Messages appendix. Parameters and keywords are dealt with in the body of this appendix and defined in the next section, About HyperTalk Commands.) There aren't enough words to go around.: the word "keyword" is being used here in a different sense than Apple's.

The information in this command appendix is as timely and as accurate as I could make it. All facts were checked and rechecked, and should be consistent with the state of HyperTalk at the time of final board check. I ran all example code through HyperCard, then pasted the properly running code directly into the text, minimizing the opportunities for errors to creep in.

It's probably impossible to write accurately about technical topics without using a lot of technical terms; at least I haven't been able to do it. If you get tripped up by any technical term or topic in this appendix, you may find clarification in one of the other technical appendixes. For more on messages, you should see the HyperTalk System Messages appendix. The HyperTalk Object Hierarchy appendix covers how messages trickle through the objects of a HyperCard stack. If you are having trouble with the concepts of objects and messages and object hierarchies, you might take another look at the Concepts section.

Taken one at a time, the concepts of command, function, property, and message may seem clear and intuitive, but in the early stages of learning HyperTalk it is not always obvious to what category a particular word belongs. The HyperTalk Vocabulary appendix can point to the appropriate appendix, and a careful comparison of the "About" sections of the Commands, Functions, Properties, and System Messages appendixes can help to clarify the differences.

About HyperTalk Commands

HyperTalk commands are the verbs of the language. They name actions that you can direct HyperCard to perform. Technically, they are a subset of the HyperTalk messages: specifically, those messages recognized by HyperCard itself. HyperTalk commands can, in general, appear in scripts or be typed into the message box, although some can only be used in scripts.

The precise specification of the ways in which you can use a command, that is, the ways in which you can construct sentences from that verb, is called the syntax of the command. Some commands, like intransitive verbs, can stand alone. The **`Beep`** command, for example, can appear alone. But most commands, like transitive verbs, require a following noun, an object upon which to act. Such an object, which may or may not be an object in the technical, HyperCard sense, is more properly called the parameter of the command. A command may have more than one parameter, and some parameters are optional.

Often it is possible to supply as a parameter either an actual value (a number, for example) or an expression that HyperCard will evaluate, producing the value that will actually be used by the command. Several kind of expressions are possible, such as variables or containers in which values are stored (startingBalance), chunking expressions that tell where to find values (word 1 of line 1 of card field "check register"), arithmetic expressions (2 + 2), combinations of these (2 + startingBalance + word 1 of line 1 of card field "check register"), and some others. Sometimes the interpretation of a parameters of a command can be ambiguous, and HyperCard has many strategies for resolving ambiguities. For example, in the command **`Put north into card field Direction`**, it will attempt to treat **`north`** as a container, placing the value of **`north`** into the field; only if this doesn't work will it place the literal string "north" into the field.

The syntax for any particular command may also require additional keywords, analogous to prepositions. For example, the **`Put`** command frequently uses the word **into**, producing command invocations such as **Put 57 into howManyVarieties**. A command's syntax may also permit adverb-like keyword modifiers, such as the words **very** and **slowly** in **Visual effect dissolve very slowly**.

Add

Syntax:

```
Add <source> to <destination>
```

Description:

The **Add** command adds the value in <source> to the value in <destination> and places the result in <destination>.

Both the <source> and <destination> parameters must contain numeric values. The <source> can be a literal, a variable, an expression, or a function, but it must evaluate to a number. The <destination> must initially contain a value (you can't add a number to a non-number). The <destination> must also be changeable, so it cannot be a literal, an expression, or a function.

There is nothing that you can do using the **Add** command that you can't do without it. You can always use **Put** <source> **+** <destination> **into** <destination> in the place of **Add** <source> **to** <destination>. You may find the **Add** command more readable in some contexts.

Examples:

```
Put 3 into theCount
Add 5 to theCount

Put 3 into theCount
Add theCount to theCount

-- A field script that totals a column of numbers
```

```
On mouseLeave
  Put 0 into line 1 of field nums
  Repeat with i=2 to the number of lines ¬
  in field nums
    Add line i of field nums to line 1 ¬
    of field nums
  End repeat
End mouseLeave
```

Answer

Syntax:

```
Answer <question>
Answer <question> with  <reply1>
Answer <question> with  <reply1> or <reply2>
Answer <question> with  <reply1> or <reply2> or <reply3>
```

Description:

The **Answer** command displays a dialog box containing the <question> and from one to three buttons, each labelled with one of the <reply> parameters. If no <reply> parameter is supplied, a button labelled "OK" will be displayed. The last of the buttons will be displayed with a double border indicating that it is the default response.

At this point, the user must click on one of the buttons. Which button the user selects determines what value will be placed in the system variable **it**. If the user presses the Return key, the default response will be placed in the variable **it**.

The <question> parameter and the <reply> parameters can be any expressions interpretable as text strings. Since HyperCard will interpret almost anything as a text string if possible, this is not very restricting. The parameters can be literal numbers, variables containing numeric values, logical values, and uninitialized variables.

The **Answer** command is a convenient way to offer a restricted set of choices to the user. Without a <reply> parameter, it can be used as an Alert box to notify the user of a situation that requires attention, or as a debugging aid by supplying a value to be monitored in the <question> parameter. The user's response, like the <reply> that it displaces, can be a string, a number, or even a logical value (true or false).

Examples:

```
Answer "Staff meeting in five minutes."

Answer "Sort cards by:" with "First name" ¬
or "Last name"
Put it into sortOrder
```

ArrowKey

The **arrowKey** command is documented in the HyperTalk System Messages appendix.

Ask

Syntax:

```
Ask <question>
Ask <question> with <default reply>

Ask password <question>
Ask password <question> with <default reply>
```

Description:

The **Ask** command displays a dialog box displaying the <question>, a text window that in turn contains the highlighted <default reply> if any, and two buttons, labelled "OK" and "Cancel."

At this point, the user must take some action. The user can click on Cancel or click on OK, and can modify the text in the text window or leave it alone. What the user does determines what value will be placed in the system variable **it**. If the user clicks on Cancel, with or without modifying the text in the text window, the special value **empty** will be placed in the variable **it**. If the user clicks on OK, the value in the text window will be placed in the variable **it**, either the default value supplied in the **Ask** command or a value keyed in by the user.

If the **Ask** command is followed by the keyword **password**, the value placed in the variable it will be encrypted as a number. The special value **empty** will not be encrypted, however.

The parameters <question> and <default reply> can be any expressions interpretable as text strings. Since HyperCard will interpret almost anything as a text string if possible, this is not very restricting. The parameters can be literal numbers, variables containing numeric values, logical values, and uninitialized variables.

The **Ask** command is the primary means for getting arbitrary input from the user. The user's response, like the <default reply> that it displaces, can be a string, a number, or even a logical value (true or false). The passworded version of the **Ask** command is, not surprisingly, appropriate for requesting a password from the user.

Although the syntax of the **Ask** command allows you to specify a <default reply> in the **Ask password** case, it really doesn't make sense to offer a default password or to encrypt a default response.

Examples:

```
Ask "Who's buried in Grant's tomb?"

Global userName
Ask "Please enter your name." with userName
Ask password "And your password."
If it is not theProperPassword then Beep

Ask "Edit the script of..." with "card button 1"
If it is not empty then Edit script of it
```

```
Ask "t/f" with true
If it then Put "Correct."
```

Beep

Syntax:

```
Beep
Beep <count>
```

Description:

The **Beep** command causes a sound to be emitted through the machine's speaker or audio port. The sound emitted is the system alert sound, typically a beep. If the command is followed by a number (the <count>), that number of identical sounds will be emitted; otherwise there will be just one sound. The <count> parameter must be a number or a variable or function or expression that evaluates to a number.

The **Beep** command is used primarily as an alert to the user; to produce a variety of sounds or to play music, you should use the **Play** command.

Examples:

```
Beep

Beep 5

Beep the ticks - 116320

Beep word 2 of card field "test"
```

Choose

Syntax:

```
Choose <toolname> tool
```

Description:

The **Choose** command is one of a number of commands that automate HyperCard actions that you would otherwise perform by pulling down menus, clicking on buttons, and so on. The **Choose** command in particular exactly mimics the action of pulling down the Tools menu and selecting one of the tools.

When using the **Choose** command, though, you refer to the tool by name rather than by icon. The parameter <toolname> must be a valid tool name. The names of the tools, in the order in which they appear in the menu, and with the acceptable alternate forms, are: browse, button, field, select, lasso, pencil, brush, eraser, line, spray or spray can, rectangle or rect, round rectangle or round rect, bucket, oval, curve, text, regular polygon or reg poly, and polygon or poly.

Examples:

```
Choose regular polygon tool

Choose reg poly tool

Choose button tool

Choose field tool
```

Click

Syntax:

```
Click at <location>
Click at <location> with <key1>
Click at <location> with <key1>,<key2>
Click at <location> with <key1>,<key2>,<key3>
```

Description:

The **Click** command is one of those commands that automate HyperCard actions that you would otherwise perform by pulling down menus, clicking on buttons, and so on. The **Click** command in particular exactly mimics the action of clicking the mouse, and allows you to specify precise HyperCard window coordinates for the click. Demands that you do, in fact.

The location is mandatory, and must consist of two numbers specifying appropriate horizontal and vertical HyperCard window coordinates, or two containers holding such numbers, or one container containing two such numbers.

You can also specify from zero to three keys from the following list: optionKey, commandKey, shiftKey. Specifying a key name simulates holding down that key while clicking the mouse.

By using the **Click** command, you can position the cursor within a field, invoke button scripts, select blocks of text, make scrolling fields scroll by clicking on their scroll bar controls, or position and use the paint tools.

Examples:

```
Put "0,0" into upLeftCorner
Click at upLeftCorner

-- Selecting a few characters of text:
Click at h,v
Click at h+24,v with shiftKey

-- Fiddling with painting tools:
```

```
Choose brush tool
Click at 500,150
-- Oh no!  Not there!
Choose eraser tool
Click at 500,150
-- Whew!
Choose browse tool
-- Don't forget that last step:
-- always restore the browse tool.
```

Close

Syntax:

```
Close printing

Close file <filename>
```

Description:

The **Close** command terminates the print job, flushing the print buffer; or it closes a file.

The keywords **file** and **printing** determine whether the **Close** command closes a file or terminates the current print job. The <filename> parameter is mandatory and must be a file name or a container holding a file name.

The commands **Open**, **Close**, and **Print** work in concert to set up and execute a print job. The **Open** command sets up the print job, the **Close** command terminates it and causes all queued cards to be printed, and between the **Open** and **Close** commands, any number of cards can be queued for printing using a **Print cards** variation of the **Print** command. (Note that the file printing variation of the **Print** command should never be used between an **Open** command and a **Close** command.) Although an individual card can be dumped to the printer by using the **Print** command without the **Open** and **Close** commands, they are necessary when you want to print a batch of cards and care about the HyperCard printing format of them.

The commands **Open**, **Close**, and either **Write** or **Read** are always used together when exporting text to or importing it from text-only external files. The **Open** command opens the text file (creating it if necessary), the **Close** command closes it and between the **Open** and **Close** commands, any number of **Read** and/or **Write** commands can be executed to copy text from and to the file. It is not possible to use the **Read** and **Write** commands to access an external file without first using **Open** to open the file. It is not possible to close a file with the **Close** command unless it has been opened with the **Open** command.

The two variations of the **Close** command in fact do very different things: wrapping up a print job is not the same as closing a disk file. But conceptually, each is the closing bracket of an I/O operation that may extend across several lines of code and for which the **Open** command is the opening bracket.

Examples:

```
Close printing

Open printing with dialog
Print this card
Print next card
Close printing

Close file myFile

Close file "HyperCard:MyStacks:Notes 5/13"

-- Note that you must close and reopen a file
-- to read back what you have written to it.
-- This is because the Write command overwrites
-- whatever was in the file and does not return
-- to the beginning of the file.
Put "Major Major" into Major
Open file Major
Write "Major" to file Major
Close file Major
```

```
Open file Major
Read from file Major until "r"
Put it
Close file Major

If printingOpen then put "printing" into whatsOpen
Else if fileOpen then put "file " & fileName ¬
into whatsOpen
Do "Close " & whatsOpen
```

Convert

Syntax:

```
Convert <time> to <format>
Covert <time> to <format1> and <format2>
```

Description:

The **Convert** command performs time and date format conversions.

HyperCard supports several formats for the time and date, and this command allows you to convert from one to another. The parameter <time> must be a container that contains a time or date value in one of the legal formats. The <format> must be a legal format name. The second syntax form permits converting date and time simultaneously to date and time formats. The names and example uses of the legal formats are:

secs, seconds:	2682460800 (seconds since 12:00:00 AM, 1/1/1904)
short time:	12:00 AM
long time:	12:00:00 AM
short date:	1/1/89
long date:	January 1, 1989
abbr date, abbrev date,	

abbreviated date:	Sun, January 1, 1989
dateItems	1989,1,1,0,0,0,1 (year, month, day, hour, minute, second, day of week, as a numeric list separated by commas).

(All of the examples above represent the same date or time: 12:00:00 AM, Sunday, January 1, 1989.)

There are two reasons to alter the format of a date or time container: because you are going to print or display it and want it to look right, or in order to perform some calculation (arithmetic or logical or string-manipulation). Before using the **Convert** command in the latter case, make sure HyperCard isn't already doing the conversion for you.

Example:

```
-- A script that computes tomorrow's date
-- from today's by converting today's date
-- into the number of seconds since a fixed
-- past time, then adding a day's worth of seconds,
-- and converting the result back to date format,
-- then packing some time data in.
-- Not something you would really want to do.
On mouseUp
  Put the date into today
  Convert today to seconds
  Put today + 60*60*24 into tomorrow
  Convert tomorrow to short date
  Put tomorrow
  Convert tomorrow to dateItems
  Put "12,30,00" into item 4 to 6 of tomorrow
  Put tomorrow
End mouseUp
```

Debug

Syntax:

```
Debug <parameters>
```

Description:

The **debug** command is an "undocumented" HyperTalk command. It sees much use by HyperCard development team, but is of little value to the general HyperTalk programmer. Before the release of version 1.2, it was used to test code written for read-only media, like CD-ROM, but version 1.2 completely eliminated this need.

Example:

```
Debug write off -- version 1.1 only.
Debug write on -- version 1.1 only.
```

Delete

Syntax:

```
Delete <text>
```

Description:

The **Delete** command deletes text from a container.

Parameter <text> must be a container; either a field or portion of a field or a variable or part thereof. You can specify a card in indicating the field; if you don't, the deletion will be done, if possible, from the current card. You can't delete across stacks.

The **Delete** command is the command to use to remove whole lines from fields. It is not equivalent to using the command **Put** with the parameter **empty**.

Examples:

```
Delete char 1 of dialNumber

Put "Robert Alice Harbinger" into name
Delete mid word of name

Repeat with i=1 to 3
  Put "testing" & return before card field 4
End repeat
Delete line 1 to 3 of card field 4

Put "testing " before card field 4
Delete word 1 of card field 4
```

Dial

Syntax:

```
Dial <phonenumber>
Dial <phonenumber> with modem
Dial <phonenumber> with modem <modem string>
```

Description:

The **Dial** command outputs the string of digits in <phonenumber> either as touch-tone telephone sounds through the Macintosh speaker or as digits through a serial port for use by a modem. In the modem case it can also send Hayes-compatible modem command strings in <modem string>.

The <phonenumber> parameter must be a string of digits or a string enclosed in quotes and including "telephone digits" (a nonce term I am using for all digits plus the characters # and * and A, B, C, and D; non-digits are ignored) or a container holding such a string. The <modem string> parameter must contain a valid modem command string.

The **Dial** command is used for to dial the telephone, either for modem or voice communication.

Examples:

```
Dial 4085551212

Dial dialNumber with modem "ATS0=0DP"

Dial line HorW of background field "Phone"

-- It can be educational to work out why and ¬
-- under what circumstances monstrosities ¬
-- such as this one work.
Dial line line line 2 of field 1 of ¬
field 1 of field 1
```

Divide

Syntax:

```
Divide <destination> by <source>
```

Description:

The **Divide** command divides the value in <destination> by the value in <source> and places the result in <destination>.

Both the <source> and <destination> parameters must contain numeric values. The <source> can be a literal, a variable, an expression, or a function, but it must evaluate to a number. The <destination> must initially contain a value (you can't divide a non-number by a number). The <destination> must also be changeable, so it cannot be a literal, an expression, or a function.

There is nothing that you can do using the **Divide** command that you can't do without it. You can always use **Put** <destination> **/** <source> **into** <destination> in the place of **Divide** <destination>

by <source>. You may find the **Divide** command more readable in some contexts.

Examples:

```
Divide theTotal by 5

If denom <> 0 then divide numer by denom

-- A field script that averages a column of numbers
On mouseLeave
  Put 0 into line 1 of field nums
  Repeat with i=2 to the number of lines ¬
  in field nums
    Add line i of field nums to line 1 ¬
    of field nums
  End repeat
  Put the number of lines of field nums - 1 ¬
  into nItems
  Divide line 1 of field nums by nItems
End mouseLeave
```

Do

Syntax:

```
Do <string>
```

Description:

The **Do** command evaluates <string> and performs it as a HyperTalk command.

The parameter <string> can be any combination of elements that evaluate to a legal HyperTalk command, including contents of fields, concatenated expressions, memory variables, and literal strings.

The **Do** command is one of a number of commands that automate HyperCard actions that you would otherwise perform by pulling down menus, clicking on buttons, and so on. The **Do** command in fact can be used to construct almost any HyperTalk command. This becomes important when you are operating on more than one level, offering a variable expression to a command that expects some literal expression.

Examples:

```
-- The following two lines produce the same effect:
Beep 7
Do "Beep 7"

-- The following lines build and execute one of
-- two commands, either this:
--   Close printing
-- or this:
--   Close file <filename>
If printingOpen then put "printing" into whatsOpen
Else if fileOpen then put "file " & fileName ¬
into whatsOpen
Do "Close " & whatsOpen

-- A script for setting properties of
-- all buttons on a card.
On mouseUp
  Ask "Set what property?" with "Style"
  If it is empty then exit to HyperCard
  Put it into prop
  Do "ask " & quote & "What value for " & ¬
  prop & "?" & quote
  If it is empty then exit to HyperCard
  Put it into setting
  Repeat with i=1 to the number of card buttons
    Do "set the " & prop & ¬
    " of card button i to " & setting
  End repeat
End mouseUp
```

DoMenu

Syntax:

```
DoMenu <menu item>
```

Description:

The **DoMenu** command performs the action indicated by <menu item>.

The parameter <menu item> can be any one of the choices under any of the HyperCard menus, or under the Apple menu. This includes desk accessories under the Apple menu, and selection of applications listed under the Apple menu when running under MultiFinder. Except that capitalization is unimportant, the spelling of <menu item> must be exact, including any ellipsis (...) at the end of the item. (Those dots are really periods. You cannot use the ellipsis characters for them.

The **DoMenu** command is used to automate HyperCard actions that you would otherwise perform by pulling down menus and making selections from them. This command can give the unwary a lesson in the non-sequential nature of object-oriented programming. Although for most purposes it suffices to treat the **DoMenu** command as actually performing the action indicated by <menu item>, it in fact merely generates a message. There are instance in which that message may be intercepted by a different handler, and it is also possible for **DoMenu** messages to reach their destinations out of the sequence in which they were generated, as in the examples given here. See the HyperTalk Object Hierarchy appendix and the discussion of object-oriented programming in the main text for more insight into how to know what HyperCard will do when. The menu item must be available at the time it is selected.

Examples:

```
DoMenu New Button
```

```
DoMenu Compact Stack
```

```
DoMenu Alarm Clock

-- This loop cycles through the cards of a stack,
-- ending up at its starting point.
Repeat for the number of cards
  DoMenu Next
End repeat

-- Invoke this mouseUp handler while running under
-- MultiFinder with an application whose name is
-- contained in the global variable otherAp.
-- The effect will not be what you'd expect.
-- First "About HyperCard..." will be invoked,
-- and then control will pass to otherAp.
-- The messages are acted upon in the order ¬
-- in which they reach their destinations, ¬
-- not in the order in which they were produced.
On mouseUp
  Global otherAp
  DoMenu otherAp
  DoMenu About HyperCard...
End mouseUp

-- Similarly, this script will produce ¬
-- a 100-tick delay BEFORE invoking ¬
-- the Key Caps desk accessory.
On mouseUp
  DoMenu Key Caps
  Wait 100
End mouseUp
```

Drag

Syntax:

```
Drag from <location1> to <location2>
Drag from <location1> to <location2> with <key1>
Drag from <location1> to <location2> with <key1>, <key2>
Drag from <location1> to <location2> with <key1>, <key2>, <key3>
```

Description:

The **Drag** command is one of those commands that automate HyperCard actions that you would otherwise perform by pulling down menus, clicking on buttons, and so on. The **Drag** command in particular exactly mimics the action of dragging the mouse, and allows you to specify precise HyperCard window starting and ending coordinates for the drag. Demands that you do, in fact.

The starting and ending locations are mandatory, and each must be one of the following: two numbers specifying appropriate horizontal and vertical HyperCard window coordinates, or two containers holding such numbers, or one container containing two such numbers. Horizontal and vertical screen coordinates are appropriate if they are within card window range.

You can also specify from zero to three keys from the following list: optionKey, commandKey, shiftKey. Specifying a key name simulates holding down that key while dragging the mouse.

By using the **Drag** command, you can select blocks of text, make scrolling fields scroll by sliding the control along the scroll bar, or draw with the paint tools.

Examples:

```
Put "30,30" into upperLeftCorner
Put "90,90" into lowerRightCorner
Drag from upperLeftCorner to lowerRightCorner

-- Fiddling with painting tools:
Choose brush tool
Drag from 450,150 to 500,200
-- Oh no!  Not there!
Choose eraser tool
Drag from 450,150 to 500,200
-- Whew!
Choose browse tool
```

Edit

Syntax:

```
Edit script of <object>
```

Description:

The **Edit** command invokes the HyperCard script editor on the script of the specified object.

The parameter <object> can be any object designator or expression evaluating to an object designator.

Why would you want to edit a script while another script is running? In fact, the script in which the **Edit** command appears halts when the editor is invoked and doesn't start up again until control leaves the editor, through clicking on either of the editor's **OK** and **Cancel** buttons. It at least makes sense to use the **Edit** command to provide more convenient access to the editor.

Examples:

```
-- Editing everything in sight:
Edit script of this stack
Repeat with j=1 to the number of cards
  Go to card j
  Edit script of this card
  Repeat with i=1 to the number of card buttons
    Edit script of card button i
  End repeat
  Repeat with i=1 to the number of card fields
    Edit script of card field i
  End repeat
End repeat
Repeat with j=1 to the number of backgrounds
Go to background j
  Edit script of this background
  Repeat with i=1 to the number of background buttons
    Edit script of background button i
  End repeat
  Repeat with i=1 to the number of background fields
```

```
    Edit script of background field i
  End repeat
End repeat

-- Script for a simple Edit button:
on mouseUp
  ask "Edit the script of..." with "card button test"
  if it is not empty then edit script of it
end mouseUp
```

EnterKey

The **enterKey** command is documented in the HyperTalk System Messages appendix.

Find

Syntax:

```
Find <target>
Find chars <target>
Find characters <target>
Find word <target>
Find whole <target>
Find string <target>

Find <target> in field <target field>
Find chars <target> in field <target field>
Find characters <target> in field <target field>
Find word <target> in field <target field>
```

Description:

The **Find** command invokes HyperCard's built-in search capability to locate the specified <target> in one or all fields of all cards of the current stack. The search is circular, proceeding from the current card through the cards to the end of the stack, then from the beginning to the starting card.

The parameter <target> can be any string or expression evaluating to a string. The parameter <target field> must be a background field designator or an expression evaluating to a background field designator. If <target field> is not specified, all fields on each card of the current stack are searched. The keywords **chars** and **characters** are interchangeable. If either of these keywords is present, the search matches <target> wherever it appears. If keyword **word** is present, the search matches only if <target> appears as a word. If neither keyword is present, the search matches only if <target> appears at the beginning of a word.

With version 1.2, the keywords **whole** and **string** were introduced. Neither of these keywords supports the specification of a target field. The form **find string** finds the specified target in any field. If the <target> contains no spaces, or a space followed by one or two characters, **find string** works like **find chars**; with three or more characters following a space, it uses HyperCard's fast search algorithm. The form **find whole** returns one or more whole words, beginning at the point where the precise string of characters in <target> (which may contain spaces) is matched.

The command is said to succeed or fail depending on whether or not <target> is found. If the command succeeds, <target> is marked; that is, is highlighted in the field and can be retrieved (for HyperCard version 1.2 and later) by the function **foundText**. If the command fails, "not found" is retrievable by the function **result**.

See also the functions **foundChunk**, **foundField**, **foundLine**, and **foundText**.

Examples:

```
Find Apple -- Will also find also Appleton.

Find chars yper -- Finds HyperTalk, HyperCard, etc.

Find word Mac -- Ignores smack, mace, Macintosh.

Find chars (415) in field phoneNumber
```

```
Find whole "ball of wax"

Find string "ple Comp"
```

FunctionKey

The **functionKey** command is documented in the HyperTalk System Messages appendix.

Get

Syntax:

```
Get <expression>
```

Description:

The **Get** command places the value of <expression> in the global variable **it**.

The parameter <expression> can be any legal expression.

The **Get** command can be convenient for evaluating complex expressions. It complements both the **Put** command and the **Set** command, retrieving what they put away. There is really nothing that it does, though, that can't be done by other means, and usually more concisely.

Examples:

```
Get word 1 of field 1

Get the sqrt of 2

Get the time
```

```
Get the visible of field 1

Get the result -- Puts what's in result into it.
If "OK" is not in it then put it -- Checks it.
```

Go

Syntax:

```
Go <destination>
Go to <destination>
```

Description:

The **Go** command transfers to a card, selected by <destination>, which can refer either to a card or a background or a stack. If <destination> refers to a background or stack, transfer is to the first card of that background or stack.

The parameter <destination> can be a recognizable reference of a stack or card, or it can be an expression that evaluates to such a reference. The keyword **to** is optional.

The **Go** command will accept any legitimate specification for a card or stack. In the case of stacks, since stacks are disk files, this includes full file specification. In the case of cards, it includes specification of the background and the use of such terms as **first**, **last, mid, this,** and **any.** The word **card** is required unless the reference is by one of the sequencing adjectives such as **first** or **next**. The logic of this is: sequence is a natural attribute of cards, but not of stacks, so if neither the keyword **card** nor the keyword **stack** is present, the expression is taken to be referring to a card if it refers to sequence, and to a stack otherwise.

In scripts that use the **Go** command to move among stacks, there is the possibility of getting trapped in a visited stack, particularly if the visited stack has a script that is triggered by an openStack message. The **Go** command, used to move to another stack, does generate an openStack message for the visited stack. The examples include a script that can be used to get around this problem.

Examples:

```
Go home -- to home STACK

Go prev -- to previous CARD

Go next -- to next CARD

Go HyperCalc -- to that STACK

-- Assuming card 2 has id 1010 and name "Info"
-- and belongs to background 1, and assuming
-- we are now at card 1, same background, and that
-- the stack is:
-- Internal 40:HyperCard:My Stacks:CmdTest
-- then all of these are equivalent:
Go card id 1010
Go card Info
Go card "Info"
Go to card two of background one of ¬
  Internal 40:HyperCard:My Stacks:CmdTest
Go to card two of background one
Go card 2 of bkgnd 1
Go to second card of this stack
Go to second card
Go to second
Go second
Go next
Go card 2
Go 2

-- This does NOT "go to" the specified field.
-- Rather, it takes the CONTENT of that field,
-- interprets it as a destination, if possible,
-- and goes to that destination.
Go to line 1 of field 1 of card 1 of this stack

-- This example is a puzzle.
-- You don't have to solve it, but if you can
```

```
-- figure out what it's doing, you'll have a solid
-- mastery of Go command syntax and HyperTalk
-- expression evaluation.
Go to card line 4 of field line 3 of field 1

-- This handler is invoked by the message setLocks.
-- It locks or unlocks certain HyperCard
-- properties, depending on the value of
-- parameter <flag>.
-- Locking messages, screen, etc. keeps your stack,
-- rather than the stack being analyzed,
-- in control.
-- You invoke it before and after a Go command,
-- thus:
--   SetLocks true
--   Go <targetStack>
--   SetLocks false
on setLocks flag
  if flag then set cursor to 4 else pop card
  if flag then set lockScreen to true else¬
  set lockScreen to false
  if flag then set lockMessages to true else¬
  set lockMessages to false
  if flag then set lockRecent to true else¬
  set lockRecent to false
  if flag then push this card else set cursor to 1
end setLocks
```

Help

Syntax:

```
Help
```

Description:

The `Help` command generates the message `Help`, which means that it transfers to the HyperCard Help stack unless the message is trapped elsewhere first.

The **Help** command has no parameters.

It is possible to create a handler for the **Help** message, and if you want to substitute your own help facility for Apple's, that's exactly what you should do. If you do, almost all actions that normally invoke Apple's help will invoke yours: command-?, the help key on some keyboards, typing the word Help into the message box. You can still get to the Help stack, though by typing **Go Help** into the message box.

Example:

```
Help
```

Hide

Syntax:

```
Hide menuBar
Hide <window>
Hide card window
Hide <object>
Hide card picture
Hide background picture
Hide picture <card>
Hide picture <background>
```

Description:

The **Hide** command hides the menubar, a window, a picture, or an object from view. The card window variation was added in Version 1.1. The four syntax variations dealing with hiding pictures were added in version 1.2. **Hide card picture** and **hide background picture** hide the picture on the current card or background; **hide picture <card>** and **hide picture <background>** hide the picture on a specified card or background.

The <window> parameter must be one of the following window descriptors:

```
pattern window,
tool window,
message window,
msg window,
message box,
msg box,
message, or
msg.
```

The last six of these mean the same thing and may be used interchangeably, and may be preceded by the keyword **the**.

The <object> parameter can be a designator of a button or field, or an expression evaluating to a designation of such an object. It can't designate any other object, such as card, stack, or HyperCard itself. The <card> and <background> parameters must evaluate to a card or background designation, respectively.

If you use the **Hide** command you should learn the syntax of the **Show** command, because you may need it to find hidden objects and windows. The **Hide** command is useful when you write stacks for others' use and want to protect them from the complexities of your stack, or your stack from the curiosity of the users. It also lets you pack more information onto a card than it could otherwise comfortably hold.

One classic use of the **Show** and **Hide** commands is in handling About boxes. An About box is a field that pops up when a button (typically labelled "About <something>") is pressed, and delivers a short message about that <something>, often programmer credit for the stack and/or copyright information. Typically, just about any action will then hide the About box, although sometimes it requires another click of the About button.

Examples:

```
Hide menuBar

Hide message box

Hide card window
```

```
-- An "About box" button handler.
On mouseUp
  If the visible of card field "About" is true
  Then
    Show card field "About"
  Else
    Hide card field "About"
  End if
End mouseUp
-- You might observe that the words "is true"
-- could be deleted from this script with impunity.
```

Lock

Syntax:

```
Lock screen
```

Description:

The **Lock** command, added in version 1.2, sets the value of the **lockScreen** property (see the HyperTalk Properties appendix) to **true**.

The keyword **screen** is required.

Locking the screen ensures that no changes will take place to the screen until an **unLock** command is performed. This is convenient if you want to go to another card or stack merely to get some information, but don't want the display to change as it normally would in moving to another card or stack.

Examples:

```
Lock screen
Push this card
Go settings
[etc.]
Pop card
```

```
Unlock screen
```

Multiply

Syntax:

```
Multiply <destination> by <source>
```

Description:

The **Multiply** command multiplies the value in <destination> by the value in <source> and places the result in <destination>.

Both the <source> and <destination> parameters must contain numeric values. The <source> can be a literal, a variable, an expression, or a function, but it must evaluate to a number. The <destination> must initially contain a value. The <destination> must also be changeable, so it cannot be a literal, an expression, or a function.

There is nothing that you can do using the **Multiply** command that you can't do without it. You can always use **Put** <destination> ***** <source> **into** <destination> in the place of **Multiply** <destination> **by** <source>. You may find the **Multiply** command more readable in some contexts.

Examples:

```
Put 3 into runningProduct
Multiply runningProduct by 5

-- A field script that computes the product
-- of a column of numbers
On mouseLeave
  Put 1 into line 1 of field nums
  Repeat with i=2 to the number of lines ¬
  in field nums
    Multiply line 1 of field nums by line i ¬
    of field nums
```

```
  End repeat
End mouseLeave
```

Open

Syntax:

```
Open printing
Open printing with dialog

Open file <document>

Open <application>
Open <apdocument> with <application>
```

Description:

The **Open** command starts a print job, so that subsequent **Print** commands will queue up cards for printing; or it opens a data file to use in importing data to or exporting data from HyperCard; or it launches an application.

The keywords **with dialog** cause the HyperCard print dialog to be presented. The <document> parameter indicates the document to be opened for I/O; it must be the name of a document or a container holding such a name. The <application> and <apdocument> parameters indicate the application program to be launched and an application to be opened with it. They must be the names of an application program and a document that can be processed by the application, respectively; or containers holding such.

The commands **Open**, **Close**, and **Print** work in concert to set up and execute a print job. The **Open** command sets up the print job, the **Close** command terminates it and causes all queued cards to be printed, and between the **Open** and **Close** commands, any number of cards can be queued for printing using a **Print cards** variation of the **Print** command. (Note that the file printing variation of the **Print** command should never be used between an **Open** command and a **Close** command.) Although an individual card can be dumped to the printer by using the **Print** command without the **Open** and **Close** commands, they are necessary when you want to print a batch of cards and care about the HyperCard printing format of them.

The commands **Open**, **Close**, and either **Write** or **Read** are always used together when exporting text to or importing it from text-only external files. The **Open** command opens the text file (creating it if necessary), the **Close** command closes it and between the **Open** and **Close** commands, any number of **Read** and/or **Write** commands can be executed to copy text from and to the file. It is not possible to use the **Read** and **Write** commands to access an external file without first using **Open** to open the file. It is not possible to close a file with the **Close** command unless it has been opened with the **Open** command.

When the command **Open** is used to launch an application, it exits from HyperCard and launches the application. On quitting the application you return to the card you were on .

The three variations of the **Open** command in fact do very different things: starting a print job is not the same as opening a disk file or launching an application. But conceptually, the first two variations are similar. Each of the first two variations can be thought of as the opening bracket of an I/O operation that may extend across several lines of code and for which the **Close** command is the closing bracket.

Examples:

```
Open printing with dialog
Print this card
Print next card
Close printing

-- Note that you must close and reopen a file
-- to read back what you have written to it.
-- This is because the Write command overwrites
-- whatever was in the file and does not return
-- to the beginning of the file.
Put "Major Major" into Major
Open file Major
```

```
Write "Major" to file Major
Close file Major
Open file Major
Read from file Major until "r"
Put it
Close file Major

Open chapter5 with MacWrite 4.6

Open PixelPaint
```

Pass

Syntax:

```
Pass <message>
```

Description:

The **Pass** command causes program flow to jump to the next handler for the message <message>. "Next" in this context means the next such handler encountered in the HyperCard hierarchy.

The parameter <message> must be a single word, and that word must be the name of the handler in which the **Pass** command appears. Quotes around the word are acceptable, but not necessary. No parameter to <message> are allowed; whatever parameters (if any) that were given to the handler in which the **Pass** command appears will be passed along with the command to the next handler. This necessitates that the parameters to the former handler be appropriate to the latter.

The **Pass** command allows you to "trap" a message that would normally be handled lower in the HyperCard hierarchy, perform some action in response to the message, and then **Pass** the message on through the hierarchy to be handled as it normally would be. It wasn't designed to send out arbitrary messages; only to pass along a message so that it can provoke more than one handler. There are two methods for sending out other messages: To generate a particular message (other than the message currently being handled) for processing by the next handler for that message, you simply use the message as you would any command. To send a particular message to a handler in the script of a particular object, you use the **Send** command.

Examples:

```
-- The following pair of handlers show how you can
-- use a specialized Beep handler to beep in
-- various voices and tempi.
-- Note that the second call to Beep
-- is syntactically illegal; the specialized
-- Beep handler must not pass it.
On mouseUp
  beep 1
  beep 1,1
End mouseUp
-- The specialized Beep handler:
on beep arg,tempo
  put the params
  if the paramCount < 2
  then
    pass beep
  else
    play line arg of field "voices",tempo
  end if
end beep

-- This handler intercepts the Help message and
-- uses it to call up a specialized Help stack.
-- The user can still get to the HyperCard
-- Help stack by holding down the command key
-- while invoking Help: by, for example,
-- holding down the command key while pressing
-- the Help key on a Mac II keyboard.
on help
  if the commandKey is down
  then
    pass help
  else
    go AddressHelp
```

```
  end if
end help
```

Play

Syntax:

```
Play <voice>
Play <voice> tempo <tempo>
Play <voice> <notes>
Play <voice> tempo <tempo> <notes>
Play stop
```

Description:

The **Play** command produces sounds through the sound synthesizer built into the Macintosh. It uses a specified stored sound resource and plays the sound according to specified tempo and note values.

The <voice> parameter must be the name of a format 2 'snd' sound resource or a container holding such a name. If a <tempo> parameter is supplied, the **tempo** keyword is mandatory. The <tempo> parameter must be a positive number.

The <notes> parameter consists of a sequence of notes, with the entire sequence surrounded by quotes and individual notes separated by spaces. If <notes> is not supplied, the default values of a quarter note at middle C are used. Each note consists of from one to five components, as follows:

- Note value: a,b,c,d,e,f,g, or silence (yields a rest). Required.
- Accidental: # or b for sharp or flat, respectively. Optional.
- Octave: a number. Use 4 for the octave based at Middle C. Optional.
- Duration: w,h,q,e,s,t,x for whole note, half, quarter, eighth, sixteenth, thirty-second, and sixty-fourth, respectively. Optional.
- Extension: either a dot (.) or a 3 for a dotted note or triple, respectively. Optional. If an extension is used, a duration is mandatory.

Note value and octave can also be specified by a single number. In this representation, 60 represents Middle C, and each half-step up or down is represented by a number one higher or lower, respectively. Some examples of legal <notes> parameter values are: **"c#"**, **"61"**, **"c e g"**, **"c3#e dq g gq."**. The command **Play silence** can be used to produce a rest. The word **silence** is used in place of a sound resource.

All parameters except for the accidentals stay in effect until changed.

The **Play** command allows you to write programs that play music, or otherwise to program sound. Any format 2 'snd' sound resource can be used. There are some eccentricities in the use of the **Play** command. Some sound resources are of long duration, and the **Play** command will continue to play them until they are finished unless cut off by the tempo setting or by the command **Play stop**. The **Play** command works in the background, so other commands can go on executing while the **Play** command is making sounds.

Examples:

```
Play harpsichord

Play silence

Play meepmeep

Play sitar tempo 400 "c3#e d3q g3q g3q. c3#e ¬
d3q g3h d3#e e3q a3q a3q. d3e e3q a3h"

Put 100 into allegro
Put line i of field "Notes" into nextMeasure
Play horns tempo allegro nextMeasure
```

Pop

Syntax:

```
Pop card
Pop card before <destination>
Pop card into <destination>
Pop card after <destination>
```

Description:

The **Pop** command retrieves card identification information from a system storage area where it was formerly placed by the **Push** command. When invoked without a <destination>, it performs a transfer to the retrieved card. When invoked with a <destination>, it places the long name of the card in <destination>. In either case, the information is removed from the system storage area.

The parameter <destination> can be any reference to a container. The keywords **before**, **into**, and **after** control whether the retrieved stack name is prepended to, replaces, or is appended to the current content of <destination>.

The "system storage area" alluded to above would be called, in any other programming language, a stack. That's what it's called in HyperTalk, too, but I avoided using the term above because of the potential for confusion in a language that also uses that word in an entirely different sense. The stack in which HyperCard stores pushed information is unrelated to HyperCard stacks. It is a last-in-first-out (LIFO) queue, a data structure in which items of information are stored sequentially and retrieved in an order exactly opposite to the order in which they were stored. Last in, first out.

The **Pop** command works in conjunction with the **Push** command to allow unwinding of movement from card to card and stack to stack. Typically, you **Push** the information for the current stack, go elsewhere, and **Pop** to return. Performing such movement within a script is dangerous, since the stack or card you're transferring to may be equipped with scripts of its own that fire up and do unpredictable things right in the middle of your script. The virtue of using **Push** and **Pop** to do this moving among cards and stacks (particularly stacks) is that the information is stored in a safe place that will not be altered no matter what goes on in that other card or stack that you've transferred to (short of catastrophe or misuse of **Push** or **Pop**). Even if scripts invoked in the stack you've transferred to also contain **Push** and **Pop** commands, the stack will normally match each **Pop** to its appropriate **Push**. The LIFO stack is an excellent device for keeping track of information under conditions of unpredictable interruptions.

Using the **Pop** command with a <destination> is at least a handy trick for keeping track of stack movements. It can also be a powerful and advanced programming technique. The ability to remove LIFO stack items to other locations means that it is possible to operate on that stack as a data structure. This is dangerous and rife with possibilities.

The cardinal rule for using **Push** is: for every **Push** there must be a **Pop**. The corresponding rule for **Pop**, for every **Pop** there must be a **Push**, is not a bad rule, but there are arguably valid reasons for wanting to perform an unmatched **Pop**; for example, to find out if there are any unmatched **Push** commands. If you use Pop with <destination> to examine the contents of the LIFO stack, you may find use for another rule: for every **Pop** <destination> there must be a **Push**.

Examples:

```
Pop card

-- Editing the LIFO stack to prevent access
-- to a secret stack.
Pop card into cardHolder
If cardHolder is the long name of secretStack
Then
  Push safeStack
Else
  Push cardHolder
End if

-- This mouseUp handler squirrels away
-- the locations of the Help and Home stacks,
-- jumps to a stack named Sounds, then visits
-- the remembered stacks in reverse (LIFO) order.
```

```
-- A Pop for every Push.
On mouseUp
  Push help
  Push home
  Go sounds
  Pop card
  Pop card
End mouseUp
```

Print

Syntax:

```
Print card
Print <card>
Print <number> cards

Print <document> with <application>
```

Description:

The **Print** command prints one or more cards, or invokes the printing facility of application program <application> to cause it to print <document>.

The <card> parameter designates the card to be printed. It must be the designator of a card. If it is not in the current stack, the stack name must be included in the designator. The <number> parameter controls the number of cards to be printed. It must be a non-negative number or an expression that evaluates to such a number or the word **all**. The parameters <application> and <document> must be, respectively, the name of an application or an expression evaluating to such a name, and the name of a document that can be processed by the application or an expression evaluating to such a name.

The commands **Open**, **Close**, and **Print** work in concert to set up and execute a print job. The **Open** command sets up the print job, the **Close** command terminates it and causes all queued cards to be printed, and between the **Open** and **Close** commands, any number of cards can be queued for printing using a **Print cards** variation of the **Print** command. (Note that the file printing variation of the **Print** command should never be used between an **Open** command and a **Close** command.) Although cards can be dumped to the printer by using the **Print** command without the **Open** and **Close** commands, they are necessary when you want to print a batch of cards and care about the HyperCard printing format of them.

When the **Print** command is used to cause an application program to print a document, control returns to HyperCard after the printing is finished.

Examples:

```
Print card
```

```
Print card 7
```

```
Print card i
```

```
Print next card
```

```
Open printing with dialog
Print this card
Print next card
Close printing
Print chapter5 with MacWrite 4.6
```

Push

Syntax:

```
Push card
Push <card>
Push recent card
```

Description:

The **Push** command stores card identification information in a system storage area for later retrieval by the **Pop** command.

The parameter <card> must be a valid reference to a card or stack, or a container holding a valid reference to a card or stack. If the reference is to a stack, it is interpreted as a reference to the first card of the stack.

The "system storage area" alluded to above would be called, in any other programming language, a stack. That's what it's called in HyperTalk, too, but I avoided using the term above because of the potential for confusion in a language that also uses that word in an entirely different sense. The stack in which HyperCard stores pushed information is unrelated to HyperCard stacks. It is a last-in-first-out (LIFO) queue, a data structure in which items of information are stored sequentially and retrieved in an order exactly opposite to the order in which they were stored. Last in, first out.

The **Push** command works in conjunction with the **Pop** command to allow unwinding of movement from card to card and stack to stack. Typically, you **Push** the information for the current stack, go elsewhere, and **Pop** to return. Performing such movement within a script is dangerous, since the stack or card you're transferring to may be equipped with scripts of their own that fire up and do unpredictable things right in the middle of your script. The virtue of using **Push** and **Pop** to do this moving among cards and stacks (particularly stacks) is that the information is stored in a safe place that will not be altered no matter what goes on in that other card or stack that you've transferred to (short of catastrophe or misuse of **Push** or **Pop**). Even if scripts invoked in the stack you've transferred to also contain **Push** and **Pop** commands, the stack will normally match each **Pop** to its appropriate **Push**. The LIFO stack is an excellent device for keeping track of information under conditions of unpredictable interruptions.

Remember: for every **Push** there must be a **Pop** .

Examples:

```
Push this card

Push card 3

Push next

Push recent card

Put "card 2 of stack Home" into line 6 of field 1
Push line 6 of field 1
Pop card

-- This mouseUp handler squirrels away
-- the locations of the Help and Home stacks,
-- jumps to a stack named Sounds, then visits
-- the remembered stacks in reverse (LIFO) order.
-- A Pop for every Push.
On mouseUp
  Push help
  Push home
  Go sounds
  Pop card
  Pop card
End mouseUp

-- This handler is invoked by the message setLocks.
-- It prevents problems in going between stacks.
-- It locks or unlocks certain properties,
-- depending on the value of flag.  It also, more
-- to the present point, executes a Push or Pop.
```

```
-- You invoke it before and after jumping to
-- another card, as follows:
--   SetLocks true
--   Go <targetStack>
--   SetLocks false
-- Note that the first call executes a Push,
-- and the second does a Pop,
-- suggesting a corollary to the above law:
-- a setLocks false for every setLocks true.
on setLocks flag
  if flag then set cursor to 4 else pop card
  if flag then set lockScreen to true else¬
  set lockScreen to false
  if flag then set lockMessages to true else¬
  set lockMessages to false
  if flag then set lockRecent to true else¬
  set lockRecent to false
  if flag then push this card else set cursor to 1
end setLocks
```

Put

Syntax:

```
Put <source>
Put <source> before <destination>
Put <source> into <destination>
Put <source> after <destination>
```

Description:

The **Put** command places the value of <source> into the container <destination>.

The parameter <source> can be any interpretable expression. The parameter <destination> must be a container designator; if <destination> is not specified, the message box is assumed. If <destination> is a single word and that word is currently undefined, a new memory variable with that name will be created and the value of <source> will be placed in it. The keywords **before, into,** and **after** determine whether the value of <source> is prepended to the content of <destination>, replaces it, or is appended to it.

The **Put** command may be the most commonly used HyperTalk command. It achieves two things: it evaluates <source> if it is not already evaluated, and it places the value into <destination>. To see how important the evaluative aspect is, and what can be achieved by evaluating an expression twice, study the background script for Dan Winkler's HyperCalc, which is supplied with HyperCard.

Examples:

```
Put the time

Put "South" into theBidder

Put North into stir

Put death before dishonor
-- What this command will do depends on whether
-- or not "death" and "dishonor" have already
-- been given values. The possibilities are:
-- Only "death" defined: value of "death" placed
-- in new variable "dishonor".
-- Only "dishonor" defined: the word "death"
-- appended to front of variable "dishonor".
-- Both defined: value of "death" appended to front
-- of variable "dishonor".
-- Neither defined: the word "death" placed
-- in new variable "dishonor".

Convert targetDate to dateItems
Put (item 3 of targetDate) mod (daysInMonth) + 1¬
  into item 3 of targetDate

-- Swapping two lines of a field:
Put line i of field 1 into temp
Put line i+1 of field 1 into line i of field 1
Put temp into line i+1 of field 1

-- A shorter and faster swap:
```

```
Put line i+1 of field 1 & return before line i ¬
of field 1
Delete line i+2 of field 1
```

Read

Syntax:

```
Read from file <file> until <character>
Read from file <file> for <number>
```

Description:

The **Read** command imports text from an external file to the variable **it**.

The <file> parameter must be the name of a file or an expression evaluating to the name of a file. The parameter <character> must be a literal character. The parameter <number> must be a non-negative number or an expression evaluating to such. The <number> and <character> parameters control the extent of the **Read** operation, <number> restricting it to a fixed number of characters, <character> causing the operation to cease when a stop character is read.

Successive **Read** commands start at the next character position in the file.

The commands **Open**, **Close**, and either **Write** or **Read** are always used together when exporting text to or importing it from text-only external files. The **Open** command opens the text file (creating it if necessary), the **Close** command closes it and between the **Open** and **Close** commands, any number of **Read** and/or **Write** commands can be executed to copy text from and to the file. It is not possible to use the **Read** and **Write** commands to access an external file without first using **Open** to open the file. It is not possible to close a file with the **Close** command unless it has been opened with the **Open** command.

Examples:

```
Open file pathStep
Read from file pathStep until ":"
Close file pathStep

-- Note that you must close and reopen a file
-- to read back what you have written to it.
-- This is because the Write command overwrites
-- whatever was in the file and does not return
-- to the beginning of the file.
Put "Major Major" into Major
Open file Major
Write "Major" to file Major
Close file Major
Open file Major
Read from file Major until "r"
Put it
Close file Major
```

Reset

Syntax:

```
Reset paint
```

Description:

The **Reset** command resets all paint properties to their default values.

The keyword **paint** is mandatory.

The paint properties and their default values are documented in the HyperTalk Properties appendix.

Example:

```
Reset paint
```

Return

Syntax:

```
Return <expression>
```

Description:

In a user-defined function or message handler, the **Return** command evaluates <expression> and causes the function or handler to terminate, returning the value of <expression> as the value of the function or, in the case of a handler, making it accessible via the function **Result**.

The parameter <expression> can be any expression. If <expression> evaluates to **empty** or if no **Return** command is supplied in the handler, the value **empty** will be returned. If a **Return** is present but no <expression> is supplied, it is an error.

The **Return** command, or something like it, is part of the normal mechanism of function processing in any programming language. Its use in message handlers is a subtle feature of HyperTalk.

Examples:

```
-- Using Return in a message handler:
On mouseUp
  CheckLoc
  Put the result
End mouseUp
On checkLoc
  Return the loc of me
End checkLoc

-- Creating Basic-style aliases for two
-- cumbersome HyperTalk functions:
Function Chr theNum
  Return numToChar(theNum)
End Chr
Function Asc theString
  Return charToNum(theString)
End Asc
```

ReturnKey

The **returnKey** command is documented in the HyperTalk System Messages appendix.

Select

Syntax:

```
Select <button>
Select <field>
Select target
Select me

Select <chunk> of <target>
Select before <chunk> of <target>
Select after <chunk> of <target>
Select text of <target>
Select before text of <target>
Select after text of <target>
Select text of target
Select text of me

Select empty
```

Description:

The **Select** command (1) chooses the appropriate tool (button or field) and selects the specified object as though it had been clicked on with the mouse, (2) selects text in a field or in the message box as though clicked on or dragged over, or (3) deselects the selected object or text. The **Select** command was added in version 1.2.

The parameters <button> and <field> must evaluate to button or field designators, respectively. Parameter <chunk> must evaluate to a chunk expression, and <target> must refer to a field or to the message box. The parameters <before> and <after> are used to set the insertion point within a field (or the message box). A special case is the use of a chunk expression of the form <char x to y> where x is greater than y. In this case, an insertion point is set between x and y. Selecting beyond the end of a field inserts carriage returns as necessary.

The keywords **me** and **target** may also be used, with their usual meanings. The form **select empty** deselects the currently selected object or text, or clears the insertion point.

The **select** command, used with buttons and fields, is especially useful for getting at covered (but not hidden) objects.

See also the functions **selection**, **selectedChunk**, **selectedField**, **selectedLine**, and **selectedText**.

Examples:

```
Select me
Select item 1 of line 1 of card field cmdTest
Select before word 1 of line 3 of field test
```

Send

Syntax:

```
Send <message>
Send <message> to <object>
```

Description:

The **Send** command causes program flow to jump to the handler for the message <message> in the script of object <object>. If no <object> is specified, the message is sent to HyperCard itself.

The parameter <message> must be the name of a handler in the script of object <object>, plus optional parameters appropriate to that handler. Quotes around the word are acceptable, but necessary only if parameters to <message> are supplied.

The **Send** command allows you to bypass the natural order of message flow in the HyperCard hierarchy. After the message <message> has been handled by a message handler, flow continues with the next command in the original script.

Examples:

```
Send mouseUp to card button 5

Send "bracketWeek" && the seconds to this card

Send idle to card button 3

-- Apple's Phone stack script has to get the Dial
-- message to HyperCard in this way because the
-- script contains its own Dial handler,
-- which would otherwise trap the Dial message
-- before HyperCard could get it.
Send "dial" && quote & dialNumber & quote && ¬
"with modem" && quote & "ATSO=ODP" & quote ¬
to HyperCard
```

Set

Syntax:

```
Set <property> of <object> to <value>
Set the <property> of <object> to <value>
Set <property> to <value>
Set the <property> to <value>
```

Description:

The **Set** command sets the global or object property designated by <property> to the value designated by <value>. The values of properties can only be adjusted via the **Set** command; the **Put** command will not work with properties.

The parameter <property> must be the name of a property appropriate to <object> if <object> is specified, or the name of a global or painting property otherwise. The parameter <object> must be an object designator or a designator of a HyperCard window. The parameter <value> must be a value appropriate to the specified property, or an expression evaluating to such a value.

HyperCard objects and windows have properties associated with them, such as the location of a button and the text font used to display its name, the rectangle bounding a field and the field's visibility. There are also global properties in HyperCard, such as the user level, and there are paint properties that determine how the paint tools work. The **Set** command can be used to adjust the properties of objects, global properties, window properties, and painting properties. All HyperTalk properties are documented in the HyperTalk Properties appendix.

Examples:

```
Set the script of card button 1 to empty

Set the textFont of card button 1 to Helvetica

Set the visible of card field "About"¬
to not the visible of card field "About"

Set the userlevel to line 3 of field 1

Set the loc of message box to 22,300

Ask "What is your name, please?"
If it is in theList then set userLevel to 5
```

Show

Syntax:

```
Show cards
Show <count> cards

Show menubar
```

```
Show <window>
Show card window
Show <object>
Show card picture
Show background picture
Show picture <card>
Show picture <background>

Show <window> at <location>
Show card window at <location>
Show <object> at <location>
```

Description:

The **Show** command displays some or all the cards of a stack; or it sets the **visible** property of a menu bar, window, or object to **visible** , and optionally sets its loc to <location>.

The four syntax variations dealing with showing pictures were added in version 1.2. **Show card picture** and **show background picture** display the picture on the current card or background; **show picture <card>** and **show picture <background>** display the picture on a specified card or background.

The <window> parameter must be one of the following window descriptors:

```
pattern window,
tool window,
message window,
msg window,
message box,
msg box,
message, or
msg.
```

The last six of these mean the same thing and may be used interchangeably, and may be preceded by the keyword **the**.

The parameter <count> must be a positive number or an expression that evaluates to a positive number or the word **all**.. The parameter <window> must be the name of a HyperCard window. The parameter <object> must be a HyperCard object. The parameter <location> must consist of two numbers specifying appropriate horizontal and vertical HyperCard window coordinates, or two containers holding such numbers, or one container containing two such numbers. In the case of the **card window**, <location> refers to screen coordinates. The <card> and <background> parameters must evaluate to a card or background designation, respectively.

The **Show** command can really be used to perform any of three different functions. **Show cards** runs a little slide show of cards. **Show** <thing> undoes the action of **Hide** <thing>, making the hidden visible. **Show** <thing> **at** <location> adjusts the location of <thing>, an object or window.

Examples:

```
Show cards

Show msg at 22,300

Show (line 3 of field 1) cards

Show card field "About"

-- Tiling auxiliary windows on a Mac II screen:
Show tool window at -69,-48
Show pattern window at¬
  (item 1 of the loc of tool window) - 3,¬
  (item 2 of the loc of tool window) + 14
```

Sort

Syntax:

```
Sort by <sort value>
Sort <sort order> by <sort value>
Sort <sort direction> by <sort value>
Sort <sort direction> <sort order> by <sort value>
```

Description:

The **Sort** command invokes the built-in HyperCard sorting facility to sort all the cards of the current stack according to one sort value.

The parameter <sort value> must be a designator of a field or part of a field. The parameter <sort direction> must be one of the following keywords: **ascending** or **descending**. The parameter <sort order> must be one of the following: **dateTime**, **international**, **numeric**, or **text**.

The <sort order> parameter determines which of the four orderings of characters is used. The default is **text**. The <sort direction> parameter determines whether the cards are ordered lowest to highest or the reverse with respect to the selected ordering. The default is **ascending**.

Examples:

```
Sort by field address

Sort descending numeric by field score

Sort by lastName & firstName
```

Subtract

Syntax:

```
Subtract <source> from <destination>
```

Description:

The **Subtract** command subtracts the value in <source> from the value in <destination> and places the result in <destination>.

Both the <source> and <destination> parameters must contain numeric values. The <source> can be a literal, a variable, an expression, or a function, but it must evaluate to a number. The

<destination> must initially contain a value. The <destination> must also be changeable, so it cannot be a literal, an expression, or a function.

There is nothing that you can do using the **Subtract** command that you can't do without it. You can always use **Put** <destination> - <source> **into** <destination> in the place of **Subtract** <source> **from** <destination>. You may find the **Subtract** command more readable in some contexts.

Examples:

```
Put 3 into theCount
Subtract 1 from theCount

Subtract theDeductions from line 13 ¬
of field taxForm
```

TabKey

The **tabKey** command is documented in the HyperTalk System Messages appendix.

Type

Syntax:

```
Type <text>
Type <text> with <key1>
Type <text> with <key1>, <key2>
Type <text> with <key1>, <key2>, <key3>
```

Description:

The **Type** command simulates typing text at the keyboard. It is one of a number of commands that automate HyperCard actions that you would otherwise perform by pulling down menus, clicking on buttons, and so on.

The parameter <text> can be a literal text string or an expression that can be evaluated to such. You can also specify from zero to three keys from the following list: optionKey, commandKey, shiftKey. Specifying a key name simulates holding down that key while clicking the mouse.

The **Type** command types its text wherever the cursor happens to be. The default location is the message box, and by using **Type** to place text there, you can simulate keyed-in commands. Employed in this way, the **Type** command is useful for supplying information required by a menu selection, after you have invoked the menu selection with the **doMenu** command. **Type** can also be used to place text into fields, but not into dialog boxes.

Examples:

```
-- This will place the number 5 at screen location
-- 0,0. If that's in a field, it will insert 5,
-- without overwriting the contents of the field.
Click at 0,0
Type "5"

Type "?" with commandKey
-- is equivalent to
DoMenu Help

-- Using Type after DoMenu.
On mouseUp
  Ask "Find what?"
  Put it into whatever
  DoMenu find...
  Type whatever & return
End mouseUp
```

UnLock

Syntax:

```
UnLock screen
UnLock screen with <effect>
UnLock screen with <effect> <speed>
UnLock screen with <effect> to <image>
UnLock screen with <effect> <speed> to <image>
```

Description:

The **unLock** command, added in version 1.2, sets the value of the **lockScreen** property (see the HyperTalk Properties appendix) to **false**.

The keyword **screen** is required. The parameter **<effect>** must be a legitimate visual effect (see the **Visual** command). If **<effect>**is supplied, the keyword **with** is required.

Unlocking the screen undoes the effect of a previous **lock** command. It is also possible to have the command perform one of a selection of visual effects. These are documented under the **Visual** command.

Examples:

```
Lock screen
Push this card
Go settings
[etc.]
Unlock screen
Pop card

UnLock screen with dissolve slowly to black
```

Visual

Syntax:

```
Visual <effect>
Visual <effect> <speed>
Visual <effect> to <image>
Visual <effect> <speed> to <image>

Visual effect <effect>
Visual effect <effect> <speed>
Visual effect <effect> to <image>
Visual effect <effect> <speed> to <image>
```

Description:

The **Visual** command performs one of a selection of visual effects. The speed at which it performs the effect is adjustable, and an image can be specified for use in performing the visual effect.

The keyword **effect** is optional. The parameter <effect> must be one of the effect names listed here. The parameter <speed> determines how fast the effect will be performed and must be one of the following: **very slow** or **very slowly**, **slow** or **slowly**, **fast**, **very fast**. The parameter <image> specifies a target image for the effect and must be one of: **white, gray, black, inverse, card**. It requires the keyword **to**.

The legal effect names are: **plain, dissolve, checkerboard, venetian blinds, scroll up, scroll down, scroll right, scroll left, iris open, iris close, wipe up, wipe down, wipe right, wipe left, zoom open, zoom close, zoom out, zoom in, barn door open, barn door close**.

The defaults for the parameters are **plain** <effect>, **fast** <speed>, and **card** <image>.

The **Visual** command is best placed before a **Go** or **Pop** command to provide a dramatic or other effect on moving from card to card. Placed anywhere else in a script, it will at best save its effect until you do a **Go** or **Pop** command. Users of Macintosh II or color-equipped

SE computers will find that the **Visual** command doesn't work with color turned on.

Examples:

```
Visual effect dissolve slowly

Visual wipe left

Visual dissolve to black
```

Wait

Syntax:

```
Wait <ticks>
Wait <ticks> ticks
Wait <seconds> seconds
Wait <seconds> secs
Wait for <ticks>
Wait for <ticks> ticks
Wait for <seconds> seconds
Wait for <seconds> secs

Wait while <condition>
Wait until <condition>
```

Description:

The **Wait** command causes HyperCard to suspend activity for some duration.

The duration is controlled by the parameters and keywords. There are two broad uses of the **Wait** command, to wait for a specified duration or to wait subject to some condition.

Waiting for a specified time requires a parameter (<ticks> or <seconds>) indicating the number of system clock ticks (1/60 second) or seconds. The keyword **ticks** is optional, but the keyword

seconds or **secs** is mandatory for the parameter to be interpreted a a number of seconds. The parameter <ticks> or <seconds> can be a non-negative number or any expression that evaluates to a non-negative number. The keyword **for** is strictly optional.

Waiting subject to some condition requires one of the two keywords **while** or **until** and a parameter <condition> that evaluates to a Boolean value; i.e., to **True** or **False**. Use of the keyword **until** results in suspension of activity until <condition> is true, **while** results in suspension while it is true.

Note that for <condition> to change during the wait, it must depend on conditions external to HyperCard, since HyperCard's execution of commands is suspended. HyperCard is still aware of external events such as keystrokes and mouse moves, however.

Examples:

```
-- These lines are equivalent:
Wait 10 secs
Wait for ten seconds

-- These lines are equivalent:
Wait for 5 ticks
Wait 5
-- And this achieves the same effect:
Put 5 into howMany
Wait howMany ticks

-- These two lines do the same thing:
Wait until the mouse is down
Wait while the mouse is up

-- In the event that you have some background
-- gremlin freeing up disk space for you,
-- and you don't want to run with less than
-- a megabyte of free space on the disk:
Wait until the diskSpace > 1048576
```

Write

Syntax:

```
Write <text> to file <file>
```

Description:

The **Write** command exports text to an external file.

The <text> parameter must be a text string or an expression evaluating to such a string or a container holding such a string. The <file> parameter must be a file name or an expression evaluating to such.

Successive **Write** commands append <text> to the contents of <file>.

The commands **Open**, **Close**, and either **Write** or **Read** are always used together when exporting text to or importing it from text-only external files. The **Open** command opens the text file (creating it if necessary), the **Close** command closes it and between the **Open** and **Close** commands, any number of **Read** and/or **Write** commands can be executed to copy text from and to the file. It is not possible to use the **Read** and **Write** commands to access an external file without first using **Open** to open the file. It is not possible to close a file with the **Close** command unless it has been opened with the **Open** command.

Examples:

```
Write chapterOne to file myNovel

Write lastName & ", " & firstName ¬
to file currentUser

-- Note that you must close and reopen a file
-- to read back what you have written to it.
-- This is because the Write command overwrites
-- whatever was in the file and does not return
-- to the beginning of the file.
Put "Major Major" into Major
Open file Major
Write "Major" to file Major
Close file Major
Open file Major
Read from file Major until "r"
Put it
Close file Major
```

Appendix E
HyperTalk Functions

About this Appendix

The following pages detail the salient facts about every HyperTalk function: its calling format, a prose description of what it does, and one or more concrete examples of its use. Like the other technical appendices, this one is intended for reference purposes. For a more tutorial presentation of the use of HyperTalk functions and the steps in writing your own user-defined functions, you should see the earlier portions of the book.

The information in this function appendix is as timely and as accurate as I could make it. All facts were checked at final board stage, and should be consistent with the state of HyperTalk at that time. I ran all example code through HyperCard, then pasted the properly running code directly into the text, minimizing the opportunities for errors to creep in.

To understand the use of functions, you need to understand some of the other language elements as well. At least these technical reference sections of this book have information relevant to understanding HyperTalk functions or user-defined functions: HyperTalk Commands, HyperTalk System Messages, HyperTalk Control Structures, and the HyperTalk Object Hierarchy.

Functions are grouped in the main body of this book according to the kind of values they expect and return. (What it means for a function to expect or return a value is discussed in the next section.) Math functions are discussed together, as are logical functions, and time/date functions, and string functions, and system functions. In this appendix, they are all listed alphabetically. My rules for deciding what to include as a distinct function in this appendix are broader than some authors' rules, and broader than my own rules used in

HyperTalk Commands appendix. I list **`abbreviated date`**, **`short date`**, **`long date`**, and **`date`** separately (and cross-referenced), even though they are all one function: each returns the date, sometimes in the same format. I do this simply to increase the likelihood of your finding what you're looking for on the first try, not for any reason rooted in the semantics of HyperTalk.

Taken one at a time, the concepts of command, function, property, and message may seem clear and intuitive, but in the early stages of learning HyperTalk it is not always obvious to what category a particular word belongs. The HyperTalk Vocabulary appendix can point to the appropriate appendix, and a careful comparison of the "About" sections of the Commands, Functions, Properties, and System Messages appendices can help to clarify the differences.

About HyperTalk Functions

HyperTalk functions have analogs in many other contexts. They are very much like functions in other programming languages, so if you have programmed and used functions, then you know what HyperTalk functions are, how to invoke them, and what to expect from them. All you need are the definitions and vital data regarding specific pre-defined HyperTalk functions, and how to define your own functions. You'll find the former in this appendix and the latter in the discussion of functions in the main body of the book. If you've learned the mathematical concept of a function, then you have the basic idea, and you only need the two things I just described and perhaps some practical experience in writing and using functions. One starting place for acquiring that is the discussion of functions in the main body of the book, but you're ultimately responsible for your own on-the-Mac experience.

If, on the other hand, like the vast majority of intelligent adults, you've never used functions in programming and (1) you're just a little shaky about the mathematical definition of a function or (2) you're pretty sure you covered functions in math class but you're equally sure you were out sick that week or (3) you don't have any idea what I'm talking about but you feel betrayed because people keep telling you that you don't need math to understand computers but all the books insist on demonstrating what appear to be key concepts by means of breezy references to cosines and third derivatives....

Here's a straightforward, practical explanation of what a function is. (If it looks like an explanation of what a function *does*, there's a good reason for that. A function is what a function does. The clearest way to define a function is by a *functional* definition, and that's not a pun, but just one of the artifacts of using words to talk about words.)

A function operates on a value to produce another value. You give it an angle, for example, and it returns the cosine of the angle. Strike that. You give it a string of characters and it returns the first character of the string. You give it your full name, it returns your initials. You give it the date, it returns the day of the week. The word *return* is, in fact, just the word mathematicians and programmers use in talking about functions. The word *parameter* is used for the value you give to the function. Some functions, like the **date** function, take no parameters; some take one or more. The important things to know about any function are what kind(s) of value(s) it expects to be given and what kind of value it will return.

You can usually test out your understanding of a function by typing it, along with any parameters it expects, into the message box. The function will be evaluated and its returned value will replace what you typed in the message box. Some few functions can't be tested in this way, but for every one that can, I have shown what to type into the message box as the first example in the function descriptions on the following pages.

If you want to write your own functions, you need to know more than this. The discussion of functions in the main body of the book describes the process and gives examples. You'll find some of the key facts more concisely and fully presented in the HyperTalk Control Structures Appendix. Different syntax rules apply for system functions and user-defined functions. Most system functions can be invoked using either a **<function name> (<parameter>)** or a **the <function name> of <parameter>** syntax (but see individual function descriptions to be sure). User-defined functions can only be invoked with the parenthesis form. You have more flexibility if you use the parenthesis form: since HyperCard will evaluate the expression in parentheses first, you avoid some ambiguities with this form that could arise using the other form.

Abbreviated Date

Calling format:

```
the abbr date
the abbrev date
the abbreviated date
abbr date()
abbrev date()
abbreviated date()
```

Description:

The **abbreviated date** function returns the current system date in an abbreviated form, such as "Thu, Jun 2, 1988."

If you use **abbreviated date** in any of the last three forms above, you may find that it does not return the abbreviated date, but rather the short date. This is a bug. By the time this book comes out, Apple will probably have fixed it, but it was still present in version 1.2 when it shipped.

See also: **Date, Long date, Short date.**

Examples:

```
-- Try this in the message box:
the abbr date

Get the abbreviated date

If the length of the long date < fldWidth
Then
  Put the long date into field "Date"
Else
  If the length of the abbrev date < fldWidth
  Then
    Put the abbrev date into field "Date"
  Else
    Put the short date into field "Date"
  End if
End if
```

Abs

Calling format:

```
the abs of <number>
abs(<number>)
```

Description:

The **abs** function returns the absolute value of its numeric parameter. That is, it returns **<number>** if **<number>** is positive or zero, and -1 * **<number>** otherwise. The **abs** function is one way to guarantee that a number will not be negative.

The parameter **<number>** must be a number or an expression that evaluates to a number.

Examples:

```
-- Try this in the message box:
the abs of -1

Put abs(10*word 1 of line 2 of field nums)

-- This user-defined function returns the
-- sign of its parameter; that is, it returns
-- -1 if the number is negative, 1 if positive,
-- and 0 if it is 0.
Function sign x
  If x=0 then return 0 else return abs(x)/x
End sign
```

Annuity

Calling format:

```
annuity(<rate>,<number of periods>)
```

Description:

The **annuity** function effectively returns the value of

(1 - (1 + <rate>) ^ (-1 * <period>)) / <rate>.

It is used to calculate the present value of a payment of an annuity with respect to the payment amount.

The parameters **<rate>** and **<number of periods>** must be numbers or expressions that evaluates to numbers. The **<rate>** parameter should fall between 0 and 1 exclusively to be meaningful; the actual calculation performed is not identical to the expression given above, but is equivalent to it for a **<rate>** parameter in this range. Outside the range, it does not necessarily return the value of that expression.

See also: **Compound**.

Examples:

```
-- Try this in the message box:
annuity(0.10,15)

Put annuity(10*word 1 of line 2 of field nums,5)
```

Atan

Calling format:

```
the atan of <number>
atan(<number>)
```

Description:

The **atan** function returns the angle whose tangent is **<number>**. It is the inverse of the function **tan**. **Atan** and **tan** refer to the trigonometric functions arctangent and tangent, respectively.

The parameter **<number>** must be a number or an expression that evaluates to a number. The parameter is in radians, not degrees.

See also: **Cos, Sin, Tan.**

Examples:

```
-- Try this in the message box:
tan(atan(5))

Put pi - the atan of 3 into diff
```

Average

Calling format:

```
average(<listOfNumbers>)
```

Description:

The **average** function returns the arithmetic mean of **<listOfNumbers>**.

The parameter **<listOfNumbers>** must be a comma-separated list of numbers or expressions evaluating to numbers.

Examples:

```
-- Try this in the message box:
average(0,10,15)

Put average(the heapSpace,the stackSpace)
```

CharToNum

Calling format:

```
the charToNum of <string>
charToNum(<string>)
```

Description:

The **charToNum** function returns the ASCII value corresponding to the first character of **<string>**. The ASCII value is a standard ordering assigned to characters.

The parameter **<string>** can be a literal string, a function returning a string, or a name or chunk expression for a container holding a string.

See also: **NumToChar**.

Examples:

```
-- Try these in the message box:
charToNum("CD ROM")
numToChar(charToNum("Z"))

Put the charToNum of currentWord into glossaryPage
```

ClickH

Calling format:

```
the clickH
clickH()
```

Description:

The **clickH** function returns the first item of the **clickLoc**: the horizontal screen coordinate of the click.

See also: **ClickLoc, ClickV, MouseH, MouseV.**

Example:

```
--  Try this in the message box:
clickH()
```

ClickLoc

Calling format:

```
the clickLoc
clickLoc()
```

Description:

The **clickLoc** function returns the card window location at which the mouse was last clicked. A location is always expressed as a pair of numbers separated by a comma.

See also: **ClickH, ClickV, Mouse, MouseClick, MouseH, MouseLoc, MouseV.**

Examples:

```
-- Try this in the message box:
clickLoc()

-- This handler should be placed in the
-- home stack's script. It puts a pseudobutton
-- in the upper lefthand corner of every card
-- of every stack. Clicking in the corner
-- of a card, as long as there is no real
-- object there to trap the mouse click,
-- causes a mouseUp message to fall through
-- to the home stack, where this handler
-- catches it.
-- Original by Jon Pugh, Livermore CA
-- Modified by Mike Swaine 6/1/88
-- Released to the public domain.
on mouseUp
  if item 1 of the clickLoc <26 ¬
  and item 2 of the clickLoc <26
  then
    -- Substitute code of your own for the
    -- following lines to make the pseudobuttons
    -- do what you want.
    ask "What do you want to edit?" ¬
    with card button 1
    if it is not empty
    then
      edit script of it
    end if
  else
    pass mouseUp
  end if
end mouseUp
```

ClickV

Calling format:

```
the clickV
clickV()
```

Description:

The **clickH** function returns the second item of the **clickLoc**: the vertical screen coordinate of the click.

See also: **ClickLoc, ClickV, MouseH, MouseV.**

Example:

```
--  Try this in the message box:
clickH()
```

CommandKey

Calling format:

```
the commandKey
commandKey()
the cmdKey
cmdKey()
```

Description:

The **commandKey** function returns "up" or "down" depending on whether the command (or apple or cloverleaf) key is up or down when the function is executed.

See also: **OptionKey**, **ShiftKey**.

Examples:

```
-- Try this in the message box:
commandKey()

Wait until the commandKey is up
```

Compound

Calling format:

```
compound(<rate>,<number of periods>)
```

Description:

The **compound** function returns the value of (**<rate>**+ 1) raised to the power **<number of periods>**. It computes compound interest for a fixed rate over a number of periods.

The parameters **<number of periods>** and **<rate>** must be numbers or expressions that evaluates to numbers.

See also: **Annuity**, **Exp1**.

Examples:

```
-- Try this in the message box:
compound(0.10,15)

Put max(compound(rate1,20),compound(rate2,15))¬
into badDeal
```

Cos

Calling format:

```
the cos of <number>
cos(<number>)
```

Description:

The **cos** function returns the cosine of the angle **<number>**. **Cos** is an implementation of the trigonometric function cosine. The value returned is in radians, not degrees.

The parameter **<number>** must be a number or an expression that evaluates to a number.

See also: **Atan, Sin, Tan.**

Examples:

```
-- Try this in the message box:
the cos of pi

If theta < 2 * pi
Then
  Put the cos of theta
Else
  Put the cos of theta - 2 * pi
End if
```

Date

Calling format:

```
the date
date()
```

Description:

The **date** function returns the current system date in the form "6/2/88." It is equivalent to the **short date** function.

See also: **Abbreviated Date, Short date, Long date.**

Examples:

```
-- Try this in the message box:
the date

If the length of the long date < fldWidth
Then
  Put the long date into field "Date"
Else
  If the length of the abbr date < fldWidth
  Then
    Put the abbr date into field "Date"
  Else
    Put the short date into field "Date"
  End if
End if
```

DiskSpace

Calling format:

```
the diskSpace
diskSpace()
```

Description:

The **diskSpace** function returns the number of bytes free on the currently logged disk.

Examples:

```
-- Try this in the message box:
diskSpace()

If the diskSpace < 1028 then beep 3
```

Exp

Calling format:

```
the exp of <number>
exp(<number>)
```

Description:

The **exp** function returns the value of the exponential function; that is, the constant *e* raised to the **<number>** power. It is the inverse of the natural log function, **ln**.

The parameter **<number>** must be a number or an expression that evaluates to a number.

See also: **Exp1, Exp2, Ln, Ln1, Log2.**

Examples:

```
-- Try these in the message box:
exp(35)
ln(exp(pi))

If exp(i*pi)+1 = 0 then put "OK"
```

Exp1

Calling format:

```
the exp1 of <number>
exp1(<number>)
```

Description:

The **exp1** function returns the value of one less than the constant *e* raised to the **<number>** power. It is the inverse of the natural log function **ln1**.

The parameter **<number>** must be a number or an expression that evaluates to a number.

See also: **Compound, Exp, Exp2, Ln, Ln1, Log2.**

Examples:

```
-- Try these in the message box:
exp1(35)
ln1(exp1(35))

Put the exp1 of line 1 of card field nums ¬
into line 2 of card field nums
```

Exp2

Calling format:

```
the exp2 of <number>
exp2(<number>)
```

Description:

The **exp2** function returns the value of 2 raised to the **<number>** power. It is the inverse of the log function, **log2**.

The parameter **<number>** must be a number or an expression that evaluates to a number.

See also: **Exp, Exp1, Ln, Ln1, Log2.**

Examples:

```
-- Try these in the message box:
exp2(35)
log2(exp2(1028))

Put exp2(numBits) into numColors
```

FoundChunk

Calling format:

```
the foundChunk
foundChunk()
```

Description:

The **foundChunk** function (added in version 1.2) returns a chunk expression for the location where the most recently executed Find command found its target string. This location is normally indicated by a box around the location on completion of the Find command.

See also: **FoundField, FoundLine, FoundText.** Compare with: **SelectedChunk.**

Examples:

```
Put the foundText into what
Put the foundChunk into where
```

FoundField

Calling format:

```
the foundField
foundField()
```

Description:

The **foundField** function (added in version 1.2) returns an expression for the field in which the most recently executed Find command found its target string. On completion of the Find command, the found text in the field normally has a box around it.

See also: **FoundChunk**, **FoundLine**, **FoundText**. Compare with: **SelectedField**.

Examples:

```
Put the foundText into what
Put the foundField into where
```

FoundLine

Calling format:

```
the foundLine
foundLine()
```

Description:

The **foundLine** function (added in version 1.2) returns an expression for the first line of the location where the most recently executed Find command found its target string. This location is normally indicated by a box around the location on completion of the Find command.

See also: **FoundChunk, FoundField, FoundText**. Compare with: **SelectedLine.**

Examples:

```
Put the foundText into what
Put the foundLine into startsWhere
```

FoundText

Calling format:

```
the foundText
foundText()
```

Description:

The **foundText** function (added in version 1.2) returns the text found by the most recent Find command. This text is normally enclosed in a box on completion of the Find command.

See also: **FoundChunk, FoundField, FoundLine**. Compare with: **SelectedText.**

Examples:

```
Put the foundText into what
Put the foundChunk into where
```

HeapSpace

Calling format:

```
the heapSpace
heapSpace()
```

Description:

The **heapSpace** function returns the number of bytes free in the system heap.

See also: **StackSpace**.

Examples:

```
-- Try this in the message box:
the heapSpace

Put average(the heapSpace,the stackSpace)
```

Length

Calling format:

```
the length of <string>
length(<string>)
```

Description:

The **length** function returns the length, in characters, of **<string>**, including any carriage return character.

The parameter **<string>** can be a quoted literal string, a function returning a string, or a name or chunk expression for a container holding a string.

See also: **Offset**.

Examples:

```
-- Try this in the message box:
the length of "The quick brown fox jumps."

Put the length of the long date into dateCharacters
```

Ln

Calling format:

```
the ln of <number>
ln(<number>)
```

Description:

The **ln** function returns the natural logarithm of **<number>**. That is, the power to which the constant *e* must be raised to yield **<number>**. It is the inverse of the exponential function, **exp**.

The parameter **<number>** must be a number or an expression that evaluates to a number.

See also: **Exp, Exp1, Exp2, Ln1, Log2.**

Examples:

```
-- Try these in the message box:
ln(35)
ln(exp(pi))

Put ln of troy + ln(wheels) into sumLns
```

Ln1

Calling format:

```
the ln1 of <number>
ln1(<number>)
```

Description:

The **ln1** function returns the natural logarithm of 1 + **<number>**. That is, the power to which the constant *e* must be raised to yield 1 + **<number>**. It is the inverse of the exponential function **exp1**.

The parameter **<number>** must be a number or an expression that evaluates to a number.

See also: **Exp, Exp1, Exp2, Ln, Log2.**

Examples:

```
-- Try these in the message box:
ln1(35)
ln1(exp1(35))

Get the ln1 of 99
```

Log2

Calling format:

```
the log2 of <number>
log2(<number>)
```

Description:

The **log2** function returns the base-2 logarithm of **<number>**. That is, the power to which 2 must be raised to yield **<number>**. It is the inverse of the exponential function **exp2**.

The parameter **<number>** must be a number or an expression that evaluates to a number.

See also: **Exp, Exp1, Exp2, Ln, Ln1.**

Examples:

```
-- Try these in the message box:
log2(35)
log2(exp2(1028))

Put log2(numColors) into numBits
```

Long Date

Calling format:

```
the long date
long date()
```

Description:

The **long date** function returns the current system date in the form "Thursday, June 2, 1988."

If you use **long date** in any of the last three forms above, you may find that it does not return the long date, but rather the short date. This is a bug. By the time this book comes out, Apple will probably have fixed it, but it was still present in version 1.2 when it shipped.

See also: **Abbreviated Date, Short date, Date.**

Examples:

```
-- Try this in the message box:
the long date

If the length of the long date ≤ fldWidth
```

```
Then
  Put the long date into field "Date"
Else
  If the length of the abbr date ≤ fldWidth
  Then
    Put the abbr date into field "Date"
  Else
    Put the short date into field "Date"
  End if
End if
```

Long Time

Calling format:

```
the long time
long time()
```

Description:

The **long time** function returns the current system time, including the seconds.

If you use **long time** in the second form above, you may find that it does not return the long time, but rather the short time. This is a bug. By the time this book comes out, Apple will probably have fixed it, but it was still present in version 1.2 when it shipped.

See also: **Seconds, Short time, Ticks, Time**.

Examples:

```
-- Try this in the message box:
the long time

Put the long time into card field "Time"
```

Long Version

Calling format:

```
the long version
the long version of HyperCard
```

Description:

The **long version** function returns the HyperCard version number in standard Macintosh version resource format. This function was added in version 1.2.

See also: **Version** .

Examples:

```
-- Try this in the message box:
the long version

If item 1 of the version of this stack ¬
<> the long version
Then
  Put "Stack created under different version."
End if
```

Max

Calling format:

```
max(<listOfNumbers>)
```

Description:

The **max** function returns the largest number in **<listOfNumbers>**.

The parameter **<listOfNumbers>** must be a comma-separated list of numbers or expressions evaluating to numbers.

See also: **Min**.

Examples:

```
-- Try this in the message box:
max(3,1,89,-144,55,21)

Put max(salaries) after item Swaine ¬
in field payroll
```

Min

Calling format:

```
min(<listOfNumbers>)
```

Description:

The **max** function returns the smallest number in **<listOfNumbers>**.

The parameter **<listOfNumbers>** must be a comma-separated list of numbers or expressions evaluating to numbers.

See also: **Max**.

Examples:

```
-- Try this in the message box:
min(3,1,89,-144,55,21)

If min(altitudes) < 1000 then put "impact imminent"
```

Mouse

Calling format:

```
the mouse
mouse()
```

Description:

The **mouse** function returns the current status of the mouse button, either "up" or "down."

See also: **ClickLoc**, **MouseClick**, **MouseH**, **MouseLoc**, **MouseV**.

Examples:

```
-- Try this in the message box:
the mouse

-- Simulating a seat-belt alarm:
Repeat until the mouse is down
  Play annoyingMusic
End repeat
```

MouseClick

Calling format:

```
the mouseClick
mouseClick()
```

Description:

The **mouseClick** function returns true if it detects a mouse click. A click involves both mouseDown and mouseUp actions. If a mouseDown has been executed without a matching mouseUp, **mouseClick** will hold up processing to wait for the mouseUp.

See also: **ClickLoc, Mouse, MouseH, MouseLoc, MouseV.**

Examples:

```
-- Try this in the message box:
mouseClick()

-- But it is only useful in scripts:
Wait until mouseClick()
```

MouseH

Calling format:

```
the mouseH
mouseH()
```

Description:

The **mouseH** function returns the horizontal component of the card window location of the mouse. A location is always expressed as a pair of numbers, first the horizontal component, then the vertical, separated by a comma.

See also: **ClickLoc, Mouse, MouseClick, MouseLoc, MouseV.**

Examples:

```
-- Try this in the message box:
the mouseH

Put the mouseV into altitude
Put the mouseH - startPoint into distanceFlown
```

MouseLoc

Calling format:

```
the mouseLoc
mouseLoc()
```

Description:

The **mouseLoc** function returns the card window location of the mouse. A location is always expressed as a pair of numbers, first the horizontal component, then the vertical, separated by a comma.

See also: **ClickLoc, Mouse, MouseClick, MouseH, MouseV.**

Examples:

```
-- Try this in the message box
-- to find out where it is:
mouseLoc()

On idle
  If the mouseLoc is not within the screenRect
  Then
    Flash
  End if
End idle
```

MouseV

Calling format:

```
the mouseV
mouseV()
```

Description:

The **mouseV** function returns the horizontal component of the card window location of the mouse. A location is always expressed as a pair of numbers, first the horizontal component, then the vertical, separated by a comma.

See also: **ClickLoc**, **Mouse**, **MouseClick**, **MouseH**, **MouseLoc**.

Examples:

```
-- Try this in the message box:
mouseV()

Put the mouseV into altitude
Put the mouseH - startPoint into distanceFlown
```

Number

Calling format:

```
the number of <object>s
number of <object>s
number(<object>s)
the number of <element>s in <source>
number of <element>s in <source>
number(<element>s in <source>)
the number of cards of <background>
number of cards of <background>
```

Description:

The **number** function returns a count of the number of objects of the specified kind, or the number of chunk elements in a specified container. The variation that returns the number of cards of a given background was added in version 1.2.

The parameter **<object>** must be a legitimate object class name from this list: button, card button, background button, field, card field, background field, card, background; or an abbreviated form of one of these, such as cd btn. The parameter **<element>** must be a legitimate chunk element name from this list: item, line, word, character; or an abbreviated form of one of these, such as wd. The parameter **<source>** must evaluate to a reference to a container. The parameter **<background>** must be a reference to a background.

Examples:

```
-- Try these in the message box:
the number of cards
the number of cards of this background
the number of cd btns

-- A slide show with pauses.
Repeat with i = 1 to the number of cards div 10
  Show 10 cards
  Wait 50
End repeat
Show the number of cards mod 10
```

NumToChar

Calling format:

```
the numToChar of <number>
numToChar(<number>)
```

Description:

The **numToChar** function returns the ASCII character corresponding to **<number>**. ASCII defines a standard ordering for characters.

The parameter **<number>** must be a number or an expression that evaluates to a number.

See also: **CharToNum**.

Examples:

```
-- Try this in the message box:
numToChar(65)

-- Putting a strange character into a name:
Put numToChar(51) & userName into userName
```

Offset

Calling format:

```
offset(<string>,<source>)
```

Description:

The **offset** function returns a number indicating the ordinal position of the first character of **<string>** in **<source>**. If **<string>** is not contained in **<source>** then 0 is returned.

The parameter **<string>** must be a string or an expression that evaluates to a string. The parameter **<source>** must evaluate to a container.

See also: **Length**.

Examples:

```
-- Try this in the message box:
offset("Inc","Lincoln Properties, Inc.")
```

OptionKey

Calling format:

```
the optionKey
optionKey()
```

Description:

The **optionKey** function returns "up" or "down" depending on whether the option key is up or down when the function is executed.

See also: **CommandKey**, **ShiftKey**.

Examples:

```
-- Try this in the message box:
the optionKey

If the optionKey is up
  Then
    Close printing
  Else
    Close file fileName
  End if
```

Param

Calling format:

```
the param of <number>
param(<number>)
```

Description:

The **param** function returns the value of the **<number>**th parameter supplied to the handler in which it appears. The 0th parameter is the name of the handler; that is, the message that invoked the handler.

The parameter **<number>** must be a number or an expression evaluating to a number.

See also: **ParamCount, Params**.

Examples:

```
Put param(0) into functionName
Put param(word 1 of line 3 of field nums)
```

ParamCount

Calling format:

```
the paramCount
paramCount()
```

Description:

The **paramCount** function returns the number of actual parameter values supplied to the handler in which this function appears, regardless of the number of parameters the handler is defined to be able to accept.

See also: **Param, Params**.

Example:

```
Put the paramCount into arity
```

Params

Calling format:

```
the params
params()
```

Description:

The **params** function returns the complete list of the actual parameter values passed to the handler in which this function appears. The 0th parameter is the name of the handler.

The parameters are returned in a distinctive format: the handler name is followed by the actual parameters, each enclosed in quotes, separated by commas. The actual parameters are enclosed in a set of parentheses if the handler is a function handler. Basically, this function rebuilds the expression that invoked the handler in which it resides.

See also: **Param**, **ParamCount**.

Examples:

```
Put item 1 of the params into functionName

-- The following code, placed in a button script...

on mouseUp
  geek 1,2
  geek a,b
  geek "c","d"
  put foo(1,2) into fooBar
  put foo(a,b) into fooBar
  put foo("c","d") into fooBar
end mouseUp

on geek x,y
  put the params
  wait 50
end geek
```

```
function foo x,y
  put the params
  wait 50
end foo

-- ...puts these values in the message box:
geek "1","2"
geek "a","b"
geek "c","d"
foo("1","2")
foo("a","b")
foo("c","d")
```

Random

Calling format:

```
the random of <number>
random(<number>)
```

Description:

The **random** function returns a random number in the range from 1 to **<number>**, inclusive.

The parameter **<number>** must be a number or an expression that evaluates to a number.

Examples:

```
-- Try these in the message box:
random(6)
random(random(2))
```

Result

Calling format:

```
the result
result()
```

Description:

The **result** function returns the status of the last command or handler. If the command was successful, it will return the value **empty**; otherwise, it will return a string identifying the nature of the failure. In the case of the **open** command, for example, it might return "no such application". The **find** command, failing to find its target string, will return "not found". A handler can specify the value that **result** will find on its termination.

Example:

```
Put the result into errorMessage
```

Round

Calling format:

```
the round of <number>
round(<number>)
```

Description:

The **round** function returns an integer, the value of **<number>** rounded to the nearest integer. If **<number>** is equidistant between integers, **round** rounds to the even integer.

The parameter **<number>** must be a number or an expression that evaluates to a number.

See also: **Trunc**.

Examples:

```
-- Try these in the message box:
round(pi)
round(1.5)
round(2.5)
```

ScreenRect

Calling format:

```
the screenRect
screenRect()
```

Description:

The **screenRect** function (added in version 1.2) returns the rect of the screen currently in use, in global coordinates.

Examples:

```
-- Try this in the message box:
the screenRect

On idle
  If the mouseLoc is not within the screenRect
  Then
    Flash
  End if
End idle
```

Seconds

Calling format:

```
the secs
secs()
the seconds
seconds()
```

Description:

The **seconds** function returns the number of seconds between midnight, January 1, 1904, and the current system time and date.

See also: **Long time, Short time, Ticks, Time.**

Examples:

```
-- Try this in the message box:
the secs

Put the secs - startTime into elapsedTime
```

SelectedChunk

Calling format:

```
the selectedChunk
selectedChunk()
```

Description:

The **selectedChunk** function (added in version 1.2) returns a chunk expression for the currently highlighted text.

See also: **SelectedField, SelectedLine, SelectedText.** Compare with: **FoundChunk.**

Example:

```
Put the selectedChunk
```

SelectedField

Calling format:

```
the selectedField
selectedField()
```

Description:

The **selectedField** function (added in version 1.2) returns an expression for the field in which the currently highlighted text is located.

See also: **SelectedChunk**, **SelectedLine**, **SelectedText**. Compare with: **FoundField**.

Example:

```
Put the selectedField
```

SelectedLine

Calling format:

```
the selectedLine
selectedLine()
```

Description:

The **selectedLine** function (added in version 1.2) returns an expression for the line in which the currently highlighted text is located.

See also: **SelectedChunk**, **SelectedField**, **SelectedText**. Compare with: **FoundLine**.

Example:

```
Put the selectedLine
```

SelectedText

Calling format:

```
the selectedText
selectedText()
```

Description:

The **selectedText** function (added in version 1.2) returns the text currently highlighted. This is a true function, unlike **the selection**, which is really a container.

See also: **SelectedChunk**, **SelectedField**, **SelectedLine**. Compare with: **FoundText**, **Selection**.

Example:

```
Put the selectedText into userSelection
```

Selection

Calling format:

```
the selection
```

Description:

The **selection** function returns the text currently highlighted. The **selection** is not a true function, because you can put values into it as well as get them out.

See also: **SelectedChunk**, **SelectedField**, **SelectedLine**, **SelectedText**.

Examples:

```
Put the selection into userSelection

If the selection is "Mike"
then
  put "Michael" into the selection
end if
```

ShiftKey

Calling format:

```
the shiftKey
shiftKey()
```

Description:

The **shiftKey** function returns "up" or "down" depending on whether the shift key is up or down when the function is executed.

See also: **CommandKey**, **OptionKey**.

Examples:

```
-- Try this in the message box:
shiftKey()

If the shiftKey is down
Then
  Put "shift" into theKey
End if
```

Short date

Calling format:

```
the short date
short date()
```

Description:

The **short date** returns the system date in the form "6/2/88." It is equivalent to the **date** function and was added as a convenient alternative form in version 1.1.

See also: **Abbreviated Date, Date, Long date.**

Examples:

```
-- Try this in the message box:
short date()

If the length of the long date < fldWidth
Then
  Put the long date into field "Date"
Else
  If the length of the abbr date < fldWidth
  Then
    Put the abbr date into field "Date"
  Else
    Put the short date into field "Date"
```

```
  End if
End if
```

Short time

Calling format:

```
the short time
short time()
```

Description:

The **short time** function returns the current system time, without the seconds. It is equivalent to the **time** function and was added as a convenient alternative form in version 1.1.

See also: **Long Time, Seconds, Ticks, Time**.

Examples:

```
-- Try this in the message box:
the short time

Put the short time into field Time
```

Sin

Calling format:

```
the sin of <number>
sin(<number>)
```

Description:

The **sin** function returns the sine of the angle **<number>**. **Sin** is an implementation of the trigonometric function sine. The value returned is in radians, not degrees.

The parameter **<number>** must be a number or an expression that evaluates to a number.

See also: **Atan, Cos, Tan.**

Examples:

```
-- Try this in the message box:
sin(pi/2)

Put sin(x^2)/cos(x) into theta
```

Sound

Calling format:

```
the sound
sound()
```

Description:

The **sound** function returns the name of the currently active sound resource; i.e., the sound that is playing, or "done" if no sound is playing.

Examples:

```
-- Try this in the message box:
sound()

If the sound is "done" then play myFavorite
```

Sqrt

Calling format:

```
the sqrt of <number>
sqrt(<number>)
```

Description:

The **sqrt** function returns the positive square root of **<number>**. The parameter **<number>** must be nonnegative.

The parameter **<number>** must be a number or an expression that evaluates to a number. If it is negative, the result will be NAN.

Examples:

```
-- Try this in the message box:
sqrt(39^2)

Put sqrt(f) && -sqrt(f) into roots
```

StackSpace

Calling format:

```
the stackSpace
stackSpace()
```

Description:

The **stackSpace** function returns the number of bytes free in the system stack (no connection with HyperCard stacks).

See also: **HeapSpace**.

Examples:

```
-- Try this in the message box:
stackSpace()

Put average(the heapSpace,the stackSpace)
```

Tan

Calling format:

```
the tan of <number>
tan(<number>)
```

Description:

The **tan** function returns the tangent of the angle **<number>**. It is the inverse of the **atan** function. **Tan** is an implementation of the trigonometric function tangent. The value returned is in radians, not degrees.

The parameter **<number>** must be a number or an expression that evaluates to a number.

See also: **Atan, Cos, Sin.**

Examples:

```
-- Try this in the message box:
tan(atan(5))

Put tan(2*pi) * sqrt(e) into newVal
```

Target

Calling format:

```
the target
target()
target
```

Description:

The **target** function (enhanced in version 1.2) returns the name of the object to which the current message was initially directed. In version 1.2, if the object is a field, the special form **target** is allowed (without the word **the**), and it refers to the contents of **the target**.

Examples:

```
-- Try this in the message box to see where
-- message box messages are directed:
the target

On mouseUp
  Put the target
End mouseUp

On openField
  Put line 1 of target
End openField
```

Ticks

Calling format:

```
the ticks
ticks()
```

Description:

The **ticks** function returns the number of clock ticks (sixtieths of a second) since the machine was last turned on or restarted.

See also: **Long time, Seconds, Short time, Time.**

Examples:

```
-- Try this in the message box:
ticks()

Put the ticks - tickStart into ticker
```

Time

Calling format:

```
the time
time()
```

Description:

The **time** function returns the current system time, not including seconds. It is equivalent to the **short time** function.

See also: **Long time, Seconds, Short time, Ticks.**

Examples:

```
-- Try this in the message box:
the time

Put the time into field Time
```

Tool

Calling format:

```
the tool
tool()
```

Description:

The **tool** function returns the name of the currently selected tool from the tools menu.

Examples:

```
-- Try this in the message box (there's only
-- one value it will ever have in the message box):
tool()

Get the tool
If it is not "browse tool" then put it
```

Trunc

Calling format:

```
the trunc of <number>
trunc(<number>)
```

Description:

The **trunc** function returns an integer, the largest integer not larger than **<number>**. In this context, larger means larger in absolute value. **Trunc** truncates positive numbers down toward zero, negative numbers up toward zero. Simply put, it chops off anything to the right of the decimal point.

The parameter **<number>** must be a number or an expression that evaluates to a number.

See also: **Round**.

Examples:

```
-- Try these in the message box:
trunc(pi)
trunc(-1.4)
trunc(-1.6)
```

Value

Calling format:

```
the value of <expression>
value(<expression>)
```

Description:

The **value** function returns the value of the expression **<expression>**. Sometimes it is necessary to explicitly force evaluation of an expression so that HyperCard does not act on it literally.

The parameter **<expression>** may be any expression.

Examples:

```
-- Try this in the message box:
the value of pi * 37 ^ 2

Put the value of word 1 of field nums ¬
into word 1 of field nums
```

Version

Calling format:

```
the version
the version of <stack>
```

Description:

The first syntax veriation listed above for the **version** function returns the version number of the currently running HyperCard, for example, **1.2**.

In version 1.2 and later, the **version of <stack>** form was added. In this form, the function returns a five-item string consisting of: the number of the version of HyperCard under which the stack was created, the number of the version of HyperCard under which the stack was last compacted, the number of the version of HyperCard under which the stack was first modified after compacting, the number of the version of HyperCard under which the stack was most recently modified, and the date of the last modification in seconds format.

In the **version of <stack>** form, the format for the version numbers is standard Macintosh version resource format; for example, **01208000**. The first four items will be set to zeros if the version to which they refer is less than 1.2. The fifth item is updated only on closing the stack.

The parameter **<stack>** must be the name of a stack or an expression that evaluates to the name of a stack.

See also: **Long version**, **Seconds**.

Examples:

```
-- Try these in the message box:
the version
the version of this stack

Put "this stack," before field misc
Put the version of item 1 of field misc

If item 1 of the version of this stack ¬
<> the long version
Then
  Put "Stack created under different version."
End if
```

Appendix F

HyperTalk Properties

About this Appendix

The following pages detail the salient facts about every HyperTalk property: the object or objects to which it belongs, its acceptable values and default value, the methods by which its values can be accessed, a prose description, and one or more concrete examples of its use. There is also a separate quick reference list of properties organized by object. Like the other technical appendixes, this one is intended for reference purposes. For a more tutorial presentation of the use of HyperTalk properties, you should see the earlier portions of the book.

The information in this property appendix is as timely and as accurate as I could make it. All facts were checked at final board stage, and should be consistent with the state of HyperTalk at that time. I ran all example code through HyperCard, then pasted the properly running code directly into the text, minimizing the opportunities for errors to creep in.

It's probably impossible to write accurately about technical topics without using a lot of technical terms; at least I haven't been able to do it. If you get tripped up by any technical term or topic in this appendix, you may find clarification in one of the other technical appendixes. For more on messages, you should see the HyperTalk System Messages appendix. The HyperTalk Object Hierarchy appendix covers how messages trickle through the objects of a HyperCard stack. If you are having trouble with the concepts of objects and messages and object hierarchies, you might take another look at the Concepts section. To work with HyperTalk properties, it is necessary to understand the **set** command, which is documented in the HyperTalk Commands appendix.

Taken one at a time, the concepts of command, function, property, and message may seem clear and intuitive, but in the early stages of learning HyperTalk it is not always obvious to what category a particular word belongs. The HyperTalk Vocabulary appendix can point to the appropriate appendix, and a careful comparison of the "About" sections of the Commands, Functions, Properties, and System Messages appendixes can help to clarify the differences.

About HyperTalk Properties

Despite the connotations of the name, HyperTalk objects are not static entities. They are imbued with changeable properties, such as **style**, **size**, and **location**. There are also global properties that pertain to the state of HyperCard itself, such as **numberFormat**, and properties that identify the state of the painting tools, such as **brush** and **pattern**. For each property there is an acceptable set of values the property can take on; for example, the **brush** property can take on numeric values from 1 to 32, representing the 32 possible brush shapes.

Although properties do take on values, they are not containers into which values can be placed via the **put** command. The only way to change a property is with the **set** command. Some properties cannot be changed at all, and there is at least one property whose value can be set but cannot be retrieved via the **get** command or by any other means. The ability to alter or to retrieve the value of a property is summarized under the heading "Access" for each command.

The keyword **the** is often required in referring to properties. The rule for the use of **the** is this: **the** is optional with all properties when used in **set** and **get** commands, optional in other commands when the property has parameters, and obligatory in commands other than **set** and **get** if the property has no parameters. Every window, stack, background, card, field, or button property has a parameter (the parameter specifies the object to which the property applies); global and painting properties have none.

A Quick Reference to HyperTalk Properties Organized by Object

Global Properties:

blindTyping	cursor	dragSpeed
editBkgnd	language	lockMessages
lockRecent	lockScreen	numberFormat
powerKeys	textArrows	userLevel
userModify		

Painting Properties:

brush	centered	filled
grid	lineSize	multiple
multiSpace	pattern	polySides
textAlign	textFont	textHeight
textSize	textStyle	

Window Properties:

bottom	bottomRight	height
left	location	rectangle
right	top	topLeft
visible	width	

Stack Properties:

cantDelete	cantModify	freeSize
name	script	size

Background Properties:

cantDelete	ID	name
number	script	showPict

Card Properties:

cantDelete	ID	name
number	script	showPict

Field Properties:

autoTab	bottom	bottomRight
height	ID	left
location	lockText	name
number	rectangle	right
script	scroll	showLines
style	textAlign	textFont
textHeight	textSize	textStyle
top	topLeft	visible
wideMargins	width	

Button Properties:

autoHilite	bottom	bottomRight
height	hilite	icon
ID	left	location
name	number	rectangle
right	script	showName
style	textAlign	textFont
textHeight	textSize	textStyle
top	topLeft	visible
width		

AutoHilite

Object: button

Values:

```
true, false.  The default is false.
```

Access:

The value can be manipulated via the **set** command from a script or from the message box, or via the Button Info dialog box. The value can be retrieved via the **get** command or by the use of the property name in an expression.

Description:

The **autoHilite** property represents highlighting of the button in response to mouse clicks. If a button's **autoHilite** is true, a **mouseDown** or **mouseUp** message sent to the button can affect the button's **hilite** property. The usual effect is to turn on the **hilite** when the button gets a **mouseDown** and to turn off the **hilite** when it gets the **mouseUp** , but if the button's **hilite** is already true, the effect will be reversed. In the case of radio buttons and check boxes, the effect is different: when the **autoHilite** property of a radio button or check box is true, the button's **hilite** property will change on every **mouseDown** message. See also **hilite** .

Example:

```
If the autoHilite of button 1 is true
Then set the autoHilite of button 1 to false
-- or, more simply,
Set the autoHilite of button 1 ¬
to not the autoHilite of button 1
```

AutoTab

Object: field

Values:

true, false. The default is **false**.

Access:

The value can be manipulated via the **set** command from a script or from the message box, or via the Field Info dialog box in version 1.2 or later. The value can be retrieved via the **get** command or by the use of the property name in an expression.

Description:

The **autoTab** property, added in version 1.2, represents the ability to use the Return key to mimic the Tab key's action in fields. If **autoTab** is true, pressing the Return key while in a field generates a tabKey message, which does what it has always done: it causes the pointer to move to the next field. "Next" in this context refers to the natural HyperCard cyclic ordering for fields, which is in increasing field number order through the fields of one layer (card or background), then in the same order through the other layer.

Example:

```
Set the autoTab of field 1 ¬
to not the autoTab of field 1
```

BlindTyping

Object: global

Values:

`true, false`. The true default is **`false`** but this property is normally set on startUp or resume to an effective default stored in the user preferences card of the Home stack.

Access:

The value can be manipulated via the **`set`** command from a script or from the message box, or via the user preferences card of the Home stack. The value can be retrieved via the **`get`** command or by the use of the property name in an expression.

Description:

The **`blindTyping`** property represents the ability to type into the message box when it is not visible. It is only available when the user level is set to 5.

Example:

```
Set blindTyping to not the blindTyping
```

Bottom

Object: window, field, button

Values:

An integer: a number of pixels. The value is relative to the card window except when applied to the card window itself, in which case it is relative to the screen.

Defaults used on creation of objects are:

button	162
field	205;

Default for windows are:

message box	335
tool window	199
pattern window	199
card window (ls)	411
card window (ss)	342.

(The notations ls and ss after card window refer to the 640 x 480 Macintosh II screen and the 512 x 342 standard Macintosh screen, respectively.)

Access:

The value can be manipulated via the **set** command from a script or from the message box, except in the case of windows. The value can be retrieved via the **get** command or by the use of the property name in an expression.

Description:

The **bottom** property, added in version 1.2, represents the bottom edge of the rectangle enclosing the object, expressed as a number of pixels relative to the card window (or the screen in the case of the card window itself). Setting this property repositions the object, and does so more efficiently than setting the **loc** property; it does not resize it. The **height** of an object is equal to the **bottom** minus the **top** of the object.

Example:

```
Set the bottom of button 1 to 100
```

BottomRight
BotRight

Object: window, field, button

Values:

A comma-separated list of two integers: a point. The value is relative to the card window except when applied to the card window itself, in which case it is relative to the screen.

Defaults used on creation of objects are:

button	306,162
field	356,205;

Default for windows are:

message box	494,335
tool window	268,199
pattern window	371,199
card window (ls)	576,411
card window (ss)	512,342.

(The notations ls and ss after card window refer to the 640 x 480 Macintosh II screen and the 512 x 342 standard Macintosh screen, respectively.)

Access:

The value can be manipulated via the **set** command from a script or from the message box, except in the case of windows. The value can be retrieved via the **get** command or by the use of the property name in an expression.

Description:

The **bottomRight** property, added in version 1.2, represents the bottom right corner of the rectangle enclosing the object, expressed in pixels relative to the card window (or the screen in the case of the card window itself). Setting this property repositions the object, and does so more efficiently than setting the **loc** property; it does not resize it. The **rectangle** of an object **<object>** is equal to **topLeft <object> & "," & bottomRight <object>**.

Example:

```
Set the botRight of button 1 to 100,100
```

Brush

Object: painting

Values:

1...32. The default is **8**.

Access:

The value can be manipulated via the **set** command from a script or from the message box, or via the brush shape dialog box. The value can be retrieved via the **get** command or by the use of the property name in an expression.

Description:

The **brush** property represents the currently selected brush shape for painting. The numeric values correspond to the brush shapes in the brush shape dialog box. This dialog box can be examined by pulling the tool window off from its normal menu location and double-clicking on the brush tool. The top left brush shape in the window is brush 1, the shape below it is brush 2, and so on.

All painting properties are reset to their default values when the **reset** command is executed.

Example:

```
Set brush to 1
```

CantDelete

Object: stack, background, card

Values:

`true, false.  The default is false.`

Access:

The value can be manipulated via the **set** command from a script or from the message box. The value can be retrieved via the **get** command or by the use of the property name in an expression.

Description:

The **cantDelete** property, script-settable since version 1.2, represents a protected state of a card, background, or stack. If **cantDelete** is true, the object cannot be deleted via the usual menu selection.

Example:

```
On openCard
   Set the cantDelete of the target to true
End openCard
```

CantModify

Object: stack

Values:

true, false. The default is **false**.

Access:

The value can be manipulated via the **set** command from a script or from the message box. The value can be retrieved via the **get** command or by the use of the property name in an expression.

Description:

The **cantModify** property, added in version 1.2, represents a locked state of a stack. If cc is true, the user cannot modify the stack, or delete or compact it.

Example:

```
Set the cantModify of this stack to true
```

Centered

Object: painting

Values:

true, false. The default is **false**.

Access:

The value can be manipulated via the **set** command from a script or from the message box, or via the options menu. The value can be retrieved via the **get** command or by the use of the property name in an expression.

Description:

The **centered** property represents the mode for drawing shapes. If **centered** is true, shapes will be drawn from the center, otherwise from the corner. Drawing from the center allows precise centering of the object on a point, while drawing from the corner facilitates lining up edges of objects with existing drawing elements.

All painting properties are reset to their default values when the **reset** command is executed.

Example:

```
Set centered to not the centered
```

Cursor

Object: global

Values:

Any ID number or name of a Macintosh 'CURS' resource in HyperCard itself or in the current stack. Resources can be added or removed using Apple's ResEdit or another resource editor. In an unmodified release version 1.2 HyperCard, the legal values are:

ID	Name	Description
1	**iBeam**	Macintosh system text cursor
2	**cross**	Macintosh system cross cursor (crosshairs)
3	**plus**	Macintosh system plus cursor (a fat cross)
4	**watch**	Macintosh system busy cursor
*	**hand**	HyperCard browse cursor
*	**arrow**	QuickDraw arrow cursor
*	**busy**	HyperCard busy cursor (the beachball cursor; 4 ID nos.)
*	**none**	HyperCard transparent cursor

The ID number is the resource ID number; it is preset in the case of the first four. There is no real default cursor; on idle, HyperCard sets the cursor to the value appropriate to its current use.

Access:

The value can be changed temporarily via the **set** command from a script. The value cannot be retrieved.

Description:

The **cursor** property, enhanced in version 1.2, represents the current value of the cursor, generally referred to in Macintosh user documentation as the pointer. The HyperCard **busy** cursor is really four cursors, each looking something like a beachball. Each successive setting of the **busy** cursor sets a different one of the beachballs, so that a script that sets the **busy** cursor inside a **repeat** structure will cause the beachball to spin. The transparent cursor **none** is useful when displaying art.

Example:

```
Set cursor to 1
Set the cursor to iBeam
```

DragSpeed

Object: global

Values:

Any non-negative integer. The default is 0, to which it is reset on idle.

Access:

The value can be manipulated via the **set** command from a script. The value can be retrieved via the **get** command or by the use of the property name in an expression.

Description:

The **dragSpeed** property represents the speed, in pixels per inch, at which the **drag** command operates. The value 0 represents the top speed possible rather than a rather boring speed of zero pixels per second. This means that the **dragSpeed** property cannot be used to halt dragging, as might or might not be expected. Even on a Macintosh II, values above 3000 are indistinguishable in effect from one another and from 0.

Example:

```
Set dragSpeed to 3
```

EditBkgnd

Object: global

Values:

`true, false`. The default is **`false`**.

Access:

The value can be manipulated via the **`set`** command from a script or from the message box, or via the Edit menu. The value can be retrieved via the **`get`** command or by the use of the property name in an expression.

Description:

The **`editBkgnd`** property represents the level at which painting and button or field creation will occur: either card or background. A value of **`true`** represents the background.

Example:

```
Set editBkgnd to not the editBkgnd
```

Filled

Object: painting

Values:

`true`, **`false`**. The default is **`false`**.

Access:

The value can be manipulated via the **`set`** command from a script or from the message box, or via the options menu. The value can be retrieved via the **`get`** command or by the use of the property name in an expression.

Description:

The **`filled`** property represents the mode of completing drawn shapes. If the value is **`true`**, shapes are drawn filled with the currently selected pattern.

All painting properties are reset to their default values when the **`reset`** command is executed.

Example:

```
Set filled to not the filled
```

FreeSize

Object: stack

Values:

Any non-negative integer. There is no default value.

Access:

The value cannot be changed directly except by compacting the stack (which sets it to 0), although it increases with each object deleted from the stack. The value can be retrieved via the **get** command or by the use of the property name in an expression.

Description:

The **freeSize** property represents the unused space, in bytes, in the stack.

Example:

```
Put the size of Home - the freeSize of Home ¬
into theRealSizeOfHome
```

Grid

Object: painting

Values:

true, false. The default is **false**.

Access:

The value can be manipulated via the **set** command from a script or from the message box, or via the options menu. The value can be retrieved via the **get** command or by the use of the property name in an expression.

Description:

The **grid** property represents the constraint on paint tool movement. If the value is true, certain paint tools are constrained to movements from point to point on an invisible eight-pixel grid that starts at card window location 0,0. The names of the tools that are affected by the **grid** property, including their alternate spellings, are: **line**, **oval**, **polygon** (or **poly**), **rectangle** (or **rect**), **regular polygon** (**regular poly**, **reg polygon**, **reg poly**), **round rectangle** (**round rect**), **select**, and **text**.

All painting properties are reset to their default values when the **reset** command is executed.

Example:

```
Set grid to not the grid
```

Height

Object: window, field, button

Values:

A non-negative integer: a number of pixels.

Defaults used on creation of objects are:

button	22
field	85;

Default for windows are:

message box	35
tool window	129
pattern window	129
card window (ls)	342

(The notations ls and ss after card window refer to the 640 x 480 Macintosh II screen and the 512 x 342 standard Macintosh screen, respectively.)

Access:

The value can be manipulated via the **set** command from a script or from the message box, except in the case of windows. The value can be retrieved via the **get** command or by the use of the property name in an expression.

Description:

The **height** property, added in version 1.2, represents the vertical extent, in pixels, of the object. Setting this property, which is only possible for fields and buttons, does not change the center point of the object; i.e., it does not change its **location** property. The object's **bottom** and **top** properties are just moved appropriately. The **height** of an object is always equal to the **bottom** minus the **top** of the object.

Example:

```
Set the height of button 1 ¬
to 2 * the height of button 1
```

Hilite
Hilight
Highlite
Highlight

Object: button

Values:

true, **false**. The default is **false**.

Access:

The value can be manipulated via the **set** command from a script or from the message box, or via the Button Info dialog box. It can also be affected by **mouseDown** and **mouseUp** messages if the **autoHilite** property for the button has the value **true**. See the **autoHilite** property description for details. The value can be retrieved via the **get** command or by the use of the property name in an expression.

Description:

The **hilite** property represents the highlighting of the button. The actual effect of highlighting varies with button style: radio buttons are highlighted by a large dot in the button's open circle, checkBox buttons are highlighted by an X in the check box, and for other buttons highlighting is reverse video. See also the **autoHilite** property.

Even though "highlight" is the only proper English spelling of the word, the spelling "hilite" is the wisest to use, since it corresponds to the spelling of the **autoHilite** property, for which there are no alternatives.

Example:

```
Set the hilite of button 1 ¬
to not the hilite of button 1
```

Icon

Object: button

Values:

Any ID number or name of a Macintosh 'ICON' resource in HyperCard itself or in the current stack. If a button has no icon, the value is 0. Resources can be added or removed using Apple's ResEdit or another resource editor. The current legal values can be viewed by clicking the Icon button in any HyperCard button's Button Info box, then clicking on each icon displayed in the resulting dialog box. The selected icon's number (and name) will appear at the top of the dialog box.

The default is `0`.

Access:

The value can be manipulated via the **set** command from a script or from the message box, or via the Button Info dialog box. The icon ID number can be retrieved via the **get** command or by the use of the property name in an expression.

Description:

The **icon** property represents the unique icon associated with a button. If the **icon** property is not zero, the button **style** property will not matter, since the icon will be displayed rather than the selected style of button.

Example:

```
On idle
   Set the icon of button 1 to 1000 + random(5)
End idle
```

Id
Abbreviated id
Abbrev id
Abbr id
Long id
Short id

Object: background, card, field, button

Values:

An integer. There is no default value.

Access:

The value is set by HyperCard on the creation of the object and cannot be changed. The value can be retrieved via the **get** command or by the use of the property name in an expression.

Description:

The **id** property represents the unique ID number associated with the object. HyperCard does the assigning and never changes an object's ID. It is unique within the stack for background and card numbers, unique within the background for background field and background button numbers, and unique within the card for card field and card button numbers. An object can be referred to unambiguously within this scope by its ID number. The alternate forms return its value in more or less abbreviated form. See also the property **number**.

Example:

```
Go to card id 1034
```

Language

Object: global

Values:

The name of a natural language supported by the translator resources in HyperCard itself or the current stack. Resources can be added or removed using Apple's ResEdit or another resource editor. In an unmodified release version 1.2 HyperCard, the only legal value is **English**, which is also the default .

Access:

The value can be manipulated via the **set** command from a script or from the message box. The value can be retrieved via the **get** command or by the use of the property name in an expression.

Description:

The **language** property represents the natural language in which scripts are interpreted and displayed. Internally, HyperTalk uses the English words and almost-words defined in this book, but translator resources are available for localizing HyperTalk to other languages, adding an automatic level of transliteration to the interpretation and display of scripts. Thus a French programmer can code with Gallicized **get**, **go**, and **global**.

Example:

```
Set Language to French
```

Left

Object: window, field, button

Values:

An integer: a number of pixels. The value is relative to the card window except when applied to the card window itself, in which case it is relative to the screen.

Defaults used on creation of objects are:

button	206
field	156;

Default for windows are:

message box	22
tool window	200
pattern window	300
card window (ls)	64
card window (ss)	0.

(The notations ls and ss after card window refer to the 640 x 480 Macintosh II screen and the 512 x 342 standard Macintosh screen, respectively.)

Access:

The value can be manipulated via the **set** command from a script or from the message box, except in the case of windows. The value can be retrieved via the **get** command or by the use of the property name in an expression.

Description:

The **left** property, added in version 1.2, represents the left edge of the rectangle enclosing the object, expressed as a number of pixels relative to the card window (or the screen in the case of the card window itself). Setting this property repositions the object, and does so more efficiently than setting the **loc** property; it does not resize it.

The **width** of an object is equal to the **right** minus the **left** of the object.

Example:

```
Set the left of field 1 to 10
```

LineSize

Object: painting

Values:

1,2,3,4,6, or **8**. The default is **1**.

Access:

The value can be manipulated via the **set** command from a script or from the message box, or via the options menu. The value can be retrieved via the **get** command or by the use of the property name in an expression.

Description:

The **lineSize** property represents the width of the line used by the line and shape drawing tools.

All painting properties are reset to their default values when the **reset** command is executed.

Example:

```
Set the lineSize to 3
```

Location
Loc

Object: window, field, button

Values:

A comma-separated list of two integers: a point. The value is relative to the card window except when applied to the card window itself, in which case it is relative to the screen.

Defaults used on creation of objects are:

button	`256,151`
field	`256,162;`

Default for windows are:

message box	`22,300`
tool window	`200,70`
pattern window	`300,70`
card window (ls)	`64,69`
card window (ss)	`0,0.`

(The notations ls and ss after card window refer to the 640 x 480 Macintosh II screen and the 512 x 342 standard Macintosh screen, respectively.)

The default locations for the tool and pattern windows refer to their placement as windows, not to their usual positions as menus. These defaults can be observed by setting the **`visible`** property for each of the windows to **`true`**.

Access:

The value can be manipulated via the **`set`** command from a script or from the message box, or by dragging the object to a new location. The value can be retrieved via the **`get`** command or by the use of the property name in an expression.

Description:

The **location** property represents, for button and field objects, the point corresponding to the center of the object in card window coordinates. For windows, it represents the point corresponding to the top left corner of the window, also in card window coordinates (that is, measured from the top left corner of the card window). In the case of the card window itself, however, it is measured relative to the top left corner of the screen. The first coordinate represents the horizontal distance from the reference point; the second, the vertical.

Example:

```
Set the loc of button 1 to 256,171
Set the loc of button 1 to -100,100
```

LockMessages

Object: global

Values:

true, false. The default is **false**, to which HyperCard returns on idle.

Access:

The value can be manipulated via the **set** command from a script. The value can be retrieved via the **get** command or by the use of the property name in an expression.

Description:

The **lockMessages** property represents a constraint on the sending of messages. When true, it inhibits the sending of automatic messages. This is useful when moving via script from stack to stack, or sometimes from card to card. It speeds processing and avoids unwanted side effects of **openStack**, **openBackground**, or **openCard** messages.

Example:

```
Set lockMessages to not the lockMessages
```

LockRecent

Object: global

Values:

true, false. The default is **false**, to which HyperCard returns on idle.

Access:

The value can be manipulated via the **set** command from a script. The value can be retrieved via the **get** command or by the use of the property name in an expression.

Description:

The **lockRecent** property represents a constraint on the recording of cards visited. When true, it inhibits such recording. This is useful when moving via script from stack to stack, or sometimes from card to card. It speeds processing.

Example:

```
Set lockRecent to not the lockRecent
```

LockScreen

Object: global

Values:

`true, false`. The default is **`false`**, to which HyperCard returns on idle.

Access:

The value can be manipulated via the **`set`** command from a script. The value can be retrieved via the **`get`** command or by the use of the property name in an expression.

Description:

The **`lockScreen`** property represents a constraint on the updating of the screen. When true, it inhibits such updating. This is useful when moving via script from stack to stack, or sometimes from card to card. It speeds processing and can mask distracting stimuli from the user.

Example:

```
Set lockScreen to not the lockScreen
```

See also the **`Lock`** and **`Unlock`** commands.

LockText

Object: field

Values:

`true, false`. The default is **`false`**.

Access:

The value can be manipulated via the **`set`** command from a script or from the message box, or via the Field Info dialog box. The value can be retrieved via the **get** command or by the use of the property name in an expression.

Description:

The **lockText** property represents a constraint on the ability to type into a field. When true, it makes it impossible to open a field for text entry by clicking in the field.

Example:

```
Set the lockText of field 1 ¬
to not the lockText of field 1
```

Multiple

Object: painting

Values:

true, **false**. The default is **false**.

Access:

The value can be manipulated via the **set** command from a script or from the message box, or via the options menu. The value can be retrieved via the **get** command or by the use of the property name in an expression.

Description:

The **multiple** property represents a style variation for drawing with shapes. When true, dragging any shape tool lays down a sequence of identical shapes.

All painting properties are reset to their default values when the **reset** command is executed.

Example:

```
Set multiple to not the multiple
```

MultiSpace

Object: painting

Values:

1...9. The default is **1**.

Access:

The value can be manipulated via the **set** command from a script or from the message box. The value can be retrieved via the **get** command or by the use of the property name in an expression.

Description:

The **multiSpace** property represents the space between edges of the individual shapes drawn by dragging a shape tool when the **multiple** property is true.

All painting properties are reset to their default values when the **reset** command is executed.

Example:

```
If the multiple
Then set multiSpace to 5
```

Name
Abbreviated name
Abbrev name
Abbr name
Long name
Short name

Object: stack, background, card, field, button

Values:

Any string made up of of letters, digits, and the underscore character. There is no default value.

Access:

The value can be manipulated via the **set** command from a script or from the message box, or via the object info dialog box. When setting the name property, only the assigned name (defined below) can be manipulated. The value can be retrieved via the **get** command or by the use of the property name in an expression. Exactly what HyperCard returns depends on the modifier that precedes the property name, if any. If there is no name in the object info dialog box, HyperCard always returns the object's ID number. (This does not apply to stacks; stacks do not have ID numbers, but every stack does have a name.)

Description:

The **name** property represents the name associated with the object. In the case of a stack, this corresponds to the stack's file name.

When setting the **name** of an object to some value, the only allowable form of the **name** property is **name**. This sets the assigned name of the object, defined below.

When retrieving its value, there are six forms of the **name** property, but the first four, **name**, **abbreviated name**, **abbrev name**, and **abbr name**, are equivalent. These four forms return a string consisting of the object identifier and the assigned name (these terms are defined below).

The form **long name** returns the object identifier, assigned name, and path name.

The form **short name** returns just the assigned name, the only form of the name that is directly manipulable.

The term "object identifier" here means one of the following strings: stack, bkgnd, card, bkgnd field, bkgnd button, card field, or card button. It indicates what *kind* of object is referred to by the name.

The term "assigned name" here means the name shown in the object's info box, or the word "id" followed by the object's id number if the name field in the object's info box is empty.

The term "path name" as used here (and only here, in the description of the **name** property), extends the concept of a Macintosh path name. Normally "path name" means the file name and all folders enclosing the file, in order from the disk name inward to the file name; separated by colons. For example, myFile:myStacks:HyperCard stuff:bootDisk. As used here, the term extends to chunk expressions as well. The path name indicates where the object resides within its stack and where the stack resides on its disk.

Examples, with sample corresponding values:

```
Set the name of this stack to cmdTest
or
Set the name of this stack to "cmdTest"
followed by
Put the name of this stack
returns
stack "cmdTest"

Put the name of this bkgnd
might return
bkgnd id 2726

Put the name of this card
might return
```

```
card "Title"

Put the name of button 1
might return
card button "tryCmd"

Put the name of field 1
might return
bkgnd field "nums"

Put the abbrev name of this stack
might return
stack "cmdTest"

Put the short name of this stack
might return
cmdTest

Put the short name of button 1
might return
tryCmd

Put the long name of this stack
might return
stack "Internal 40:HyperCard:My Stacks:cmdTest"

Put the long name of button 1
might return
card button "tryCmd" of card "Title" of ¬
stack "Internal 40:HyperCard:My Stacks:cmdTest"
```

Number

Object: background, card, field, button

Values:

A non-negative integer. There is no default value.

Access:

The value can be manipulated only via the **send farther** and the **bring closer** menu commands (in the case of buttons and fields), or by adding or deleting objects of the same kind (for buttons, fields, cards, or backgrounds). In the case of buttons and fields, added or deleted objects must belong to the same card or background. In the case of cards, the value can also be changed by sorting the cards. The value can be retrieved via the **get** command or by the use of the property name in an expression.

Description:

The **number** property represents the unique ordering number associated with the object. It is unique within the stack for background and card numbers, unique within the background for background field and background button numbers, and unique within the card for card field and card button numbers. It is set by HyperCard and adjusted by HyperCard in the course of adding or deleting other objects. Because HyperCard can change an object's number without notice, it is not a reliable method for referring to a specific object within a script, but it is ideal for itemizing objects within a **repeat** structure; to, say, set the **style** property for all buttons of a card. See also the **id** property.

Example:

```
Put the number of button 1 - the number of ¬
button 2 into the Difference
```

NumberFormat

Object: global

Values:

```
0
0.0
0.#
```

Any number of **0**s can be substituted for any **0** in the above examples, and any number of **#**s for the **#**. If the format contains a **#** character, it must be enclosed in quotes. The default is **0.######**, to which HyperCard returns on idle. Setting the **numberFormat** property to more digits of precision than the Macintosh numeric package supports will result in numbers being displayed in the full supported precision.

Access:

The value can be manipulated via the **set** command from a script. The value can be retrieved via the **get** command or by the use of the property name in an expression.

Description:

The **numberFormat** property represents the format in which HyperCard displays numbers. It does not affect the precision with which calculations are carried out. However, since HyperCard prefers to interpret values as string whenever possible, surprises lie in wait for the unwary programmer. A literal number remains a string and is unaffected by **numberFormat** until it is used in calculations. Try typing the examples below into the message box.

Examples:

```
Set numberFormat to 00.00
Put 135.246

Set numberFormat to 00.00
Put 135.246 + 1
```

Pattern

Object: painting

Values:

`1...40`. The default is `12`.

Access:

The value can be manipulated via the **`set`** command from a script or from the message box, or via the pattern palette. The value can be retrieved via the **`get`** command or by the use of the property name in an expression.

Description:

The **`pattern`** property represents the currently selected painting pattern. The numeric values correspond to the patterns in the pattern window. The top left pattern in the window is pattern 1, the pattern below it is pattern 2, and so on.

All painting properties are reset to their default values when the **`reset`** command is executed.

Example:

```
Set pattern to 25
```

PolySides

Object: painting

Values:

`3...50` or **`0`**. The default is **`4`**.

Access:

The value can be manipulated via the **`set`** command from a script or from the message box, or via the options menu. The value can be retrieved via the **`get`** command or by the use of the property name in an expression.

Description:

The **`polySides`** property represents the number of sides of any polygon produced via the polygon tool. If a script sets it to a value below 3 or above 50, it reverts to 3 or 50 respectively; if set via the options menu, a value of 0 (representing a circle) is possible, but 0 cannot be set from a script.

All painting properties are reset to their default values when the **`reset`** command is executed.

Example:

```
Set polySides to 25
```

PowerKeys

Object: global

Values:

`true, false`. The true default is **`false`** but this property is normally set on startUp or resume to an effective default stored in the user preferences card of the Home stack.

Access:

The value can be manipulated via the **set** command from a script or from the message box, or via the user preferences card of the Home stack. The value can be retrieved via the **get** command or by the use of the property name in an expression.

Description:

The **powerKeys** property represents a set of keystroke shortcuts for painting actions. If it is true, the shortcuts are enabled. The shortcuts are defined in the HyperCard Quick Reference Card supplied with the product.

Example:

```
Set powerKeys to not the powerKeys
```

Rectangle
Rect

Object: window, field, button

Values:

A comma-separated list of four integers: two points. The value is relative to the card window except when applied to the card window itself, in which case it is relative to the screen.

Defaults used on creation of objects are:

button	206,140,306,162
field	156,120,356,205;

Default for windows are:

message box	22,300,494,335
tool window	200,70,268,199
pattern window	300,70,371,199

card window (ls) `64,69,576,411`
card window (ss) `0,0,512,342.`

(The notations ls and ss after card window refer to the 640 x 480 Macintosh II screen and the 512 x 342 standard Macintosh screen, respectively.)

Access:

The value for fields and buttons can be manipulated via the **set** command from a script or from the message box, or by dragging the top left or bottom right corner of the object. The value cannot be changed in the case of a window. The value can always be retrieved via the **get** command or by the use of the property name in an expression.

Description:

The **rectangle** property represents the rectangle bounding the object. It consists of four numbers, the first two representing the upper left corner of the rectangle, the last two the lower right, expressed as a number of pixels relative to the card window (or the screen in the case of the card window itself). The **rectangle** of an object **<object>** is equal to **topLeft <object> & "," & bottomRight <object>**.

Example:

```
Set the rect of button 1 to 0,0,512,342
```

Right

Object: window, field, button

Values:

An integer: a number of pixels. The value is relative to the card window except when applied to the card window itself, in which case it is relative to the screen.

Defaults used on creation of objects are:

button	306
field	356;

Default for windows are:

message box	494
tool window	268
pattern window	371
card window (ls)	576
card window (ss)	512.

(The notations ls and ss after card window refer to the 640 x 480 Macintosh II screen and the 512 x 342 standard Macintosh screen, respectively.)

Access:

The value can be manipulated via the **set** command from a script or from the message box, except in the case of windows. The value can be retrieved via the **get** command or by the use of the property name in an expression.

Description:

The **right** property, added in version 1.2, represents right edge of the object, expressed as a number of pixels relative to the card window (or the screen in the case of the card window itself). Setting this property repositions the object, and does so more efficiently than setting the **loc** property; it does not resize it. The **width** of an object is equal to the **right** minus the **left** of the object.

Example:

```
Set the right of field 1 to 256
```

Script

Object: stack, background, card, field, button

Values:

A string constituting zero or more legal HyperTalk message or function handlers. HyperCard sets the script of every newly-created button to the default value of:

```
on mouseUp

end mouseUp
```

Access:

The value can be manipulated via the **set** command from a script or from the message box, or via the script editor. If an executing script is modified, the modification does not take effect until the next time it is invoked. The value can be retrieved via the **get** command or by the use of the property name in an expression, including a chunk expression.

Description:

The **script** property is the object's script: the (possibly empty) set of HyperTalk handlers invoked by messages received by the object.

Example:

```
Put the script of button "New Button" into newOne
Put "Beep 27" into line 2 of newOne
Set the script of button "New Button" to newOne
```

Scroll

Object: field

Values:

A non-negative integer. There is no default value.

Access:

The value can be manipulated via the **set** command from a script or from the message box, or by clicking or dragging in the field's scroll bar. The value can be retrieved via the **get** command or by the use of the property name in an expression.

Description:

The **scroll** property represents the number of pixels that have scrolled off the top of a scrolling field. It has no meaning with non-scrolling fields.

Example:

```
Set the scroll of field 1 ¬
to the textHeight of field 1
```

ShowLines

Object: field

Values:

true, false. The default is **false**.

Access:

The value can be manipulated via the **set** command from a script or from the message box, or via the Field Info dialog box. The value can be retrieved via the **get** command or by the use of the property name in an expression.

Description:

The **showLines** property represents the visibility of text baselines in the field. If it is true, the baselines are shown.

Example:

```
Set the showLines of field 1 ¬
to not the showLines of field 1
```

ShowName

Object: button

Values:

true, false. The default is **false**.

Access:

The value can be manipulated via the **set** command from a script or from the message box, or via the Button Info dialog box. The value can be retrieved via the **get** command or by the use of the property name in an expression.

Description:

The **showName** property represents the visibility of the button's name. If it is true, the name is displayed.

Example:

```
Set the showName of button 1 ¬
to not the showName of button 1
```

ShowPict

Object: background, card

Values:

`true, false`. The default is **`true`**.

Access:

The value can be manipulated via the **`set`** command from a script or from the message box. The value can be retrieved via the **`get`** command or by the use of the property name in an expression.

Description:

The **`showPict`** property, added in version 1.2, represents the visibility of whatever is drawn on a card or background. If showPict is false for a card (or background), the visible card (or background) buttons and fields will be shown, but card (or background) art will not.

Example:

```
Set the showPict of card 1 ¬
to not the showPict of bkgnd 1
```

Size

Object: stack

Values:

`4096...536870912`. There is no default value.

Access:

The value cannot be changed directly. It grows with additions of objects to the stack and shrinks with compaction following the deletion of objects. The value can be retrieved via the **get** command or by the use of the property name in an expression.

Description:

The **size** property represents the size, in bytes, of the stack.

Example:

```
Put the size of Home - the freeSize of Home ¬
into theRealSizeOfHome
```

Style

Object: field, button

Values:

Fields can take on the style values **transparent**, **opaque**, **rectangle**, **shadow**, and **scrolling**. Buttons can take on the style values **transparent**, **opaque**, **rectangle**, **roundRect**, **checkBox**, and **radioButton**. The default for fields is **transparent** and for buttons is **roundRect**.

Access:

The value can be manipulated via the **set** command from a script or from the message box, or via the object info dialog box. The value can be retrieved via the **get** command or by the use of the property name in an expression.

Description:

The **style** property represents the display style of the object. Fields and buttons have overlapping sets of **style** values.

Example:

```
Set the style of button 1 to radioButton
```

TextAlign

Object: painting, field, button

Values:

`left, right, center`. The default is **`left`**.

Access:

The value can be manipulated via the **`set`** command from a script or from the message box. For fields, the value can also be changed via the Field Info dialog box. The value for the painting property can be changed via menu selection. The value can be retrieved via the **`get`** command or by the use of the property name in an expression.

Description:

The **`textAlign`** property represents the horizontal alignment or justification of text: left justified, centered, or right justified (full justification, which would be useful for fields, is not yet supported). The text properties of individual buttons, fields, and the painting text properties are all independent.

All painting properties are reset to their default values when the **`reset`** command is executed.

Example:

```
Set the textAlign of button 1 to left
Set the textAlign of field 1 to center
Set textAlign to right
```

TextArrows

Object: global

Values:

`true, false`. The default is **`false`** but this property is normally set on startUp or resume to an effective default stored in the user preferences card of the Home stack.

Access:

The value can be manipulated via the **`set`** command from a script or from the message box, or via the user preferences card of the Home stack. The value can be retrieved via the **`get`** command or by the use of the property name in an expression.

Description:

The **`textArrows`** property, added in version 1.1, represents the interpretation of the four arrow keys on the keyboard. If is true, the arrow keys move the text insertion points in the indicated direction within fields or the message box (the Up and Down arrows move to the beginning and end, respectively, of the text string in the message box). If **`textArrows`** is true, holding down the Option key temporarily restores the default (false) actions of the arrow keys: Left and Right transfer to the previous and next cards in the stack, Up and Down transfer forward and backward through recent cards.

Example:

```
Set textArrows to not the textArrows
```

TextFont

Object: painting, field, button

Values:

Any name of a Macintosh 'FONT' resource in HyperCard itself or in the current stack. Resources can be added or removed using Apple's ResEdit or another resource editor. The names of recognized fonts can be viewed via menu. The initial default is **Geneva**, but HyperCard will use **Chicago** font when a nonexistent font is specified.

Access:

The value can be manipulated via the **set** command from a script or from the message box. For fields, the value can also be changed via the Field Info dialog box. The value for the painting property can be changed via menu selection. The value can be retrieved via the **get** command or by the use of the property name in an expression.

Description:

The **textFont** property represents the font in which text will be displayed. The text properties of individual buttons, fields, and the painting text properties are all independent.

All painting properties are reset to their default values when the **reset** command is executed.

Example:

```
Set the textFont of button 1 to the textFont
Set textFont to the textFont of button 1
```

TextHeight

Object: painting, field, button

Values:

A non-negative integer. The default is 1.5 * **textSize**, and attempts to set **textHeight** less than the current value of **textSize** for the same object (or for painting) will result in **textHeight** being set to the **textSize** value.

Access:

The value can be manipulated via the **set** command from a script or from the message box. For fields, the value can also be changed via the Field Info dialog box. The value for the painting property can be changed via menu selection. The value can be retrieved via the **get** command or by the use of the property name in an expression.

Description:

The **textHeight** property represents the distance, in pixels, between baselines of text. The text properties of individual buttons, fields, and the painting text properties are all independent.

All painting properties are reset to their default values when the **reset** command is executed.

Example:

```
Set the textHeight of button 1 to the userLevel
-- Seems odd, but the textHeight of a button
-- is currently only useful as a place to hide
-- a value, since a button has at most one line
-- of text (its name).
```

TextSize

Object: painting, field, button

Values:

A non-negative integer. The default is **12**.

Access:

The value can be manipulated via the **set** command from a script or from the message box. For fields, the value can also be changed via the Field Info dialog box. The value for the painting property can be changed via menu selection. The value can be retrieved via the **get** command or by the use of the property name in an expression.

Description:

The **textSize** property represents the height, in pixels, of the standard character for the current font. The text properties of individual buttons, fields, and the painting text properties are all independent.

All painting properties are reset to their default values when the **reset** command is executed.

Example:

```
Set the textSize of field 2 ¬
to 2 * the textSize of field 1
```

TextStyle

Object: painting, field, button

Values:

Legal values are **plain, bold, italic, underline, outline, shadow, condense, extend,** and any combination of these. The default is **plain**.

Access:

The value can be manipulated via the **set** command from a script or from the message box. For fields, the value can also be changed via the Field Info dialog box. The value for the painting property can be changed via menu selection. The value can be retrieved via the **get** command or by the use of the property name in an expression.

Description:

The **textStyle** property represents the style in which text is displayed. The value **plain** used in combination with any other values overrides them. The text properties of individual buttons, fields, and the painting text properties are all independent.

All painting properties are reset to their default values when the **reset** command is executed.

Example:

```
Set the textStyle of field 1 to bold, italic
Set the textStyle to the textStyle & ",condense"
```

Top

Object: window, field, button

Values:

An integer: a number of pixels. The value is relative to the card window except when applied to the card window itself, in which case it is relative to the screen.

Defaults used on creation of objects are:

button	140
field	120;

Default for windows are:

message box	300
tool window	70
pattern window	70
card window (ls)	69
card window (ss)	0.

(The notations ls and ss after card window refer to the 640 x 480 Macintosh II screen and the 512 x 342 standard Macintosh screen, respectively.)

Access:

The value can be manipulated via the **set** command from a script or from the message box, except in the case of windows. The value can be retrieved via the **get** command or by the use of the property name in an expression.

Description:

The **top** property, added in version 1.2, represents the top edge of the rectangle enclosing the object, expressed as a number of pixels relative to the card window (or the screen in the case of the card window itself). Setting this property repositions the object, and does so more efficiently than setting the **loc** property; it does not resize it. The **height** of an object is equal to the **bottom** minus the **top** of the object.

Example:

```
Set the top of button 1 to the top of field 1
```

TopLeft

Object: window, field, button

Values:

A comma-separated list of two integers: a point. The value is relative to the card window except when applied to the card window itself, in which case it is relative to the screen. Defaults used on creation of objects are button: 206,140, field: 156,120.

Defaults used on creation of objects are:

button	`206,140`
field	`156,120;`

Default for windows are:

message box	`22,300`
tool window	`200,70`
pattern window	`300,70`
card window (ls)	`64,69`
card window (ss)	`0,0.`

(The notations ls and ss after card window refer to the 640 x 480 Macintosh II screen and the 512 x 342 standard Macintosh screen, respectively.)

Access:

The value can be manipulated via the **set** command from a script or from the message box, except in the case of windows. The value can be retrieved via the **get** command or by the use of the property name in an expression.

Description:

The **topLeft** property, added in version 1.2, represents the top left corner of the rectangle enclosing the object, expressed in pixels relative to the card window (or the screen in the case of the card window itself). Setting this property repositions the object, and does so more efficiently than setting the **loc** property; it does not resize it. The

rectangle of an object **<object>** is equal to **topLeft <object> & "," & bottomRight <object>**.

Example:

```
Set the topLeft of button 1 ¬
to the loc of pattern window
```

UserLevel

Object: global

Values:

`1...5`. Attempts to set to higher or lower values will result in the highest or lowest value, respectively, being set. The true default is **2** but this property is normally set on startUp or resume to an effective default stored in the user preferences card of the Home stack.

Access:

The value can be manipulated via the **set** command from a script or from the message box, or via the user preferences card of the Home stack. The value can be retrieved via the **get** command or by the use of the property name in an expression.

Description:

The **userLevel** property represents the level of access to the capabilities of HyperCard. The levels have names. Level 1 is the Browsing level. Level 2 is the Typing level. Level 3 is the Painting level. Level 4 is the Authoring level. Level 5 is the Scripting level. Users of this book should **set userLevel to 5**, but may want to set a lower user level in stacks they develop for others or for their own limited use.

Example:

```
If the userLevel < 5
Then set userLevel to the userLevel + 1
```

UserModify

Object: global

Values:

true, false. The default is **false**.

Access:

The value can be manipulated via the **set** command from a script or from the message box. It is automatically set to false on leaving a stack. The value can be retrieved via the **get** command or by the use of the property name in an expression.

Description:

The **userModify** property, added in version 1.2, represents a capability of HyperCard allowing users to make temporary, local modifications to a locked stack. When userModify is true, painting and text entry actions are allowed, but their effects will be discarded on the user's leaving the card.

Example:

```
Set userModify to not the userModify
```

Visible

Object: window, field, button

Values:

`true, false`. The default is **`true`** for newly-created objects and for the card window, and **`false`** for other windows.

Access:

The value can be manipulated via the **`set`** command from a script or from the message box, or via the **`show`** and **`hide`** commands. The Tool and Pattern palettes can be made visible by tearing them off from the menu bar, the message box and menu bar can be toggled to visibility or invisibility via Cmd-M and Cmd-Space respectively, and any window with a close box can be made invisible by clicking that control. The value can be retrieved via the **`get`** command or by the use of the property name in an expression.

Description:

The **`visible`** property represents the visibility of the object. If it is true, the object can be seen unless obscured by other objects in front of it.

Example:

```
Set the visible of button 1 ¬
to not the visible of button 1
```

WideMargins

Object: field

Values:

`true, false`. The default is **`false`**.

Access:

The value can be manipulated via the **`set`** command from a script or from the message box, or via the Field Info dialog box. The value can be retrieved via the **`get`** command or by the use of the property name in an expression.

Description:

The **`wideMargins`** property represents the width of margins in a field. If it is true, field text is constrained to an area several pixels narrower, resulting in a wider margin and generally a more appealing display of the text.

Example:

```
Set the wideMargins of field 1 ¬
to not the wideMargins of field 1
```

Width

Object: window, field, button

Values:

A non-negative integer: a number of pixels.

Defaults used on creation of objects are:

button	`100`
field	`200;`

Default for windows are:

message box	472
tool window	68
pattern window	71
card window (ls)	512
card window (ss)	512.

(The notations ls and ss after card window refer to the 640 x 480 Macintosh II screen and the 512 x 342 standard Macintosh screen, respectively.)

Access:

The value can be manipulated via the **`set`** command from a script or from the message box, except in the case of windows. The value can be retrieved via the **`get`** command or by the use of the property name in an expression.

Description:

The **`width`** property, added in version 1.2, represents the horizontal extent, in pixels, of the object. Setting this property, which is only possible for fields and buttons, does not change the center point of the object; i.e., it does not change its **`location`** property. The object's **`right`** and **`left`** properties are just moved appropriately. The **`width`** of an object is always equal to the **`right`** minus the **`left`** of the object.

Example:

```
If the scroll of field 1 > 0
Then set the width of field 1 ¬
to 2 * the width of field 1
```

Appendix G

HyperTalk System Messages

About this Appendix

The following pages detail the salient facts about every HyperTalk system message: its syntax, its entry point, and a prose description of what it does. Like the other technical appendixes, this one is intended for reference purposes. For a more tutorial presentation of the use of HyperTalk messages, you should see the earlier portions of the book.

The information in this message appendix is as timely and as accurate as I could make it. All facts were checked at final board stage, and should be consistent with the state of HyperTalk at that time. I ran all example code through HyperCard, then pasted the properly running code directly into the text, minimizing the opportunities for errors to creep in.

It's probably impossible to write accurately about technical topics without using a lot of technical terms; at least I haven't been able to do it. If you get tripped up by any technical term or topic in this appendix, you may find clarification in one of the other technical appendixes. The HyperTalk Object Hierarchy appendix covers how messages trickle through the objects of a HyperCard stack. If you are having trouble with the concepts of objects and messages and object hierarchies, you might take another look at the Concepts section.

Taken one at a time, the concepts of command, function, property, and message may seem clear and intuitive, but in the early stages of learning HyperTalk it is not always obvious to what category a particular word belongs. The HyperTalk Vocabulary appendix can point to the appropriate appendix, and a careful comparison of the "About" sections of the Commands, Functions, Properties, and System Messages appendixes can help to clarify the differences.

About HyperTalk System Messages

Things happen. The system responds. That's the essence of event-driven programming, and it's explained with more words in the concepts chapter. The medium of event-driven programming is the *message*, a news flash sent to an object. Objects in an object-oriented, event-driven world like HyperCard exist to respond to events, to send messages to other objects, receive messages from other objects, and to handle those messages with their message handlers.

Certain messages are pre-defined in HyperCard and are documented in this appendix. Each message has a class of object to which it is normally directed, called the entry point for the message. The system message **closeField**, for example, is normally directed to a field. The entry point for each message is listed here, and the HyperTalk Hierarchy appendix explains how messages move through the system and what happens if the message's entry point doesn't have a handler for the message.

Messages are informational; the event that a message reports can't in general be intercepted by a handler for the message. Such a handler should instead take appropriate action in response to the event. Some messages are also commands, though, and this can cause confusion. The following example may be helpful.

The system message **openStack** reports to a stack that it has just been opened. An **openStack** handler placed in the stack's script can perform some action every time this message is received by the stack; that is, every time the stack is opened. But what such a script can't do is to affect the opening of the stack; the fact that the message has arrived is evidence that the **openStack** event has already occurred. The message is not a command that can be intercepted and redefined to do something else, but a signal informing its entry point object that an event has occurred.

Now contrast this with the use of the system message **doMenu "Open Stack..."**. A handler *can* be placed in the script of a stack to intercept this construction, doing something entirely different from opening a stack. Why the difference? Here is what's happening: as a message, **doMenu** is reporting that a particular menu selection has been made. That can't be altered; it's history. But any menu selection invokes a command, and such a command always has the name **doMenu**. **DoMenu** is both a message and a command, and it is as a command that its action can be redefined. The message **doMenu** alerts its entry point object that a menu selection has occurred, and the resulting **doMenu** command is available for redefinition.

ArrowKey

Syntax:

```
arrowKey <direction>
```

Entry point: current card

Description:

The system message **arrowKey** is sent when one of the arrow keys is pressed. The parameter **<direction>** is one of the constants **left**, **right**, **up**, or **down**, depending on which of the left, right, up, and down arrow keys was pressed. ArrowKey is also a command. As a command, it produces one of the following effects:

```
arrowKey left      go to previous card
arrowKey right     go to next card
arrowKey up        go forward through recent cards
arrowKey down      go back through recent cards
```

CloseBackground

Syntax:

```
closeBackground
```

Entry point: current card

Description:

The system message **closeBackground** is sent when the current background is closed. Putting a **closeBackground** handler in the script of the card makes it possible to perform certain actions just before closing, but not to prevent the closing (unless one of the actions, such as quitting HyperCard, makes the closing impossible).

CloseCard

Syntax:

```
closeCard
```

Entry point: current card

Description:

The system message **closeCard** is sent to the card when it is closed. Putting a **closeCard** handler in the script of the card makes it possible to perform certain actions just before closing, but not to prevent the closing (unless one of the actions, such as quitting HyperCard, makes the closing impossible).

CloseField

Syntax:

```
closeField
```

Entry point: field

Description:

The system message **closeCard** is sent to the field when it is closed. It is only sent if the field is unlocked and text was changed in it since entering it. This message can be generated by clicking the mouse outside the field, pressing the Tab or Enter key, or leaving the current card. See also the system message **enterInField**.

CloseStack

Syntax:

```
closeStack
```

Entry point: current card

Description:

The system message **closeStack** is sent when the stack is closed. Putting a **closeStack** handler in the script of the card makes it possible to perform certain actions just before closing, but not to prevent the closing (unless one of the actions, such as quitting HyperCard, makes the closing impossible).

ControlKey

Syntax:

```
controlKey  <key>
```

Entry point: current card

Description:

The system message **controlKey** is sent when the control key and another key are depressed. The parameter **<key>** is a numeral from 0 to 255. Many controlKey sequences have predefined meanings, but any can be trapped by a handler and redefined.

DeleteBackground

Syntax:

```
deleteBackground
```

Entry point: current card

Description:

The system message **deleteBackground** is sent when a background is being deleted. Putting a **deleteBackground** handler in the script of the card makes it possible to perform certain actions just before deletion, but not to prevent the deletion (unless one of the actions, such as quitting HyperCard, makes the deletion impossible).

DeleteButton

Syntax:

```
deleteButton
```

Entry point: button

Description:

The system message **deleteButton** is sent when the button is being deleted. Putting a **deleteButton** handler in the script of the button makes it possible to perform certain actions just before deletion, but not to prevent the deletion (unless one of the actions, such as quitting HyperCard, makes the deletion impossible).

DeleteCard

Syntax:

```
deleteCard
```

Entry point: current card

Description:

The system message **deleteCard** is sent when the card is being deleted. Putting a **deleteCard** handler in the script of the card makes it possible to perform certain actions just before deletion, but not to prevent the deletion (unless one of the actions, such as quitting HyperCard, makes the deletion impossible).

DeleteField

Syntax:

```
deleteField
```

Entry point: field

Description:

The system message **deleteField** is sent when the field is being deleted. Putting a **deleteField** handler in the script of the field makes it possible to perform certain actions just before deletion, but not to prevent the deletion (unless one of the actions, such as quitting HyperCard, makes the deletion impossible).

DeleteStack

Syntax:

```
deleteStack
```

Entry point: current card

Description:

The system message **deleteStack** is sent when a stack is being deleted. Putting a **deleteStack** handler in the script of the card makes it possible to perform certain actions just before deletion, but not to prevent the deletion (unless one of the actions, such as quitting HyperCard, makes the deletion impossible).

EnterInField

Syntax:

```
enterInField
```

Entry point: field

Description:

The system message **enterInField** is sent when the enter key is pressed, and there is an insertion point or selection in a field. Normally, this will result in a **closeField** message being generated, but this can be intercepted. This message was added in version 1.2. See also system message **enterKey**.

EnterKey

Syntax:

```
enterKey
```

Entry point: current card

Description:

The system message **enterKey**is sent when the enter key is pressed, unless there is an insertion point or selection in a field. **EnterKey** is also a command, and as a command it either sends the contents of the message box to the current card or, if there is an insertion point in a field, closes the field without sending the **closeField** message. See also system message **enterInField**.

FunctionKey

Syntax:

```
functionKey  <key>
```

Entry point: current card

Description:

The system message **functionKey** is sent when a function key is pressed. The parameter **<key>** is a numeral in the range from 1 to 15, representing the number of the function key pressed. **FunctionKey** is also a command. Unless it is intercepted, command **functionKey 1** through **functionKey 4** will be interpreted as the **undo**, **cut**, **copy**, and **paste** commands; but all 15 **functionKey** values can be redefined.

Help

Syntax:

```
help
```

Entry point: current card

Description:

The system message **help** is sent when **Help** is selected from the menu or Command-H is typed, or the Help key on an extended keyboard is pressed. **Help** is also a command; unless intercepted, it acts just like the command **Go to stack Help**.

Idle

Syntax:

```
idle
```

Entry point: current card

Description:

The system message **idle** is sent repeatedly when no other handler is active. An **idle** handler in the card script will permit actions to happen seemingly in the background; one common use is to put the current time in a field. One caution offered by Apple is this: the hander just described could interfere with user interaction by removing the insertion point from the field in which the user is typing. **Idle** handlers should do their best to leave the status of everything as they found it.

MouseDown

Syntax:

```
mouseDown
```

Entry point: button, field, card

Description:

The system message **mouseDown** is sent to a button or field when the mouse button is pressed down while the pointer is inside the rectangle of the object, or to the current card if the pointer is not within the rectangle of any button or field. If button or field rectangles overlap, the frontmost object gets the message. In this instance, all card objects are construed as being in front of all background objects. Invisible objects don't count, nor do fields that are not locked, but an unlocked field can receive a mouse message if the Command key is held down during the mouse action.

MouseEnter

Syntax:

```
mouseEnter
```

Entry point: button, field

Description:

The system message **mouseEnter** is sent to a button or field when the pointer moves inside the rectangle of the object. The mouse button status is unimportant. If button or field rectangles overlap, the frontmost object gets the message. In this instance, all card objects are construed as being in front of all background objects. Invisible objects don't count.

MouseLeave

Syntax:

`mouseLeave`

Entry point: button, field

Description:

The system message **mouseLeave** is sent to a button or field when the pointer moves outside the rectangle of the object. The mouse button status is unimportant. If button or field rectangles overlap, the frontmost object gets the message. In this instance, all card objects are construed as being in front of all background objects. Invisible objects don't count.

MouseStillDown

Syntax:

`mouseStillDown`

Entry point: button, field, card

Description:

The system message **mouseStillDown** is repeatedly sent to a button or field when the mouse button is held down while the pointer is inside the rectangle of the object, or to the current card if the mouse button is being held down while the pointer is not within the rectangle of any button or field. If button or field rectangles overlap, the frontmost object gets the message. In this instance, all card objects are construed as being in front of all background objects. Invisible objects don't count, nor do fields that are not locked.

MouseUp

Syntax:

```
mouseUp
```

Entry point: button, field, card

Description:

The system message **mouseUp** is sent to a button or field when the mouse button is released while the pointer is inside the rectangle of the object, or to the current card if the pointer is not within the rectangle of any button or field. The message is only sent if the mouse release occurs in the rectangle of the object that received the last **mouseDown** message, or if both events occurred outside any object rectangles. If button or field rectangles overlap, the frontmost object gets the message. In this instance, all card objects are construed as being in front of all background objects. Invisible objects don't count, nor do fields that are not locked, nor does the scroll bar of a scrolling field.

MouseWithin

Syntax:

```
mouseWithin
```

Entry point: button, field

Description:

The system message **mouseWithin** is repeatedly sent to a button or field while the pointer is within the rectangle of the object. The mouse button status is unimportant. If button or field rectangles overlap, the frontmost object gets the message. In this instance, all card objects are construed as being in front of all background objects. Invisible objects don't count.

NewBackground

Syntax:

```
newBackground
```

Entry point: current card

Description:

The system message **newBackground** is sent when a background is created. The logical place for a handler for this message is the stack, since the message is sent to the card that is created along with the background.

NewButton

Syntax:

```
newButton
```

Entry point: button

Description:

The system message **newButton** is sent when a new button is created. The logical place for a handler for this message is the current card, since the button to which the message is sent was just created.

NewCard

Syntax:

```
newCard
```

Entry point: current card

Description:

The system message **newCard** is sent when a new card is created. The logical place for a handler for this message is the current stack, since the card to which the message is sent was just created.

NewField

Syntax:

```
newField
```

Entry point: field

Description:

The system message **newField** is sent when a new field is created. The logical place for a handler for this message is the current card, since the field to which the message is sent was just created.

NewStack

Syntax:

```
newStack
```

Entry point: current card

Description:

The system message **newStack** is sent when a new stack is created. The logical place for a handler for this message is the Home stack, since the stack to which the message is sent was just created.

OpenBackground

Syntax:

```
openBackground
```

Entry point: current card

Description:

The system message **openBackground** is sent when a background is opened. A handler for this message, placed in a background script, is a convenient way to ensure that certain actions will be performed the first time any of a group of cards (all those of the background) is opened.

OpenCard

Syntax:

```
openCard
```

Entry point: current card

Description:

The system message **`openCard`** is sent when a card is opened. A handler for this message, placed in a card script, ensures that certain actions will be performed whenever the card is opened.

OpenField

Syntax:

```
openField
```

Entry point: field

Description:

The system message **`openField`** is sent when a field is opened. The field must be unlocked. A handler for this message, placed in a field script, ensures that certain actions will be performed whenever the field is opened for text entry.

OpenStack

Syntax:

```
openStack
```

Entry point: current card

Description:

The system message **openStack** is sent when a stack is opened. A handler for this message, placed in a stack script, ensures that certain actions will be performed whenever the stack is opened.

Quit

Syntax:

```
quit
```

Entry point: current card

Description:

The system message **quit** is sent when HyperCard is about to shut down. This message is generated when "Quit HyperCard" is selected from the menu, or Command-Q is typed. A handler for this message can effect a "graceful" shutdown.

Resume

Syntax:

```
resume
```

Entry point: current card

Description:

The system message **resume** is sent when HyperCard resumes action after being suspended.

ReturnInField

Syntax:

```
returnInField
```

Entry point: field

Description:

The system message **returnInField** is sent when the Return key is pressed while there is an insertion point or selection in a field. If the insertion point or selection is on the last line of the field and the value of the field's **autoTab** property is **true**, then HyperCard sends a **tabKey** message. Otherwise, the system message **returnInField** just places a carriage return in the field. The net effect is to permit using the Return key to jump to the next field if on the last line of the current field. See also system message **returnKey**. This message was added in version 1.2.

ReturnKey

Syntax:

```
returnKey
```

Entry point: current card

Description:

The system message **returnKey** is sent when the Return key is pressed. It is not sent if there is an insertion point or a selection in a field. As a command, it sends the contents of the message box to the current card, if there is no insertion point in a field. See also system message **returnInField**.

StartUp

Syntax:

```
startUp
```

Entry point: current card

Description:

The system message **startUp** is sent to the first card opened when HyperCard is launched. Apple has supplied a **startUp** handler in its Home stack, but you can augment it or write others.

Suspend

Syntax:

```
suspend
```

Entry point: current card

Description:

The system message **suspend** is sent when HyperCard is suspended, normally on launching another application.

TabKey

Syntax:

```
tabKey
```

Entry point: current card, field

Description:

The system message **tabKey** is sent when the tab key is pressed. If it is sent while there is an insertion point or selection in a field, its entry point is the field and the effect will normally be to move the insertion point to the next field ("next" is defined in terms of a circular ordering of visible unlocked fields by ID number). This effect can be overriden by putting a **tabKey** handler in the script of the card. If there is no insertion point, its entry point is the curent card and its effect is to select the contents of the first visible unlocked field.

Appendix H

HyperTalk Operators

About this Appendix

The following pages detail the salient facts about HyperTalk operators: their syntax, precedence, prose descriptions of what they do, and one or more concrete examples of the use of each. Most examples are designed to be able to be typed into the message box verbatim for testing their effects. Like the other technical appendixes, this one is intended for reference purposes. To see operators in meaningful context, you should see the earlier portions of the book. In describing individual operators I have used some terminology, such as the word "parameter," defined in the HyperTalk Functions appendix, so it may be helpful to refer to that appendix if the usage is not clear. Operators are a special kind of function. In general, if you need an explanation of any HyperTalk term not explained in this appendix, the HyperTalk Vocabulary appendix should point you to the appropriate place.

About HyperTalk Operators

HyperTalk operators are symbols, like those used in elementary arithmetic, and they perform the same kinds of functions, such as adding two numbers together. Often the HyperCard operators are expressed using the same symbols used to express arithmetic operations: +, -, =. Some operators look like words and some are used to form logical or string expressions rather than arithmetic expressions, but all are used to construct expressions of some kind.

Generally, anywhere an expression can appear, an operator can appear as part of the expression. Different types of operators are appropriate in different contexts, however. You cannot in general use a string operator in the same expressions in which you can use an arithmetic operator.

The precise specification of the ways in which you can use an operator, that is, the ways in which you can construct expressions from it, is called here the syntax of the operator. Some operators stand between the things they operate on, as you put the + sign between two numbers to add them. Some operators precede the thing they operate on, as the - sign does with negative numbers. The syntax templates used here to describe operators show how the operator fits into an expression.

An expression can contain more than one operator, and the value of the expression may differ based on the order in which the operators are applied. What, for example, is the value of the expression **3 + 4 * 2** ? If the addition is performed before the multiplication, the expression is the same as **7 * 2** or **14**. If the multiplication is performed first, the value is **3 + 8** or **11**. On the other hand, in the expression **3 + 4 + 2** , it doesn't matter which addition is performed first.

To resolve such ambiguities, HyperTalk has a set of rules governing the order of evaluation of components of expressions. The key elements of the rules are: parentheses, operator precedence classes, and left-to-right evaluation.

Parentheses are considered first in evaluating expressions. If a part of an expression is enclosed in parentheses, it is evaluated as a unit, and the value of that unit is combined with other parts of the overall expression. Parentheses are described more fully later in this appendix.

Operator precedence classes come next. Operators are grouped into classes according to the order in which they should be evaluated. Multiplications, for example, are performed before additions. The precedence classes are defined fully in this appendix, and the description of each operator includes an indication of its precedence class. (The above-mentioned priority of parentheses can be thought of as one case of operator precedence.)

HyperTalk Operator Precedence Classes

Precedence class	Operator	Function
1	( )	grouping
2	-	arithmetic negation
	not	logical negation
3	^	exponentiation
4	*	multiplication
	/	division
	div	integer division
	mod	modulo
5	+	addition
	-	subtraction
6	&	concatenation
	&&	concatenation
7	<	less than
	>	greater than
	<= ≤	less than or equal to
	>= ≥	greater than or equal to
	contains	string inclusion
	is in	string inclusion
	is not in	string exclusion
	is within	point inclusion
	is not within	point exclusion
8	=	equality
	is	equality
	<> ≠	inequality
	is not	inequality
9	and	logical and
10	or	logical or

Other things (i.e., parentheses and precedence class) being equal, operators are evaluated by HyperTalk as it encounters them in a left-to-right reading of the expression. Thus, **9 - 4 + 2** has the value **5 + 2** or **7** rather than the value **9 - 6** or **3**. Exponentiation, the raising of a number to a power, is evaluated right-to-left, so **2^3^2** is **512**, not **64** This should not be an issue unless you are in the habit of raising numbers to powers that are themselves powers.

Parentheses can *always* be used to control order of evaluation, or even simply to clarify it for a reader of the code.

Note that the same symbol, -, is used for two different operators of different precedence. Context disambiguates.

HyperTalk Operators

()

Syntax:

```
(<expression>)
```

Precedence: 1

Description:

The left and right parentheses operators (and), are grouping operators. They can be used to override the order of evaluation of operators in a complex expression. Parentheses are always evaluated in pairs, and must be used in pairs. They can be nested; that is, a pair of parentheses can be used inside a pair of parentheses, as shown below. When parentheses are nested, the individual pairs of parentheses are evaluated from the innermost pair outward, and from left to right among pairs at the same level of nesting.

Parentheses also have some special, related purposes, such as being used to enclose the parameters when invoking a function.

The parameter **<expression>**can be any expression.

Examples:

```
-- Try these in the message box:
(3 + 4) * 5
3 + (4 * 5)

-- The following code:

on mouseUp
```

```
  put f(2,3)
end mouseUp

function f a,b
  return params()
end f

-- puts this in the message box:
f("2","3")
```

-

Syntax:

```
- <number1>
<number1> - <number2>
```

Precedence: 2 and 5

Description:

There are two operators each represented by the same symbol, -. One is arithmetic negation, the other subtraction. Negation is a precedence-2 unary operator; that is, it applies to just one parameter (and precedes it). It turns positive numbers negative, negative numbers positive. Subtraction returns its first parameter minus its second, and has precedence 5.

The parameters **<number1>**and **<number2>** can be any expressions that evaluate to numeric values.

Examples:

```
12 - item 1 of field nums
-- In this example, the space between the two -
-- operators is necessary to keep them from
-- being interpreted as the comment symbol (--).
1 - -1
```

```
-- Try these in the message box:
(12 - 5) - 3
12 - (5 - 3)
-(4 - 5)
```

+

Syntax:

```
<number1> + <number2>
```

Precedence: 5

Description:

The addition operator, **+**, returns the sum of its parameters. Note that there is no unary plus corresponding to unary negation.

The parameters **<number1>**and **<number2>** can be any expressions that evaluate to numeric values.

Examples:

```
3 + word 1 of field nums

-- Try these in the message box:
(3 + 4) * 5
3 + (4 * 5)
```

*

Syntax:

```
<number1> * <number2>
```

Precedence: 4

Description:

The multiplication operator, *, returns the product of its two parameters.

The parameters **<number1>**and **<number2>** can be any expressions that evaluate to numeric values.

Examples:

```
3 * item 2 of field nums

-- Try these in the message box:
(3 + 4) * 5
3 + (4 * 5)
3 * 4 * 5
```

/

Syntax:

```
<number1> / <number2>
```

Precedence: 4

Description:

The division operator, /, returns its first parameter divided by its second.

The parameters **<number1>**and **<number2>** can be any expressions that evaluate to numeric values.

Examples:

```
3 / word 2 of field nums

-- Try these in the message box:
(3 / 4) * 5
3 / (4 * 5)
3 / 4 / 5
```

div

Syntax:

```
<number1> div <number2>
```

Precedence: 4

Description:

The integer division operator, **div**, returns the integer part of the quotient of its parameters; that is, it divides its first parameter by its second and truncates the result.

The parameters **<number1>**and **<number2>** can be any expressions that evaluate to numeric values.

Examples:

```
-- Try these in the message box:
12 div 3
13 div 3
13 div 3 div 3
```

mod

Syntax:

```
<number1> mod <number2>
```

Precedence: 4

Description:

The modulo operator, **mod**, returns the remainder when its first parameter is divided by its second.

The parameters **<number1>**and **<number2>** can be any expressions that evaluate to numeric values.

Examples:

```
-- Try these in the message box:
10 mod 3
11 mod 3
12 mod 3
18 mod 7 mod 3
```

^

Syntax:

```
<number1> ^ <number2>
```

Precedence: 3

Description:

The exponentiation operator, **^**, returns its first parameter raised to the power of its second.

The parameters **<number1>**and **<number2>** can be any expressions that evaluate to numeric values. If the first parameter is negative and the second is not an integer, the result will be NAN.

Examples:

```
-- Try these in the message box:
3 ^ 2
pi ^ -1
-1 ^ 0
```

not

Syntax:

```
not <logical value>
```

Precedence: 3

Description:

The logical operator **not** returns the logical negation of the value of its parameter. The parameter **<logical value>** must evaluate to a logical value: true or false. The result is the opposite value.

Examples:

```
-- Try these in the message box:
not true
not (1 = 1)
```

and

Syntax:

```
<logical value1> and <logical value2>
```

Precedence: 9

Description:

The logical operator **and** returns the logical **and** of its parameters. The parameters **<logical value1>** and **<logical value2>** must evaluate to logical values: true or false. It returns true if both parameters evaluate to true, and false otherwise.

Examples:

```
-- Try these in the message box:
true and false
(1 = 1) and (2 = 7)
```

or

Syntax:

```
<logical value1> or <logical value2>
```

Precedence: 10

Description:

The logical operator **or** returns the logical **or** of its parameters. The parameters **<logical value1>** and **<logical value2>** must evaluate to logical values: true or false. It returns true if either or both parameters evaluate to true, and false if neither does.

Examples:

```
-- Try these in the message box:
true or false
(1 = 1) or (2 = 7)
(1 = 1) or not (2 = 7)
```

=

Syntax:

```
<expression1> = <expression2>
```

Precedence: 8

Description:

The equality operator = returns true if its parameters evaluate to the same value, and false otherwise. It is equivalent to the **is** operator.

The parameters **<expression1>**and **<expression2>** can be any expressions.

Examples:

```
-- Try these in the message box:
1 = 1
(1 = 1) or (2 = 7)
(1 = 1) and (2 = 7)
```

is

Syntax:

```
<expression1> is <expression2>
```

Precedence: 8

Description:

The equality operator **is** returns true if its parameters evaluate to the same value, and false otherwise. It is equivalent to the = operator.

The parameters **<expression1>**and **<expression2>** can be any expressions.

Examples:

```
-- Try these in the message box:
1 is 1
(1 is 1) or (2 is 7)
(1 is 1) and (2 is 7)
false is true
```

<> (or ≠)

Syntax:

```
<expression1> <> <expression2>
<expression1> ≠ <expression2>
```

Precedence: 8

Description:

The inequality operator **<>** or ≠ returns false if its parameters evaluate to the same value, and true otherwise. Either form produces the same effect. It is equivalent to the **is not** operator.

The parameters **<expression1>**and **<expression2>** can be any expressions.

Examples:

```
-- Try these in the message box:
1 ≠ 1
(1 <> 1) or (2 <> 7)
(1<> 1) and (2 <> 7)
```

is not

Syntax:

```
<expression1> is not <expression2>
```

Precedence: 8

Description:

The equality operator **is not** returns false if its parameters evaluate to the same value, and true otherwise. It is equivalent to the **<>** or ≠ operator.

The parameters **<expression1>**and **<expression2>** can be any expressions.

Examples:

```
-- Try these in the message box:
1 is not 1
(1 is not 1) or (2 is not 7)
(1 is not 1) and (2 is not 7)
false is not true
```

<

Syntax:

```
<expression1> < <expression2>
```

Precedence: 7

Description:

The inequality operator **<** returns true if its first parameter is strictly less than its second. For expressions evaluating to numeric values, "less than" is defined in the obvious way. For expressions evaluating to strings, "less than" refers to alphabetical order, using the ASCII alphabet sorting order.

The parameters **<expression1>**and **<expression2>** can be any expressions evaluating to numbers or strings.

Examples:

```
-- Try these in the message box:
3 < 7
"Bluto" < "Bo3b"
```

>

Syntax:

```
<expression1> > <expression2>
```

Precedence: 7

Description:

The inequality operator **>** returns true if its first parameter is strictly greater than its second. For expressions evaluating to numeric values, "greater than" is defined in the obvious way. For expressions evaluating to strings, "greater than" refers to alphabetical order, using the ASCII alphabet sorting order.

The parameters **<expression1>**and **<expression2>** can be any expressions evaluating to numbers or strings.

Examples:

```
-- Try these in the message box:
3 > 7
"Bluto" > "Bo3b"
```

<= (or ≤)

Syntax:

```
<expression1> <= <expression2>
<expression1> ≤ <expression2>
```

Precedence: 7

Description:

The inequality operator **<=** or ≤ returns true if its first parameter is less than or equal to its second. The two forms are equivalent. For expressions evaluating to numeric values, "less than" is defined in the obvious way. For expressions evaluating to strings, "less than" refers to alphabetical order, using the ASCII alphabet sorting order.

The parameters **<expression1>**and **<expression2>** can be any expressions evaluating to numbers or strings.

Examples:

```
-- Try these in the message box:
3 ≤ 7
"Bluto" <= "Bo3b"
```

>= (or ≥)

Syntax:

```
<expression1> >= <expression2>
<expression1> ≥ <expression2>
```

Precedence: 7

Description:

The inequality operator **>=** or ≥ returns true if its first parameter is greater than or equal to its second. The two forms are equivalent. For

For expressions evaluating to numeric values, "greater than" is defined in the obvious way. For expressions evaluating to strings, "greater than" refers to alphabetical order, using the ASCII alphabet sorting order.

The parameters **<expression1>**and **<expression2>** can be any expressions evaluating to numbers or strings.

Examples:

```
-- Try these in the message box:
3 ≥ 7
"Bluto" >= "Bo3b"
```

contains

Syntax:

```
<expression1> contains <expression2>
```

Precedence: 7

Description:

The operator **contains** returns true if its first argument contains its second; that is, if the string represented by the first parameter is a substring of the string represented by the second. It returns false otherwise.

The parameters **<expression1>**and **<expression2>** can be any expressions interpretable as strings, including names of containers.

Examples:

```
item 1 of field nums contains "1"
"12345" contains item 1 of field nums
line 1 of card field trycmd ¬
contains line 2 of field nums
```

```
-- Try these in the message box:
"12345" contains "23"
12345 contains 23
54321 contains 23
```

is in

Syntax:

```
<expression1> is in <expression2>
```

Precedence: 7

Description:

The operator **is in** returns true if its first argument is contained in its second; that is, if the string represented by the second parameter is a substring of the string represented by the first. It returns false otherwise.

The parameters **<expression1>**and **<expression2>** can be any expressions interpretable as strings, including names of containers.

Examples:

```
1 is in item 1 of field nums
item 1 of field nums is in "12345"
line 2 of field nums ¬
is in line 1 of card field tryCmd

-- Try these in the message box:
"23" is in "12345"
23 is in 12345
23 is in 54321
```

is not in

Syntax:

```
<expression1> is not in <expression2>
```

Precedence: 7

Description:

The operator **is not in** returns false if its first argument is contained in its second; that is, if the string represented by the second parameter is a substring of the string represented by the first. It returns true otherwise.

The parameters **<expression1>**and **<expression2>** can be any expressions interpretable as strings, including names of containers.

Examples:

```
1 is not in item 1 of field nums
item 1 of field nums is not in "12345"
line 2 of field nums ¬
is not in line 1 of card field tryCmd

-- Try these in the message box:
"23" is not in "12345"
23 is not in 12345
23 is not in 54321
```

&

Syntax:

```
<string1> & <string2>
```

Precedence: 6

Description:

The concatenation operator **&** returns the string formed by concatenating its string parameters. For example,

> **"Mike" & "Swaine"** yields
> **MikeSwaine.**

The parameters **<string1>** and **<string2>** can be any expressions that can be evaluated as strings.

Examples:

```
-- Try these in the message box:
"abc" & "def"
1 & 2
```

&&

Syntax:

```
<string1> && <string2>
```

Precedence: 6

Description:

The concatenation operator **&&** returns the string formed by concatenating its string parameters with a space between them. For example,

> "Mike" && "Swaine" yields
> Mike Swaine.

The parameters **<string1>** and **<string2>** can be any expressions that can be evaluated as strings.

Examples:

```
-- Try these in the message box:
"abc" && "def"
1 && 2
```

within

Syntax:

```
<point> is within <rectangle>
<point> is not within <rectangle>
```

Precedence: 7

Description:

The operator **within** returns true if the point represented by its first parameter lies within the rectangle represented by its second. The operator **within** was added with Version 1.2.

The parameters **<point>** and **<rectangle>** must evaluate to a point and a rectangle, respectively.

Examples:

```
wait until the mouseLoc ¬
is not within the rect of me
```

Appendix I

HyperTalk Constants

About this Appendix

The following pages detail the salient facts about every HyperTalk constant, including a prose description of its use and one or more concrete examples. There is also a separate complete list of the HyperTalk constants. Like the other technical appendixes, this one is intended for reference purposes. For a more tutorial presentation of the use of HyperTalk constants, you should see the earlier portions of the book. For a clue as to where to find information about any troubling term of HyperTalk, see the HyperTalk Vocabulary appendix.

About HyperTalk Constants

HyperTalk Constants are words of the HyperTalk language that refer to fixed, unalterable values, as proper nouns in a natural language like English refer to specific individuals.

HyperTalk constants are different from variables or containers on one hand, and from literal values on the other. For example, the HyperTalk constant **ten** represents the value of the decimal number ten. It is possible to use the number ten directly in a script, by simply typing the numeral 10; this is called using a literal value. It is also possible to refer to the number ten by using the name of a variable or container, like **theNumber** or **item i of field "theNumbers"** if the variable or container currently holds the value ten. HyperTalk constants differ from literal values in that the constant is not the value, but merely refers to it. They differ from variables or containers in that the value to which the constant refers cannot be changed.

Some constants, such as the constants **zero** to **ten** that represent the numbers zero to ten, are chiefly for convenience or readability in writing scripts. Others are essential scripting tools. An example of this is the **Quote** constant, which refers to the double-quote character ("). When this literal character appears in a script it is interpreted as signalling the beginning or end of a quoted string. There is no way to use the double-quote character directly in a script without its being interpreted, hence there is no way to use it to refer to itself. That also means that it cannot be used in a command putting it into a variable or container. But if you can't construct a valid command to put the quote character into a variable or container, a variable or container cannot be used to refer to it. The only way out of this dilemma is to refer to the double-quote character in a HyperTalk script by means of the **Quote** constant.

Two entities that are not HyperTalk constants but that certainly look like constants, and that may creep up in calculations are NaN and Infinity. These are literal values that can be generated by Apple's numeric processing firmware (NaN is pronounced "not a number"). Years ago, division by zero on a computer caused the program to crash. Today, dividing by zero on a Mac produces the value Infinity. It's still almost certainly an error, but Apple's arithmetic extensions make it easier to write error-handling code and bring computer arithmetic a little closer to real math. Good for Apple.

A List of the HyperTalk Constants

```
Up
Down
True
False
Empty
Quote
Space
Return
Tab
FormFeed
LineFeed
Pi
Zero
One
Two
Three
Four
Five
Six
Seven
Eight
Nine
Ten
```

The HyperTalk Constants

The remainder of this appendix defines and demonstrates the use of each HyperTalk constant.

Down

Description:

The constant **down** represents one of the two possible status conditions of a key or mouse button, the condition of being depressed (but not necessarily sad).

Example:

```
If the commandKey is down then exit to HyperCard
```

Eight

Description:

The constant **eight** represents the decimal number eight.

Example:

```
Put eight into foldWay
```

Empty

Description:

The constant **empty** represents the empty string. Putting **empty** into a chuck or container deletes its contents. Note, however, that this does not remove the chuck delimiter characters. Putting **empty** into a line leaves the Return character behimnd; putting **empty** into an item leaves the comma. See also the **delete** command..

Examples:

```
Put empty into mid word of fullName

If userName is not empty then put it after greeting
```

False

Description:

The constant **false** represents the Boolean value false. It is used in logical expressions and tests.

Examples:

```
Put false into printNow

SetLocks false -- (See the examples for the Go command.)
```

Five

Description:

The constant **five** represents the decimal number five.

Example:

```
Subtract five from minutesLeft
```

FormFeed

Description:

The constant **formFeed** represents the formfeed character, an ASCII character (decimal value 12) defined to be used to advance the printer to the next page.

Examples:

```
Put formFeed after mySignature

if lineCount > 60 then put formFeed into nextLine
```

Four

Description:

The constant **four** represents the decimal number four.

Example:

```
Put four into suits
```

LineFeed

Description:

The constant **lineFeed** represents the linefeed character, an ASCII character (decimal value 10) defined to be used to advance the printer to the next line.

Example:

```
If numChars > 80 then put lineFeed after theLine
```

Nine

Description:

The constant **nine** represents the decimal number nine.

Example:

```
Put nine into lives
```

One

Description:

The constant **one** represents the decimal number one.

Example:

```
Add one to theCount
```

Pi

Description:

The constant **pi** represents the mathematical constant pi, all too often defined as the ratio of the circumference to the diameter of a circle. Pi is more interesting than that. The constant **pi** actually only represents the transcendental number pi to twenty decimal places, or 3.14159265358979323846. If you need more precision than that, you'll have to calculate it yourself.

Example:

```
Put pi * diameter into circumference
```

Quote

Description:

The constant **quote** represents the double-quote character (").

Example:

```
Put "He said " & quote & ¬
  "You can quote me." & quote into attribOK
```

Return

Description:

The constant **return** represents the carriage return character, an ASCII character (decimal value 13) defined to be used to return the printer to the left margin. It more commonly represents the end of a line or paragraph in text files or line in scripts.

Examples:

```
If nextChar is not return then put it after theString

Read from file fileName until return
```

Seven

Description:

The constant **seven** represents the decimal number seven.

Example:

```
Put seven into item seven of line seven of field seven
```

Six

Description:

The constant **six** represents the decimal number six.

Example:

```
Put six into sides
```

Space

Description:

The constant **space** represents the space character (ASCII value 32).

Example:

```
Put "Mike" & space & "Swaine" into myName
```

Tab

Description:

The constant **tab** represents the tab character (ASCII calue 9).

Example:

```
If nextChar is tab
Then
  Put space & space & space & space after theString
End if
```

Ten

Description:

The constant **ten** represents the decimal number ten.

Example:

```
Put ten into numberBase
```

Three

Description:

The constant **three** represents the decimal number three.

Example:

```
Subtract three from minutesLeft
```

True

Description:

The constant **true** represents the Boolean value true. It is used in logical expressions and tests.

Examples:

```
Put true into finished
```

```
SetLocks true -- (See the examples for the Go command.)
```

Two

Description:

The constant **two** represents the decimal number two.

Example:

```
Put two into howManyTimes
```

Up

Description:

The constant **up** represents one of the two possible status conditions of a key or mouse button, the condition of not being depressed.

Example:

```
If the commandKey is up then exit to HyperCard
```

Zero

Description:

The constant **zero** represents the decimal number zero.

Examples:

```
If minutesLeft is zero then exit to HyperCard

If denominator is not zero
Then
  Divide numerator by denominator
End if
```

Appendix J

HyperTalk Special Words

About this Appendix

HyperTalk uses a number of words and symbols in special ways, such as to name visual effects or tools, or as adverbs or other modifiers. The following pages lists HyperTalk language elements not explicitly defined elsewhere in these appendixes. Special words are generally used in just one context, and you will often find more information about a special word in one of the other appendixes, under the description of the command, function, or other word that defines its context. The HyperTalk Vocabulary appendix may be helpful in directing you to other source of information in this reference section. To see a special word in a more meaningful context, you should see the earlier portions of the book.

Three Special Characters

" The double-quote character marks the beginning or end of a character string.

-- The double-hyphen character marks the beginning of a comment. The end of the comment is marked by the end of the line. Comments can appear on lines by themselves or at the end of lines of code, but all characters between the double-hyphen and the end of the line are treated as commentary and are not interpreted.

¬ This character is produced by the key combination Option-Return in the HyperTalk script editor, Option-L in text editors. It signals a continuation of the current line onto the next line. Long lines can be continued onto succeeding lines by ending each partial line with the continuation character. Lines should not be broken inside a pair of double-quotes.

Adjectives

The following words, placed before the word date or time, select different forms of the date or time: **abbr**, **abbrev**, **abbreviated**, **long**, **short**.

Chunk Parts

The following words name parts of chunk expressions: **char**, **character**, **chars**, **characters**, **item**, **items**, **line**, **lines**, **word**, **words**.

Cursors

These are the names of the cursors that HyperCard usually recognizes: **Watch**, **hand**, **arrow**, **iBeam**, **plus**, **cross**, **busy**, **none**.

Identifiers, Ordinals, Selectors

The following words serve to identify a card or other item out of many. The first five are used with the **go** command to identify the card to which to transfer. The rest pick out one item, except for the last (**all**). **back**, **forth**, **next**, **prev**, **previous**, **first**, **second**, **third**, **fourth**, **fifth**, **sixth**, **seventh**, **eighth**, **ninth**, **tenth**, **any**, **mid**, **middle**, **last**, **all**.

Objects and Windows

The following words identify HyperCard objects and windows: **background**, **backgrounds**, **bk**, **bks**, **bkgnd**, **bkgnds**, **btn**, **btns**, **button**, **buttons**, **card**, **cards**, **cd**, **cds**, **field**, **fields**, **fld**, **flds**, **hypercard**, **menubar**, **message box**, **message window**, **message**, **msg box**, **msg window**, **msg**, **pattern window**, **tool window**, **stack**.

Prepositions

The following words are used in putting data into containers: **after, before, into.** The prepositions **in** and **of** are synonyms, whether used to connect parts of a chunk expression, in referring to a property of an object, or in a function call. The prepositions **from** and **to** specify ranges: **to** appears alone in **go** commands and chunk expressions; they appear together in the **drag** command. The preposition **at** is used to specify a point, as in the **click** command. The preposition **by** is used with the **sort** command to specify the string on which to sort.

Pronouns

Three words are the pronouns of the HyperTalk language. **It** holds the value of the most recent operation that acquires a value. **Me** allows a script to refer to its object. This <object> refers to the current object. These last two are not equivalent to the noun **target**: **the target** refers to the object to which the current message was initially directed. If that object is a field, **target** refers to its contents (a version1.2 feature).

Search Types

There are four: **Chars, string, whole, word.**

Sort Types

There are four: **DateTime, international, numeric, text.**

Sort Orders

There are two: **`Ascending, descending.`**

Time, Months, and Days

These words and abbreviations are needed in expressions including the date and time: **`AM, PM, January, Jan, February, Feb, March, Mar, April, Apr, May, June, Jun, July, Jul, August, Aug, September, Sep, October, Oct, November, Nov, December, Dec, Sunday, Sun, Monday, Mon, Tuesday, Tue, Wednesday, Wed, Thursday, Thu, Friday, Fri, Saturday, Sat.`**

Tool Names

These are the names of the tools, in order: **`Browse, button, field, select, lasso, pencil, brush, eraser, line, spray can, rectangle, rect, round rectangle, round rect, bucket, oval, curve, text, regular polygon, regular poly, reg polygon, reg poly, polygon, poly.`**

Visual Effects

The visual command accepts three parameters: an effect name, a speed, and an image name. The effect names are: **`plain, dissolve, checkerboard, venetian blinds, scroll up, scroll down, scroll right, scroll left, iris open, iris close, wipe up, wipe down, wipe right, wipe left, zoom open, zoom close, zoom out, zoom in, barn door open, barn door close.`**

Visual Speeds

These are also used by the **visual** command: **very slow** or **very slowly**, **slow** or **slowly**, **fast**, **very fast**.

Visual Images

As are these: **white, gray, grey, black, inverse, card**.

Appendix K
Writing Stacks

About this Appendix

This appendix is all about how to make your stacks usable by as many people as possible. It tells what HyperTalk features are supported and not supported under HyperDA, a desk accessory that allows 512K Macintosh user to browse HyperCard stacks. It gives advice on writing stacks that will work on any size of screen, but also provides scripts designed to take advantage of the large screen and color capabilities of the Macintosh II. It gives advice on developing stacks for use on CD-ROM and other locked media. And it discusses the main issues in developing software for non-English-speaking markets.

About HyperDA

HyperDA is not an Apple product, but a desk accessory from Symmetry Corporation. At present, HyperDA is the only tool available for permitting Macintoshes with only 512K of memory to read HyperCard stacks. HyperDA implements much of the browse-mode ability of HyperCard and runs in surprisingly little memory as a desk accessory. If you create an art or information stack for broad distribution, and if the consumers of the stack need only look at the cards, HyperDA extends your reach to Mac users who don't have a megabyte of memory. But not all HyperTalk commands are supported by HyperDA. Reading this appendix will give you an idea about how to design stacks so they can be read by all Mac users.

HyperDA, in my opinion, fills a need. It may not fill one for you, but if it does, this appendix will give you some information about developing for HyperDA compatibility. HyperDA was written by Bill Appleton and the Symmetry Design Team, and is available from

Symmetry Corporation, 761 East University Drive, Mesa AZ 85203, (602) 844-2199.

HyperCard Features Supported by HyperDA

HyperDA allows any Macintosh with at least 512K memory to access HyperCard stacks, navigate through the cards, copy information from them, and to do so while running other applications.

HyperDA's own menu presents the user with the following menu choices, most of which are equivalent to HyperCard menu choices:

```
Open Stack...
Close Stack...
Page Setup...
Print Card...
First
Prev
Next
Last
Find...
Window
Quit HyperDA
```

HyperDA supports references to instances of all five HyperCard object classes and to the message box. It also recognizes and handles appropriately the following language elements in the scripts of the stacks it browses.

System messages:

```
closeBackground
closeCard
closeStack
enterKey
idle
mouseDown
mouseStillDown
mouseUp
openBackground
openCard
```

```
openStack
returnKey
tabKey
```

Commands:

```
beep
doMenu, for the following menu items:
   Find...
   First
   Last
   Message
   Next
   Open Stack...
   Page Setup...
   Print Card
find
go
hide
pop
push
show
```

Property:

```
id
```

Other words:

```
zero,one,...,ten
first,...,tenth
all, any, back,last,mid,next,prev,recent,this
```

HyperCard Features Not Supported by HyperDA

There is a great body of HyperCard capability that is not supported by HyperDA. This includes all commands, functions, properties, and other language elements not explicitly mentioned in the preceding section. It also includes all external commands and functions (XCMDs and XFCNs), mathematical operations, sounds and visual effects, self-modifying code, and any stack-resident resources like specialized fonts and icons.

That sounds pretty awful, but what it really adds up to is this: A HyperDA user can browse just about any stack, examining the contents of the cards. All information statically held in the cards—stored in fields, painted on the background or card picture, and so on—should be accessible. Only if your stack makes the access to its information dependent on a non-supported feature will a HyperDA user have trouble browsing your stack. Symmetry publishes a technical note with tips on how to design stacks so that you don't preclude smooth HyperDA browsing.

About HyperCard, CD-ROM, and Networks

In versions prior to version 1.2, HyperCard did not work on locked or read-only media, because of its propensity to save changes automatically. Version 1.2 did not alter the propensity, but it did provide some checks on it. Under version 1.2, stacks can be written so that they will function on locked media, but the way in which they function will in some cases be markedly different from the way in which they function on unlocked media. The changes make HyperCard much more useful on networks and for CD-ROM (compact disk, read-only memory) applications, but the HyperTalk programmer needs to know what works and what doesn't.

HyperCard Behavior on Locked Media

The general picture is this: users can now act on read-only stacks as though they were not read-only, but any changes they make will not stick.

There are five ways to make a stack read-only. You can put it on a CD-ROM, put it on a locked diskette, lock the stack via its Get Info window under the finder, limit access privileges on a network, or set its **cantModify** property to true.

CantModify, **cantDelete**, and **userModify** are three properties added in version 1.2 to allow your scripts some control over the user's ability to modify stacks. If any of the first four read-only cases is true, HyperCard will automatically set **cantModify** and **cantDelete** to true, but a script can set these properties to true as well. **UserModify**, when true, allows the user to paint and type in fields when the stack is locked. This could be an exercise in futility, since any such changes will be discarded when the user leaves the card.

Several users can read the same stack if it is truly locked (read-only). Setting **cantModify** to true is not sufficient to allow multiuser access.

It is possible to copy information from a locked stack, print from it, and to save information from it into global variables. Global variables provide a means for capturing information keyed into fields of locked but **userModify**-able stacks.

Temporary changes made to the current card in a stack residing on a locked medium are discarded on leaving the card by any method, entering or leaving the background mode, or choosing any of the following File menu options: New Stack..., Open Stack..., Save a Copy..., Print Stack..., or Print Report.... Also, setting **cantModify** to false if it's true discards changes.

HyperCard Features Not Supported on Locked Media

When using a HyperCard stack that resides on a locked medium such as CD-ROM, neither your script nor your user can: sort, delete, compact, or change the name of the stack; create backgrounds; create, delete, cut, or paste cards; edit patterns; or edit scripts.

The Mac II: Big Screen and Color

HyperCard was not designed for the Macintosh II. It uses a fixed card size that is precisely the size of the screen on a Mac SE or Plus, and it does not support color (nor will it in the near future, according to Bill Atkinson). On a Mac II, the menu bar is fixed at the top of the screen and the card window floats some distance below it. If you own a Macintosh II, there are a dozen or so techniques for coloring various aspects of your desktop; none of these do anything for the black-on-white box of HyperCard.

The larger Mac II screen lets you move the auxiliary windows (the pattern, tool, and message box windows) alongside the card window out of the way. Slightly more of the card window is also visible because the menu bar does not hide it. This is all fine if you own a Mac II, but you should be careful not to count on these benefits in designing stacks that might be used on other Macs. The best procedure if you will be distributing stacks to others is to check the stacks on machines with each of the two standard screen sizes before distributing them.

If you own a Mac II and are developing stacks for your own use, you might as well make the most of it. The following script, first published in *The Macintosh II Report*, lets you hide the card window in the corner of a Mac II screen when running under MultiFinder.

```
-- Picture Mount Relocate Grabber 1.0
-- 5/1/88
-- A public domain handler from Macreations.
-- Use and modify it freely.

-- This handler repositions the HyperCard window
-- on the Mac II screen. Put this handler into each
-- of four buttons, and place the buttons in or
-- near the corners of the card. Clicking on one of
-- the buttons will move the window toward the
-- appropriate corner of the screen if it is
-- currently in the center of the screen & back to
-- the center otherwise.

  On mouseUp
    -- Defining the interesting screen locations.
    -- Change these to suit your needs:
    Put "620,470"  into lowerRightLoc
    Put "-500,470" into lowerLeftLoc
    Put "620,0"    into upperRightLoc
    Put "0,20"     into upperLeftLoc
    -- Don't change these:
    Put "22,300"   into msgLoc
    Put "64,69"    into centerLoc
```

```
    Put centerLoc  into windowLoc
    -- Deciding where to put the card window
    -- based on where the button is.
    If the loc of card window=centerLoc
    Then
      Put the loc of me into myLoc
      Put item 1 of myLoc into h
      Put item 2 of myLoc into v
      If h>64 and v>69
      Then put lowerRightLoc into windowLoc
      If h<64 and v>69
      Then put lowerLeftLoc into windowLoc
      If h>64 and v<69
      Then put upperRightLoc into windowLoc
      If h<64 and v<69
      Then put upperLeftLoc into windowLoc
      -- Otherwise it's in the center,
      -- so by default windowLoc = centerLoc.
    End if
    -- Positioning the window,
    -- and the message box relative to it.
    Set the loc of card window to windowLoc
    Set the loc of message box to msgLoc
  End mouseUp
```

The Macintosh II Report is a newsletter for Mac II owners. I happen to be coeditor of this newsletter, which is published by Macreations, 329 Horizon Way, Pacifica, CA 94044.

Although HyperCard doesn't support color, it is possible with some effort to make it seem to. A product called Color for HC from Imaginetic Neovision (CompuServe: 72356,253; GEnie: B.Tuttle; product also available on MacNET) allows the use of color in limited ways in HyperCard stacks, via an XCMD called **color**. It's clever and free for noncommercial uses. The following handlers are helpful in making use of **color**. They include a modified Home stack handler, a new Home stack handler, and the complete script for the User Preferences card of the Home stack. The User Preferences card needs a set of 16 radio buttons for the 8 possible foreground and background colors, and a field in which to store the selected colors. (If it is big enough to accommodate the string "magenta, magenta," it will be fine. But I can't recommend that color combination.)

```
-- These are the Home stack handlers:
  On startUp
    -- Handler modified by Mike Swaine, 5/88.
    GetColor -- the 5/88 modification.
    GetHomeInfo
    Pass startUp -- to a startUp XCMD, if present
  End startUp

  On getColor
    -- Handler added by Mike Swaine, 5/88.
    -- This handler uses Color for HC from
    -- Imaginetics Neovision.
    -- It gets foreground and background colors
    -- from a User Preference field,
    -- puts them into global variables,
    -- and uses the Color XCMD
    -- to make them the current fg & bg colors.
    Global fgColor,bgColor
    Put item 1 of card field "colors" ¬
    of card "User Preferences" into fgColor
    Put item 2 of card field "colors" ¬
    of card "User Preferences" into bgColor
    Color fgColor,bgColor -- The color XCMD.
  End getColor

-- This is the User Preferences card script:
  On closeCard
    -- Handler added by Mike Swaine, 5/88.
    Global fgColor, bgColor, fgPrefColor, ¬
    bgPrefColor, colors
    -- NB: you can't really break this next line
    -- as I have done here inside a string:
    Put "red, green, ¬
    blue, cyan, magenta, yellow, black, white" ¬
    into colors
    If fgColor is empty
    Then put "blue" into fgColor
    If bgColor is empty
    Then put "white" into bgColor
    If fgPrefColor is not empty
    Then put fgPrefColor into fgColor
    If bgPrefColor is not empty
```

```
  Then put bgPrefColor into bgColor
  Color fgColor,bgColor
End closeCard

On mouseUp
  -- Handler added by Mike Swaine, 5/88.
  Global fgColor,bgColor,fgPrefColor,bgPrefColor
  If "color" is in the short name of the target
  Then
    Put the short name of the target ¬
    into theButton
    Set the hilite of button theButton to true
    If word 1 of theButton is "fg"
    Then
      Put word 3 of theButton into fgPrefColor
      Put fgPrefColor into item 1 ¬
      of card field colors
    End if
    If word 1 of theButton is "bg"
    Then
      Put word 3 of theButton into bgPrefColor
      Put space & bgPrefColor into item 2 ¬
      of card field colors
    End if
    Repeat with i=1 to the number of buttons
      If word 1 of the short name of button i ¬
      = word 1 of theButton ¬
      and word 2 of the short name of button i ¬
      = word 2 of theButton ¬
      and word 3 of the short name of button i ¬
      <> word 3 of theButton
      Then set the hilite of button i to false
    End repeat
  End if
End mouseUp

On openCard
  SetUserLevel the userLevel
  If card field "User Name" is empty
  Then click at the loc of card field "User Name"
End openCard
```

```
On setUserLevel whatLevel
  Set userLevel to whatLevel
  If the userLevel is whatLevel then
    Put the userLevel ¬
    into card field "User Level"
    Set hilite of button "Browsing" ¬
    to the userLevel = 1
    Set hilite of button "Typing" ¬
    to the userLevel = 2
    Set hilite of button "Painting" ¬
    to the userLevel = 3
    Set hilite of button "Authoring" ¬
    to the userLevel = 4
    Set hilite of button "Scripting" ¬
    to the userLevel = 5
    Set visible of button "Text Arrows" ¬
    to the userlevel >= 2
    Set visible of button "Power Keys" ¬
    to the userLevel >= 3
    Set visible of button "Blind Typing" ¬
    to the userLevel = 5
    Set hilite of button "Text Arrows" ¬
    to the textArrows
    Set hilite of button "Power Keys" ¬
    to the powerKeys
    Set hilite of button "Blind Typing" ¬
    to the blindTyping
  Else
    Set hilite of the target to false
  End if
End setUserLevel
```

Internationalizing Your Stacks

If you design stacks for international distribution there are some things that Apple has done that will make your job easier, but there are some things to watch out for, too. Here are the highlights:

HyperTalk itself is multilingual. Or at least there are translator resources that allow non-English-speaking programmers to use words from their language in the place of the English words of HyperTalk; internally, the HyperTalk vocabulary remains English-like.

Sorting, the **doMenu** command, date and time operations, and the **convert** command all work through the international utilities package to do the right thing, whatever that may be, in foreign countries. It won't be the right thing if you make clever assumptions about the results of a sort or do clever operations on date and time values.

Most text will get longer when translated. Leave room for this possibility in fields of text.

Appendix L

Resources, XCMDs, and XFCNs

About this Appendix

This appendix provides some basic information on resources, the use of the resource utility ResEdit, and external commands and functions.

About Resources

Every Macintosh applications makes use of what are called resource. Fonts, icons, and menus are resources, but the code that makes up an application also resides in one or more resources. The purpose of putting parts of an application in different resources is modularity: the ability to replace a menu, say, without recompiling the entire program.

Resources reside in files; every Macintosh file has the ability to contain resources and data. The portion of a file that can hold resources is called the resource fork, the portion that can contain data is the data fork. Every application file has a resource fork and may have a data fork, while every document has a data fork and perhaps a resource fork. Your stacks can have resources, as can your Home stack, and the HyperCard application itself.

Resources that are especially useful in HyperCard stacks include sound resources, icons, fonts, XCMDs, and XFCNs. The sound resources used by HyperCard are format 2 'snd" resources, described in Volume V of *Inside the Macintosh*.

Most users of resources will merely copy existing resources from one file to another; after all, resources are intended to be read-only compiled plug-in modules. This scheme permits stack developers to incorporate compiled code modules, sounds, and other resources into their stacks without programming in other languages. On coming across something in a script that could be a reference to a resource, HyperTalk will check, in the course of following the hierarchy, the current stack's resource fork, the Home stack's resource fork, HyperCard's resource fork, and finally the resource fork of the system file, if necessary.

The most readily available tool for copying resources is the ResEdit utility supplied with the system by Apple. You should use it carefully, since it does allow you to corrupt system files, but if you never work on the only copy of an important file and don't act without thinking, you should stay out of trouble. On invoking ResEdit, simply follow the folder path down to the file you're interested in, and open the file to see the types of resources in its resource fork (if any). Open a resource type to see individual resources; clicking on a resource may give you further information about it, as will picking the **`Get Info`** menu selection.

You can copy a resource to the clipboard with Command-c and paste it into another file with Command-v. You can copy all fonts at once or just one font depending on what you select. It's helpful if copying more than one resource to move the windows around so you can see two at once.

Another way to copy resources is via my Programmer's Pegboard stack. It's on the disk you can order to accompany this book.

About XCMDs and XFCNs

Two resource types important for stack developers are external commands and functions (XCMDs and XFCNs). These resources are small programs written in some language other than HyperTalk. When installed in a HyperCard stack, they act just like HyperTalk commands and functions. The **`Flash`** command, supplied with HyperCard, is the most obvious example, and is indistinguishable in operation from a "real" HyperTalk command, but it is in fact an XCMD.

You can use external routines in place of HyperTalk code when you need speed. You can use them to gain access to parts of the Mac that

HyperTalk doesn't know about—ejecting disk, accessing the toolbox. You can add features to HyperCard, like new menus. And you can protect proprietary algorithms by putting them in opaque compiled code. Many external commands and functions now exist, many of them floating around on electronic bulletin boards, free but for the downloading cost.

Most HyperTalk programmers will be consumers, not producers, of XCMDs and XFCNs. For them, XCMDs and XFCNs are straightforward: you install and remove them just like any other resource. Keep in mind the hierarchy and install them where they will do the most good: either in your stack, your Home stack, or in HyperCard itself. Once an XCMD or XFCN is installed, you only need to remember its syntax and to use it appropriately in your scripts. That's not entirely a trivial problem, since XCMDs may come into your life without documentation.

Some HyperTalk programmers will not be content merely to use XCMDs and XFCNs written by others, and will want to develop their own. I will only here point out the basic sources of information.

Developing an XCMD or XFCN involves many of the concerns of general Macintosh software development. Books on Macintosh programming in C or Pascal or almost any language except HyperTalk routinely recommend at least a nodding familiarity with the contents of *Inside Macintosh*, Volumes 1-5. There are easier ways to get started in Mac programming, but every Mac programmer has to have *Inside Macintosh*, both to answer the questions that aren't answered anywhere else and to keep him or her out of trouble.

But XCMDs and XFCNs are special Macintosh programs, and have some special restrictions. You'll need to know how to make your external routines support the HyperCard metaphor and how to make them communicate with HyperCard. The only book I know of on external routines, and a good one, is Gary Bond's *XCMD's for HyperCard*, 1988, MIS Press, Portland, OR. You should get it.

Then there's APDA. The Apple Programmer's and Developer's Association, 290 SW 43rd Street, Renton, WA 98055, is an Apple user's group licensed to distribute developer tools to software developers. APDA has both code and documentation for members who are developing HyperCard externals commands and functions. And membership is not expensive.

The Programmer's Pegboard and Other Scripts

This part of the book contains scripts. Some of these were originally published in this or another form in my column "Card Tricks" in *MacUser* magazine or in *The Macintosh II Report*. A few others are scripts used as examples in this book, here expanded, generalized, or just repeated for convenient reference. Some have never appeared before in any form.

Since the book was already long enough, I give only scripts, not stack specifications, so your implementation of these scripts probably won't look much like mine. Feel free to use these scripts, modify them as you wish, pass them on to others, or incorporate them into commercial products you may develop. I am placing them all in the public domain. If you do implement any of these scripts and pass them on to others, do me these two favors: (1) if you leave anything of me in the code, leave my name there too; and (2) add your own name in any case. I'll be grateful for reports of bugs in any of this code, but the only way I'll be able to deal with bugs is by fixing them in the next edition of the book. To be useful, a bug report should include at least a listing of the script and an indication of any input supplied and the exact error message or erroneous output produced. But bear in mind that there probably *are* errors—these scripts were written for tutorial purposes, not as commercial software.

All the scripts in this section, plus the examples from the body of the book, are available on disk [disk info].

About the Programmer's Pegboard

The first scripts in this code part of the book implement something I call Programmer's Pegboard, Version 1.0. Programmer's Pegboard is a stack developer's utility that should make all the rest of the scripts more useful. It also makes it easier to work with resources, like XCMDs, XFCNs, fonts, icons, and sounds.

Programmer's Pegboard is an installer and database for reusable software components. It maintains a library of commonly used buttons, scripts, and resources, and it allows you to select those you wish to install in any stack. Whatever you install is automatically recorded in the database, making it easy to tell the reusable components from the specialized ones in a stack. If you ask it to remove any installed components, Programmer's Pegboard will first check its database to ensure that it doesn't remove something it did not install.

That's the idea, at least. The present version of Programmer's Pegboard has some rough edges, chiefly in its merely serviceable user interaction. In fact, the version printed here won't even install resources, although it will let you record in its database where *you* have installed them. The version on disk, though, *does* support resource installation. (This feature requires a compiled-code module that is hard to distribute on paper.) When I make those improvements and add several dozen other features I have in mind, the result will be pretty nifty, will be called Programmer's Pegboard Version 2.0, and will, I'm afraid, be a commercial product.

Scripts Included in this Section

Programmer's Pegboard (1)
Home stack handler
Programmer's Pegboard (2)
stack script
Script Analyzer Version 2.0
button script
Editing Tools
button scripts
Script Formatter
button script
DimSum
Home stack handlers
Autocompacter
Home stack handlers
TileButton
button script
Button Properties
button script
GetColor
Home stack script
Special preferences
User Preferences card script
Self-linking buttons
Home card script
Typing test
stack, card, field, button scripts
Calculator
field script
Circles
button scripts
Moiré effect
card script
Recursive factorial
button script
Picture Mount Relocate Grabber
button script

Programmer's Pegboard (1)

This script is the Home stack component of the stack development utility Programmer's Pegboard. Installing this handler in your Home stack script makes the pseudocommand **pb** available to you in any stack at any time. When you type **pb**, you will be transported to the Pegboard stack, assuming you have created such a stack. Its script is included here as Programmer's Pegboard (2).

```
On pb
  -- This handler is the Home stack component of
  -- Mike Swaine's stack development utility called
  -- •••••     PROGRAMMER'S PEGBOARD     ••••• --
  -- The other component is stack PegBoard (q.v.).
  Global pbTargetStack
  Put the long name of this stack ¬
  into pbTargetStack
  Push card
  Go to stack "Pegboard"
  Pop card
End pb
```

Programmer's Pegboard (2)

This script should be installed in a stack named Pegboard. It implements the stack development utility Programmer's Pegboard, which allows you to keep track of reusable software components and where you have installed them.

```
-- Programmer's Pegboard Version 1.0, July, 1988
-- Written by Michael Swaine
-- Designed for tutorial purposes and released
-- to the public domain. May be used freely.

-- This script maintains a library of reusable
-- software components, installing them in scripts,
-- removing them, and keeping track of where they
-- are installed. The components can be resources,
-- scripts, or buttons.
```

```
-- To keep track of the components, this script
-- requires that the stack in which it is
-- installed contain four scrolling card fields
-- named Stacks, Resources, Scripts, and Buttons.
-- These hold the names of stacks in which you
-- install the components and the names of the
-- resources, scripts, and buttons that you've
-- chosen to treat as reusable software components.

On openStack
  -- This handler is invoked when stack is opened.
  -- It directly maintains the field of stacknames.
  -- The full path name of the stack is stored.
  -- This handler messages two other handlers to
  -- maintain the fields of resource, script, and
  -- button names and to perform the installation
  -- and removal of components.
  Hide message box
  Global pbTargetStack, pbFieldNames, userLevel
  If pbTargetStack is empty then exit to HyperCard
  Put the userLevel into oldUserLevel
  Set the userLevel to 5
  Put "Stacks,Resources,Scripts,Buttons" ¬
  into pbFieldNames
  Put item 1 of pbFieldNames into pbFld
  -- If current stack is not in database, add it.
  If pbTargetStack is not in card field pbFld
  Then
    Put 1+ the number of lines of card field pbFld¬
    into pbLine
    Put pbTargetStack into line pbLine of card ¬
    field pbFld
    Repeat with i=1 to 3
      Put item i+1 of pbFieldNames into line ¬
      pbLine+i of card field pbFld
    End repeat
  End if
  -- Find the entry in the database
  -- for the current stack.
  Repeat with i=1 to ¬
    (the number of lines of card field pbFld)
    If pbTargetStack is in line i ¬
    of card field pbFld
    Then
      Put i into pbLine
      Repeat with j=1 to 3
```

```
        Put line pbLine + j of card field ¬
        (item 1 of pbFieldNames) ¬
        into line j of prevList
      End repeat
      Exit repeat
    End if
  End repeat
  -- For each type of reusable component,
  -- offer to insert/remove items in database.
  Repeat with i=1 to 3
    DbUpdate i,pbLine
  End repeat
  StackUpdate pbLine,prevList
  Set the userLevel to oldUserLevel
  Put empty into pbTargetStack
End openStack

-- Handler for maintaining the database.
-- This handlers keeps track of where the reusable
-- software components have been installed.
-- It does not install or remove components.

On dbUpdate n,pbStack
  -- This handler conducts a dialog with the user,
  -- offering to add items to or remove items from
  -- the stack specified by parameter pbStack.
  -- The items are components read off from
  -- one of the files containing the names of the
  -- reusable components.
  -- The parameter n indicates which of the files.
  Global pbFieldNames
  Put empty into pbList
  Put item n+1 of pbFieldNames into pbTool
  -- Allow user to skip any type of component.
  Answer "Do you want to see" && pbTool & "?" ¬
  with "Yes" or "No"
  If it is "Yes"
  Then
    -- The interaction with the user is not
    -- sophisticated. Each item from the field
    -- (each resource, script, or button) is
    -- presented; if it's already installed in the
    -- stack, the user is asked if it should be
    -- removed; otherwise, the user is asked if it
    -- should be installed.
    Repeat with i=1 to the number of lines ¬
```

```
    of card field pbTool
    Put 0 into pbFound
    Repeat with j=2 to the number of items of ¬
      line pbStack+n of card field ¬
      (item 1 of pbFieldNames)
      If item 1 of line i of card field pbTool ¬
      = item j of line pbStack+n of card field ¬
      (item 1 of pbFieldNames)
      Then put j into pbFound
    End repeat
    If pbFound=0 then put "Add" into action
    else put "Remove" into action
    Answer item 2 of line i of card field ¬
    pbTool with action or "Skip"
    -- If the user requests an installation or
    -- removal, add the item to a list.
    If it is not "Skip"
    Then
      If pbList is empty
      Then
        Put item 1 of line i of card field ¬
        pbTool into pbList
      Else
        Put "," & item 1 of line i of ¬
        card field pbTool after pbList
      End if
    End if
  End repeat
  -- Handle all the items in the list.
  Repeat with i=1 to the number of items ¬
    of pbList
    Put 0 into pbFound
    Repeat with j=2 to the number of items of ¬
      line pbStack+n of card field ¬
      (item 1 of pbFieldNames)
      If item j of line pbStack+n of card field ¬
      (item 1 of pbFieldNames) = item i of pbList
      Then put j into pbFound
    End repeat
    If pbFound>0
    Then
      Delete item pbFound of line pbStack+n of ¬
      card field (item 1 of pbFieldNames)
    Else
      Put "," & item i of pbList after line ¬
      pbStack+n of card field ¬
```

```
        (item 1 of pbFieldNames)
      End if
    End repeat
  End if
End dbUpdate

-- Handlers for the installation and removal
-- of reusable software components in stacks.

-- These handlers manage resources, handlers
-- for special messages, and buttons that you
-- find yourself installing often in your stacks.
-- They turn the Pegboard stack into a real
-- library of reusable software components.

On stackUpdate pointer, oldList
  -- This handler takes care of the installation
  -- and removal of the components.
  Put item 1 of line pointer of card field 1 ¬
  into stackName
  Repeat with i = 1 to 3
    Put line (pointer + i) of card field 1 ¬
    into line i of newList
  End repeat
  If line 1 of oldList ≠ line 1 of newList
  Then ResrceUpdate stackName, line 1 of oldList, ¬
  line 1 of newList
  If line 2 of oldList ≠ line 2 of newList
  Then ScriptUpdate stackName, line 2 of oldList, ¬
  line 2 of newList
  If line 3 of oldList ≠ line 3 of newList
  Then ButtonUpdate stackName, line 3 of oldList, ¬
  line 3 of newList
End stackUpdate

On resrceUpdate stackName,l1,l2
  -- This handler installs and removes resources
  -- (fonts, XCMDs, sounds, pictures, icons, etc.).
  Set lockMessages to true
  Lock screen
  -- Format source and destination stack names.
  put (long name of this stack) into sourceStack
  delete first word of sourceStack
  delete first character of sourceStack
  delete last character of sourceStack
  put stackName into destStack
```

```
delete first word of destStack
delete first character of destStack
delete last character of destStack
-- Compare before & after lists to see what
-- to install and remove.
Put empty into cutList
Put empty into addList
Repeat with i=2 to (the number of items of l1)
  If item i of l1 is not in l2
  Then put item i of l1 & "," after cutList
End repeat
Repeat with i=2 to (the number of items of l2)
  If item i of l2 is not in l1
  Then put item i of l2 & "," after addList
End repeat
-- Perform the installations.
Repeat with i=1 to the number of items of addList
  -- Look up the name of the resource.
  Repeat with j=1 to the number of lines of ¬
    card field "Resources"
    Put empty into theResource
    If item 1 of line j of card field ¬
    "Resources" = item i of addList
    Then
      Put item 2 of line j of card field ¬
      "Resources" into theResource
      Exit repeat
    End if
  End repeat
  -- Invoke the resource mover to copy it to
  --the target stack.
  put the value of word 1 of theResource ¬
  into rType
  put the value of word 2 of theResource ¬
  into rName
  ModResCopy sourceStack,destStack,rType,rName
End repeat
-- Perform the removals.
Repeat with i=1 to the number of items of cutList
  -- Look up the name of the resource.
  Repeat with j=1 to the number of lines of ¬
    card field "Resources"
    Put empty into theResource
    If item 1 of line j of card field ¬
    "Resources" = item i of cutList
    Then
```

```
        Put item 2 of line j of card field ¬
        "Resources" into theResource
        Exit repeat
      End if
    End repeat
    -- Invoke the resource deleter to cut it.
    put the value of word 1 of theResource ¬
    into rType
    put the value of word 2 of theResource ¬
    into rName
    resDelete destStack,rName,rType
  End repeat
  Set lockMessages to false
  Unlock screen
End resrceUpdate

On scriptUpdate stackName,l1,l2
  -- This handler installs and removes scripts
  -- (actually, handlers for special messages).
  Set lockMessages to true
  Lock screen
  -- Compare before & after lists to see what
  -- to install and remove.
  Put empty into cutList
  Put empty into addList
  Repeat with i=2 to (the number of items of l1)
    If item i of l1 is not in l2
    Then put item i of l1 & "," after cutList
  End repeat
  Repeat with i=2 to (the number of items of l2)
    If item i of l2 is not in l1
    Then put item i of l2 & "," after addList
  End repeat
  -- Perform the installations.
  Repeat with i=1 to the number of items of addList
    -- Look up the name of the script.
    Repeat with j=1 to the number of lines of ¬
      card field "Scripts"
      Put empty into theScript
      If item 1 of line j of card field "Scripts" ¬
      = item i of addList
      Then
        Put item 2 of line j of card field ¬
        "Scripts" into theScript
        Exit repeat
      End if
```

```
End repeat
-- Copy the script from card 2.
If theScript is not empty
Then
  Push this card
  Go to card 2
  Put empty into theHandler
  Put 0 into handlerStart
  Put the script of this card into ¬
  theCardScript
  Repeat with i=1 to the number of lines of ¬
    theCardScript
    Put line i of theCardScript into theLine
    If (word 1 of theLine is "On" ¬
    or  word 1 of theLine is "Function") ¬
    and word 2 of theLine is in theScript
    Then
      Put i into handlerStart
      Exit repeat
    End if
  End repeat
  If handlerStart is not 0
  Then
    Repeat with i=handlerStart to the number ¬
      of lines of theCardScript
      Put line i of theCardScript into theLine
      If  word 1 of theLine is "End" ¬
      and word 2 of theLine is in theScript
      Then
        Put line i of theCardScript & return ¬
        after theHandler
        Exit repeat
      Else
        Put line i of theCardScript & return ¬
        after theHandler
      End if
    End repeat
  End if
  -- Go to the target stack and paste it there.
  Push this card
  Go to stackName
  put the script of this stack into ¬
  theStackScript
  put theHandler & return before ¬
  theStackScript
  set the script of this stack to ¬
```

```
    theStackScript
    Pop card
    Pop card
  End if
End repeat
-- Perform the removals.
Repeat with i=1 to the number of items of cutList
  -- Look up the name of the script.
  Repeat with j=1 to the number of lines of ¬
    card field "Scripts"
    Put empty into theScript
    If item 1 of line j of card field "Scripts" ¬
    = item i of cutList
    Then
      Put item 2 of line j of card field ¬
      "Scripts" into theScript
      Exit repeat
    End if
  End repeat
  If theScript is not empty
  Then
    -- Go to the target stack and cut it.
    Push this card
    Go to card 2
    Push this card
    Go to stackName
    Put the script of this stack into ¬
    theStackScript
    Put false into inHandler
    Put empty into newStackScript
    Repeat with i=1 to the number of lines of ¬
      theStackScript
      Put line i of theStackScript into theLine
      If not inHandler
      Then
        If (word 1 of theLine is "On" ¬
        or  word 1 of theLine is "Function") ¬
        and word 2 of theLine is in theScript
        Then
          Put true into inHandler
        Else
          Put theLine & return after ¬
          newStackScript
        End if
      Else
        If  word 1 of theLine is "End" ¬
```

```
          and word 2 of theLine is in theScript
          Then
            Put false into inHandler
          End if
        End if
      End repeat
      Set the script of this stack to ¬
      newStackScript
      Pop card
      Pop card
    End if
  End repeat
  Set lockMessages to false
  Unlock screen
End scriptUpdate

On buttonUpdate stackName,l1,l2
  -- This handler installs and removes buttons
  -- (including their scripts and properties,
  -- but won't install icons; you'll need to
  -- use rsrceUpdate for that).
  Set lockMessages to true
  Lock screen
  -- Compare before & after lists to see what
  -- to install and remove.
  Put empty into cutList
  Put empty into addList
  Repeat with i=2 to (the number of items of l1)
    If item i of l1 is not in l2
    Then put item i of l1 & "," after cutList
  End repeat
  Repeat with i=2 to (the number of items of l2)
    If item i of l2 is not in l1
    Then put item i of l2 & "," after addList
  End repeat
  -- Perform the installations.
  Repeat with i=1 to the number of items of addList
    -- Look up the name of the button.
    Repeat with j=1 to the number of lines of ¬
      card field "Buttons"
      Put empty into theButton
      If item 1 of line j of card field "Buttons" ¬
      = item i of addList
      Then
        Put item 2 of line j of card field ¬
        "Buttons" into theButton
```

```
        Exit repeat
      End if
    End repeat
    -- Copy the button from card 2.
    If theButton is not empty
    Then
      Push this card
      Go to card 2
      Select card button theButton
      DoMenu Copy Button
      -- Go to the target stack and paste it there.
      Push this card
      Go to stackName
      DoMenu Paste Button
      Pop card
      Pop card
    End if
  End repeat
  -- Perform the removals.
  Repeat with i=1 to the number of items of cutList
    -- Look up the name of the button.
    Repeat with j=1 to the number of lines of ¬
      card field "Buttons"
      Put empty into theButton
      If item 1 of line j of card field "Buttons" ¬
      = item i of cutList
      Then
        Put item 2 of line j of card field ¬
        "Buttons" into theButton
        Exit repeat
      End if
    End repeat
    If theButton is not empty
    Then
      -- Go to the target stack and cut it.
      Push this card
      Go to card 2
      Push this card
      Go to stackName
      Select card button theButton
      DoMenu Cut Button
      Pop card
      Pop card
    End if
  End repeat
  Set lockMessages to false
```

```
  Unlock screen
  Choose browse tool
End buttonUpdate
```

Stack Analyzer Version 2.0

This script produces a report on a selected stack, tracking down all its scripts. It was originally published in *MacUser* magazine in May 1988.

```
-- Script   Stack Analyzer
-- Author:  Mike Swaine
-- Version: 1.0 2/1/88
-- This script describes the structure of a
-- HyperCard stack. It reports all messages handled
-- by any script in the stack, and any messages
-- passed or sent by the handlers. It lists the
-- scripts, if desired, and tells which buttons and
-- fields belong to which cards and backgrounds.
-- Its intended use is as a learning and debugging
-- tool for present and future HyperCard stack
-- developers. It should be attached to a button on
-- its own card, and it requires one (scrolling)
-- card field for output. Script Stack Analyzer is
-- placed in the public domain and may be used freely.

-- This handler is invoked when the mouse is
-- clicked. It prompts the user for some
-- information, performs some setup, then messages
-- another handler to do the real stack analysis.

on mouseUp
  -- Initialization details.
  global userName, showScripts, showEvents, ¬
  analysis, theScripts
  put empty into analysis
  put empty into theScripts
  put empty into card field 1
  put empty into user
  -- Get name of stack (politely) from user.
  if userName is not empty then put ", " & word 1 ¬
  of userName into user
  ask "Analyze what stack" & user & "?" ¬
  with the short name of this stack
  -- Proceed only if user has given you a name.
  if it is not empty then
```

```
    put it into theStack
    -- Offer choices in information to be reported.
    answer "Do message tracking?" ¬
    with "Yes" or "No"
    put (it="Yes") into showEvents
    answer "Do script extraction?" ¬
    with "Yes" or "No"
    put (it="Yes") into showScripts
    -- The report will be built in a container
    -- called analysis. Start building by putting
    -- the report title into analysis.
    if user is not empty then put ¬
    " for " &userName into user
    put "Analysis of " &theStack &" stack" & user ¬
    into analysis
    if showEvents or showScripts then put ¬
    " with" after analysis
    if showEvents then put " message tracking" ¬
    after analysis
    if showEvents and showScripts then put " and" ¬
    after analysis
    if showScripts then put " script extraction
    after analysis
    put return &return after analysis
    -- Do some initialization, including locking
    -- certain global properties to keep the stack
    -- from running away from you.
    setLocks true
    -- Now analyze the stack.
    analyze theStack,0
    -- Now it's safe to unlock what you locked.
    setLocks false
    -- Display the analysis and tidy things up.
    put analysis & theScripts & return & ¬
    "End of analysis" into card field 1
    put empty into analysis
    put empty into theScripts
    hide message box
  end if
end mouseUp
--
-- This handler is invoked by the message setLocks
```

```
-- in handler mouseUp.  It either locks or unlocks
-- certain HyperCard properties, depending on the
-- value of flag.
on setLocks flag
  -- Locking messages, screen, etc. keeps your
  -- stack, rather than the stack being analyzed,
  -- in control.
  if flag then set cursor to 4 else pop card
  if flag then set lockScreen to true else¬
  set lockScreen to false
  if flag then set lockMessages to true else¬
  set lockMessages to false
  if flag then set lockRecent to true else¬
  set lockRecent to false
  if flag then push this card else set cursor to 1
end setLocks

-- This handler does the analysis. It uses
-- recursion to dig through the stack hierarchy.
-- One invocation of this handler digs one level
-- deep (e.g., looks at the stack but not at its
-- component cards), then it messages itself to
-- look at each component object.
on analyze thing,lev
  -- Analyze something: a stack, background, card,
  -- field, or button; i.e., report its name, the
  -- events it handles, and its components. Then,
  -- if it HAS components, analyze them.
  global analysis, showScripts, showEvents, theScripts
  put the name of thing into itsName
  -- Give the user some on-screen feedback.
  put "Now examining " &itsName
  -- Report the object's name.
  put indent(lev) &itsName &return after analysis
  if lev<2 then go to thing
  put word 1 of itsName into object
  -- Determine what kind of components it has.
  if object="stack" then put "bkgnd,card" into sub
  if object="bkgnd" or object="card" then put ¬
object & " field," & object & " button" into sub
  -- If a card, say what background it belongs to.
  if object="card" and lev=1 then
```

```
    put indent(lev) &"  of " after analysis
    put the name of this bkgnd &return ¬
    after analysis
  end if
  -- If the user asked to see scripts, report
  -- object's script.
  if showScripts then
    put the script of thing into itsScript
    if itsScript is not empty then
      put return & "Script of " & itsName ¬
      & return after theScripts
      put itsScript &return after theScripts
    end if
  end if
  -- If user asked for message tracking, report it.
  if showEvents then
    put the script of thing into itsScript
    put the number of lines of itsScript into ¬
    nlines
    if nlines>2 then
      -- This takes time, so tell what's happening.
      put "Now examining the script of " & itsName
      put indent(lev) ¬
      & "- handles these message(s):" & ¬
      return after analysis
      -- Examine each line of the script.
      repeat with i=1 to nlines
        put line i of itsScript into linei
        put word 1 of linei into word1
        -- The word "on" signals a handler.
        if (word1="on") then put indent(lev)¬
        & "  " & (word 2 of linei) & return after ¬
        analysis
        -- The words "pass" and "send" signal
        -- deviations from normal message flow.
        if (word1="pass") then put indent(lev) & ¬
        " (which it passes)" ¬
        & return after analysis
        if (word1="send") then put indent(lev) & ¬
        " (It sends message "¬
        & (word 2 of linei) & " to " & ¬
        (word 4 of linei) & " )" ¬
```

```
        & return after analysis
      end repeat
    end if
  end if
  -- Determine what components the object has, if
  -- any. (Stacks have backgrounds & cards, cards
  -- have buttons, etc.)
  if lev<2 then
    do "put the number of " & (item 1 of sub) & ¬
    "s into n1"
    do "put the number of " & (item 2 of sub) & ¬
    "s into n2"
    if n1<>1 then put "s" into s1 else put "" ¬
    into s1
    if n2<>1 then put "s" into s2 else put "" ¬
    into s2
    -- Report its components.
    if n1+n2>0 then
      put indent(lev) & " contains " & n1 & " " ¬
      & (item 1 of sub) after analysis
      put s1 & " and " & n2 & " " & ¬
      (item 2 of sub) & s2 & return after analysis
      -- Then, for each kind of component...
      repeat with i=1 to 2
        do "put the number of " & (item i of sub) ¬
        &"s into n"
        -- and for each component of that kind...
        repeat with j=1 to n
          put (item i of sub) &" " &j into m
          -- analyze IT.
          analyze m,lev+1
        end repeat
      end repeat
    end if
  end if
end analyze

function indent level
  -- This produces a tab for indentation
  -- based on recursion level.
  repeat with i=1 to level+1
    put "    " after s
```

```
  end repeat
  return(s)
end indent
```

Editing Tools

This set of scripts demonstrates the edit script command, and one demonstrates self-modifying code. They all invoke the script editor on the script of a user-specified object, and are pretty much superfluous except for tutorial purposes for anyone who has version 1.2 (or greater) of HyperCard, with its improved script editing capabilities. They were first published in *MacUser* magazine in June 1988.

```
-- This handler invokes the script editor
-- on the script of a user-specified object.
on mouseUp
  ask "Edit the script of..." with "card button 1"
  if it is not empty then edit script of it
end mouseUp

-- This handler invokes the script editor
-- on the script of a user-specified object.
-- It uses a global variable to save the
-- last-specified object.
on mouseUp
  -- This line declares the global variable.
  global targetObject
  if targetObject is empty then put ¬
  "card button 1" into targetObject
  ask "Edit the script of..." with targetObject
  if it is not empty then
    -- Save the user's choice for the next time.
    put it into targetObject
    edit script of targetObject
  end if
end mouseUp

-- This handler invokes the script editor
-- on the script of a user-specified object.
-- It uses self-modifying code rather than
-- a global variable.
on mouseUp
  -- The following line is part of
  -- the self-modifying code.
  put the script of me into thisScript
  ask "Edit the script of..." with ¬
```

```
  "card button edit4"
  if it is not empty then
    put it into targetObject
    -- The main self-modifying block begins here.
    -- It searches for the line to modify,
    -- then modifies it or signals an error.
    put false into foundLine
    put 0 into lineNo
    repeat until foundLine
      put lineNo+1 into lineNo
      if lineNo>the number of lines of thisScript
      then
        beep 1
        put "Error in edit script."
        wait 100
        edit thisScript
      else
        if word 1 of line lineNo of ¬
        thisScript = "ask" then
          put "ask " & quote & "Edit the script ¬
          of..." & quote & " with " & quote ¬
          & targetObject & quote into line lineNo ¬
          of thisScript
          put true into foundLine
        end if
      end if
    end repeat
    set the script of me to thisScript
    -- The main self-modifying block ends here.
    edit script of targetObject
  end if
end mouseUp
```

Script Formatter

This script was originally published in *MacUser* magazine in July 1988. It is an aid to formatting scripts for printing. The comment lines should be understood to be long lines, rather than syntactically incorrect short lines without comment markers. One of the things that this script does is to break such long lines, putting in necessary comment markers.

```
-- Script:  Script Formatter
-- Author:  Mike Swaine
-- Version: 1.0 4/1/88

--   This script formats HyperTalk scripts. It breaks
lines at a specified length and suggests places to add
comments. Its intended use is as a learning and
documenting tool for present and future HyperCard stack
developers.
--   It produces output that should both run and look
good when printed, and it provides means for testing both
the function and the appearance of the code.
--   It should be attached to a button, and it requires a
second card button and a scrolling background field (with
a monospace font) for testing. Both of these should be
named "test".
--   Script Formatter is placed in the public domain and
may be used freely.

-- Formatter's known flaws and how to deal with them:
-- •A concatenate operator mooshed up against a string
("home" &"run") may cause it to break the line in the
middle of the string. Bad.
--  Solution: leave spaces between components.
-- •It can't reformat formatted scripts.
--  Solution: always return to the original.
-- •It doesn't work across stacks.
--  Solution: copy the button (and its test button and
field) to any stack where you want to use it.
-- •It doesn't rewrap successive comment lines.
--  Solution: enter each paragraph of commentary as one
long line.
```

```
--   This handler drives the script formatting. It takes
care of the user interaction and invokes other handlers
to do the actual formatting and output.

on mouseUp
  -- Ask the user for the name of the script to format,
the maximum number of characters desired per line, and
whether the user wants the program to suggest places to
insert comments.
  ask "Format the script of.." with "card button 1"
  if it is not empty
  then
    put script of it into theScript
    ask "Width desired:" with 55
    if it is empty then exit to HyperCard
    put it into theWidth
    answer "Comment help?" with "Quit" or ¬
    "Yes" or "No"
    if it is "Quit" then exit to HyperCard
    put it into commentHelp
    -- Format the specified script as specified.
    put format(theScript,theWidth,commentHelp) ¬
    into fmt
    -- Show the result both in a field
    -- and as a script.
    output(fmt)
  end if
end mouseUp


--   This handler formats a script, breaking lines at a
specified length, suggesting places to add comments.

function format theScript,theWidth,commentHelp
  -- This will take time, so show the watch cursor.
  set cursor to 4
  -- Convert theScript into a formattedScript, one line
at a time.
  repeat with i=1 to the number of lines ¬
  in theScript
    put line i of theScript into theLine
```

```
    -- Insert line breaks into any too-long line, making
it a sort of multiline line.
    if the length of theLine > theWidth then ¬
    put break(theLine,theWidth) into theLine
    -- The comment help feature is trivial, but is
intended as a suggestion for how you can develop your own
commenting aids.
    if commentHelp is "Yes" and first word of ¬
    theLine is in "on,repeat,if" then ¬
    put "-- [add comment here]" & ¬
    return before theLine
    -- Stick theLine onto the end of the formattedScript
you're building.
    put theLine & return after formattedScript
  end repeat
  return formattedScript
end format


--   This handler outputs a formatted script. It puts the
script into a field so the user can see how it will look
when printed, and into a button script for editing and
testing.

on output formattedScript
  -- Put the formattedScript into a field and a script.
  put formattedScript into background field test
  set the script of card button test to ¬
  formattedScript
  -- Reset the cursor and invoke the script editor on the
formatted script.
  set cursor to 1
  edit script of card button test
end output


--   This handler returns a new version of the Line, with
HyperTalk-style line breaks inserted to turn it into a
continued line, no component of which exceeds theWidth
characters.

function break theLine,theWidth
```

```
  put numToChar(194) into continuedMark
  -- Extract the longest coherent piece of theLine
shorter than theWidth. Leave this in theLine and put the
rest in theRest.
  repeat while the length of theLine > theWidth
    -- If it can't be broken, say why and bail out.
    if the length of last word of ¬
    theLine > theWidth
    then
      beep
      put "Wider than " & theWidth & " characters:"
      wait 100
      put last word of theLine into the message box
      exit to HyperCard
    end if
    -- Find the character position at which the line can
safely be broken.
    put the length of theLine - the length of ¬
    last word of theLine - 1 into breakChar
    -- Break it there.
    put char (breakChar + 1) to ¬
    (the length of theLine) of theLine ¬
    before theRest
    put char 1 to breakChar of theLine ¬
    into theLine
  end repeat
  -- If theLine is a comment, mark theRest as one. Don't
use the continuedMark with comments.
  if char 1 to 2 of first word of theLine = "--"
  then
    put "--" before theRest
    put empty into continuedMark
  end if
  -- Indent theRest according to the number of
leadingSpaces in theLine. If theRest is (now) longer than
theWidth, break it as well.
  put leadingSpaces(theLine) before theRest
  if the length of theRest > theWidth then put ¬
  break(theRest,theWidth) into theRest
  -- Put theLine back together. It now has continuedMarks
and returns within it, and is a kind of multiline line.
  return theLine & continuedMark & return & ¬
```

```
  theRest
end break


--   This handler returns the number of spaces at the
beginning of theLine.

function leadingSpaces theLine
  put 1 into i
  put empty into spaces
  repeat while char i of theLine = " "
    put " " after spaces
    add 1 to i
  end repeat
  return spaces
end leadingSpaces
```

DimSum

This script consists of two handlers, to be placed in the Home Stack script. It gives the message box a memory. It is described in Chapter 8.

```
On functionKey k
  -- DimSum functionKey handler added by MS 6/88.
  -- Puts the contents of the global variable
  -- dimSum into the message box. One of a pair
  -- of handlers for short-term msg memory.
  Global dimSum
  If k=12 then put dimSum into msg
End functionKey

On returnKey
  -- DimSum returnKey handler added by MS 6/88.
  -- Puts the contents of the message box into
  -- global variable dimSum. One of a pair of
  -- handlers implementing short-term msg memory.
  Global dimSum
  Put msg into dimSum
  Pass returnKey
End returnKey
```

Autocompacter

This script consists of two Home stack handlers that automate the process of compacting stacks. It is useful when upgrading from one version of HyperCard to another. Typing "compact on" or "compact off" into the message box enables or disables the automatic compacting of stacks.

```
On compact flag
  -- Compact handler added by MS 6/88.
  Global autoCompact
  If flag is "on"  then put true into autoCompact
  If flag is "off" then put false into autoCompact
  If flag is not "on" and flag is not "off" then put ¬
"on/off, please"
End compact

On idle
  -- AutoCompact handler added by MS 6/88.
  Global autoCompact
  If the freeSize of this stack > 100 and ¬
  autoCompact is true
  Then
    DoMenu "compact stack"
    DoMenu "compact stack"
    Put "FreeSize:" && the freesize of this stack
  End if
End idle
```

TileButton

This script is a button script that "tiles" buttons on the screen, fitting them into a grid. It positions a target button with respect to a reference button, adjusting its dimensions to those of the reference button. It uses only "early" HyperTalk vocabulary; it could be simplified with new words introduced in version 1.2.

```
On mouseUp
  Ask "Target button:"
  If it is empty then exit to HyperCard
  Put it into target
  Answer "Target button type:" ¬
  with "Background" or "Card"
  Put it into targetType
  Ask "Reference button:" with "Help"
  If it is empty then exit to HyperCard
  Put it into ref
  Answer "Reference button type:" ¬
  with "Background" or "Card"
  Put it into refType
  Ask "Steps to the right:" with 0
  If it is empty then exit to HyperCard
  Put it into stepsRight
  Ask "Steps downward:" with 0
  If it is empty then exit to HyperCard
  Put it into stepsDown
  -- Find the location and dimensions
  -- of the reference button.
  Do "put the rect of " & refType & ¬
  " button ref into theRect"
  Put first item of theRect into l
  Put second item of theRect into u
  Put third item of theRect into r
  Put fourth item of theRect into d
  Put r-l+1 into width
  Put d-u+1 into height
  -- Calculate location for target button.
  Put l+stepsRight*width into l
  Put r+stepsRight*width into r
  Put u+stepsDown*height into u
  Put d+stepsDown*height into d
```

```
    Put l into first item of theRect
    Put u into second item of theRect
    Put r into third item of theRect
    Put d into fourth item of theRect
    Do "set the rect of " & targetType & ¬
    " button target to theRect"
  End mouseUp
```

Button Properties

This script is a button script that sets a specified property to a specified value for *all* card buttons of a card. It is described only a little more fully in Chapter 7.

```
On mouseUp
  Ask "Set what property?" with "Style"
  If it is empty then exit to HyperCard
  Put it into prop
  Do "put the " & prop & " of me into default"
  Do "ask " & quote & "What value for " & prop ¬
  & "?" & quote ¬
  & " with " & default
  If it is empty then exit to HyperCard
  Put it into propSetting
  Repeat with i=1 to the number of card buttons
    Do "set the " & prop & " of card button i ¬
  to " & propSetting
  End repeat
End mouseUp
```

GetColor

This script and the next are helpful in making use of **color**. They include a modified Home stack handler, a new Home stack handler, and the complete script for the User Preferences card of the Home stack. The User Preferences card needs a set of 16 radio buttons for the 8 possible foreground and background colors, and a field in which to store the selected colors. (

They require a product called Color for HC from Imaginetic Neovision.

```
-- These are the Home stack handlers:
  On startUp
    -- Handler modified by Mike Swaine, 5/88.
    GetColor -- the 5/88 modification.
    GetHomeInfo
    Pass startUp -- to a startUp XCMD, if present
  End startUp

  On getColor
    -- Handler added by Mike Swaine, 5/88.
    -- This handler uses Color for HC from
    -- Imaginetics Neovision.
    -- It gets foreground and background colors
    -- from a User Preference field,
    -- puts them into global variables,
    -- and uses the Color XCMD
    -- to make them the current fg & bg colors.
    Global fgColor,bgColor
    Put item 1 of card field "colors" ¬
    of card "User Preferences" into fgColor
    Put item 2 of card field "colors" ¬
    of card "User Preferences" into bgColor
    Color fgColor,bgColor -- The color XCMD.
  End getColor
```

Special Preferences

This script is a full script for the User Preferences card of the Home Stack, modified to accommodate setting of color preferences. Like the preceding script, it requires a product called Color for HC from Imaginetic Neovision.

```
-- This is the User Preferences card script:
  On closeCard
    -- Handler added by Mike Swaine, 5/88.
    Global fgColor, bgColor, fgPrefColor, ¬
    bgPrefColor, colors
    -- NB: you can't really break this next line
    -- as I have done here inside a string:
    Put "red, green, ¬
    blue, cyan, magenta, yellow, black, white" ¬
    into colors
    If fgColor is empty
    Then put "blue" into fgColor
    If bgColor is empty
    Then put "white" into bgColor
    If fgPrefColor is not empty
    Then put fgPrefColor into fgColor
    If bgPrefColor is not empty
    Then put bgPrefColor into bgColor
    Color fgColor,bgColor
  End closeCard

  On mouseUp
    -- Handler added by Mike Swaine, 5/88.
    Global fgColor,bgColor,fgPrefColor,bgPrefColor
    If "color" is in the short name of the target
    Then
      Put the short name of the target ¬
      into theButton
      Set the hilite of button theButton to true
      If word 1 of theButton is "fg"
      Then
        Put word 3 of theButton into fgPrefColor
        Put fgPrefColor into item 1 ¬
        of card field colors
      End if
```

```
      If word 1 of theButton is "bg"
      Then
        Put word 3 of theButton into bgPrefColor
        Put space & bgPrefColor into item 2 ¬
        of card field colors
      End if
      Repeat with i=1 to the number of buttons
        If word 1 of the short name of button i ¬
        = word 1 of theButton ¬
        and word 2 of the short name of button i ¬
        = word 2 of theButton ¬
        and word 3 of the short name of button i ¬
        <> word 3 of theButton
        Then set the hilite of button i to false
      End repeat
    End if
End mouseUp

On openCard
  SetUserLevel the userLevel
  If card field "User Name" is empty
  Then click at the loc of card field "User Name"
End openCard

On setUserLevel whatLevel
  Set userLevel to whatLevel
  If the userLevel is whatLevel then
    Put the userLevel ¬
    into card field "User Level"
    Set hilite of button "Browsing" ¬
    to the userLevel = 1
    Set hilite of button "Typing" ¬
    to the userLevel = 2
    Set hilite of button "Painting" ¬
    to the userLevel = 3
    Set hilite of button "Authoring" ¬
    to the userLevel = 4
    Set hilite of button "Scripting" ¬
    to the userLevel = 5
    Set visible of button "Text Arrows" ¬
    to the userlevel >= 2
    Set visible of button "Power Keys" ¬
```

```
    to the userLevel >= 3
    Set visible of button "Blind Typing" ¬
    to the userLevel = 5
    Set hilite of button "Text Arrows" ¬
    to the textArrows
    Set hilite of button "Power Keys" ¬
    to the powerKeys
    Set hilite of button "Blind Typing" ¬
    to the blindTyping
  Else
    Set hilite of the target to false
  End if
End setUserLevel
```

Self-linking Buttons

This handler, placed in the Home card script, will make it unnecessary to explicitly link a button to the stack to which it is supposed to send you. This handler is pretty inefficient as it stands, and was originally intended as a demonstration of building a script within a script.

```
On openCard
  -- Create script for self-linking button.
  Put "on mouseUp" &return into goScript
  Put "go (the short name of me)" &return ¬
  after goScript
  Put "end mouseUp" &return after goScript
  -- Attach that script to any scriptless button.
  Repeat with i=1 to the number of card buttons
    If (the number of lines of the ¬
    script of card button i) <3 then
      Set script of card button i to goScript
    End if
  End repeat
End openCard
```

Typing Test

This set of scripts, with appropriate buttons and fields, implements a simple HyperCard application: a typing test. It allows you to type as long as you like, and reports your speed and number of words typed on completion. It requires card buttons named "Start" and "Stop" and background fields named "Typing" (should be large and scrolling), "Results," and "Errors," although the last of these fields is more a joke than anything else.

```
-- Stack script
On openStack
  Repeat with i=1 to the number ¬
  of background fields
    Put empty into background field i
  End repeat
  -- Note: the next line can't be broken as shown.
  Put "--Press 'Start' to start, then type, then ¬
  press Enter or 'Stop' to stop.--"
End openStack

-- Field script for field "Typing"
On enterInField
  Send mouseUp to card button "stop"
End enterInField

-- Start button script
On mouseUp
  Global startTime
  Set the lockText of background field "Typing" ¬
  to false
  Put empty into background field "Typing"
  Click at the loc of background field "Typing"
  Put the seconds into startTime
End mouseUp

-- Stop button script
On mouseUp
  Global startTime
  Put empty into field "Errors"
  Set the lockText of background field "Typing" ¬
  to true
```

```
  Put the seconds-startTime into secondsTyped
  Put "Seconds typed: " &secondsTyped ¬
  into background field "Results"
  Put the number of words in background field ¬
  "Typing" into wordsTyped
  Put "    Words typed: " &wordsTyped after ¬
  background field "Results"
  If secondsTyped>0 then
    Put 60*wordsTyped/secondsTyped into wpm
  Else
    Put "unmeasurable" into wpm
  End if
  Put return & "Words per minute: " & round(wpm) ¬
  after background field "Results"
  Put "Not tracking errors yet." into field ¬
  "errors"
End mouseUp
```

Calculator

This field script turns its field into a simple adding machine. It would make more sense to implement this as an **enterInField** handler, but as implemented it's a little more flashy.

```
On mouseLeave
  Put 0 into last line of field nums
  Repeat with i=1 to the number of lines ¬
  in field nums - 2
    Add line i of field nums to last line ¬
    of field nums
  End repeat
End mouseLeave
```

Circles

These three button scripts present three approaches to drawing a circle. The results are presented in Chapter 6.

```
On mouseUp
  -- Draws a circle using trig functions.
  -- Not an efficient method.
  Put the seconds into secStart
  Put 256 into H
  Put 171 into V
  Choose pencil tool
  Repeat with D=1 to 360
    Put D*2*pi/360 into R
    Put 100*cos(R) into Hdelta
    Put 100*sin(R) into Vdelta
    Click at round(H+Hdelta),round(V+Vdelta)
  End repeat
  Choose browse tool
  Put the seconds-secStart
End mouseUp

On mouseUp
  -- Draws a circle using Bresenham's algorithm.
  -- An efficient method.
  Put the seconds into secStart
  Put 256 into H
  Put 171 into V
  Choose pencil tool
  Put 0 into ix
  Put 100 into iy
  Put 0 into ie
  Repeat while ix ≤ iy
    If ie < 0
    Then
      Add iy+iy-1 to ie
      Subtract 1 from iy
    End if
    Subtract ix+ix+1 from ie
    Add 1 to ix
    Click at H+ix,V+iy
    Click at H-ix,V+iy
```

```
    Click at H+ix,V-iy
    Click at H-ix,V-iy
    Click at H+iy,V+ix
    Click at H-iy,V+ix
    Click at H+iy,V-ix
    Click at H-iy,V-ix
  End repeat
  Choose browse tool
  Put the seconds-secStart
End mouseUp

On mouseUp
  -- Draws a circle using the oval tool.
  -- When you have the tools,
  -- it's wise to use them.
  Put the seconds into secStart
  Put 256 into H
  Put 171 into V
  Set centered to true
  Choose oval tool
  Drag from H,V to H+100,V+100
  Choose browse tool
  Put the seconds-secStart
End mouseUp
```

Moiré Effect

This script draws pretty pictures. It has no practical value.

```
On openCard
  -- This handler produces moiré patterns.
  -- It's halted by holding the mouse button
  -- down. A quick click of the mouse button will
  -- not stop it, but will force it to select a
  -- new pattern to use in its drawing.
  Put 256 into h
  Put 171 into v
  Choose brush tool
  Set brush to 32
  Put 3 into gap
  Put 0 into pat
  Repeat until the mouse is down
    Put pat into oldPat
    Repeat until pat is not oldPat
      Put random(31)+1 into pat
    End repeat
    Set pattern to pat
    Put 0 into i
    Repeat until i=87 or the mouse is down
      Put i*gap into j
      Drag from h,v to h+j,v-h+j
      Drag from h,v to h-j,v-h+j
      Drag from h,v to h+j,v+h-j
      Drag from h,v to h-j,v+h-j
      Add 1 to i
    End repeat
  End repeat
  Choose browse tool
End openCard
```

Recursive Factorial

This script demonstrates the use of recursion—and its limitations. It computes factorials.

```
On mouseUp
  Ask "Compute the factorial of what number?"
  Put it into theNumber
  If theNumber ≥0 then put factorial(theNumber)
End mouseUp

Function factorial num
  If num=1
  Then return num
  Else return num*factorial(num-1)
End factorial
```

Picture Mount Relocate Grabber

This script, first published in *The Macintosh II Report*, lets you hide the card window in the corner of a Mac II screen when running under MultiFinder.

```
-- Picture Mount Relocate Grabber 1.0
-- 5/1/88
-- A public domain handler from Macreations.
-- Use and modify it freely.

-- This handler repositions the HyperCard window
-- on the Mac II screen. Put this handler into each
-- of four buttons, and place the buttons in or
-- near the corners of the card. Clicking on one of
-- the buttons will move the window toward the
-- appropriate corner of the screen if it is
-- currently in the center of the screen & back to
-- the center otherwise.

 On mouseUp
   -- Defining the interesting screen locations.
   -- Change these to suit your needs:
   Put "620,470"  into lowerRightLoc
   Put "-500,470" into lowerLeftLoc
   Put "620,0"    into upperRightLoc
   Put "0,20"     into upperLeftLoc
   -- Don't change these:.
   Put "22,300"   into msgLoc
   Put "64,69"    into centerLoc
   Put centerLoc  into windowLoc
   -- Deciding where to put the card window
   -- based on where the button is.
   If the loc of card window=centerLoc
   Then
     Put the loc of me into myLoc
     Put item 1 of myLoc into h
     Put item 2 of myLoc into v
     If h>64 and v>69
     Then put lowerRightLoc into windowLoc
     If h<64 and v>69
     Then put lowerLeftLoc into windowLoc
```

```
    If h>64 and v<69
    Then put upperRightLoc into windowLoc
    If h<64 and v<69
    Then put upperLeftLoc into windowLoc
    -- Otherwise it's in the center,
    -- so by default windowLoc = centerLoc.
  End if
  -- Positioning the window,
  -- and the message box relative to it.
  Set the loc of card window to windowLoc
  Set the loc of message box to msgLoc
End mouseUp
```

About the Author

Michael Swaine is currently editor-at-large of *Dr. Dobb's Journal of Software Tools* and a columnist for *MacUser*. Swaine has been programming for more than twenty years. During this time he has served as senior editor for new technologies at *InfoWorld*, and as editor-in-chief and associate publisher for *Dr. Dobb's Journal of Software Tools*. He has written hundreds of articles for various technical publications and is coauthor of the book *Fire in the Valley*, a history of the making of the personal computer.

Index

More Programming Tools from M&T Books

Programming Languages

C

Graphics Programming in C
Roger T. Stevens
Item #019-2 $39.95 (book/disk)
Item #018-4 $24.95 (book)
Details the fundamentals of graphics processes for the IBM PC family and its clones. All the information needed to program graphics in C, including source code, is presented. The provided source code will enable the user to easily modify graphics functions to suit specific needs. Both Turbo C and Microsoft C are supported. Available September 1988.

C Chest and Other C Treasures from *Dr. Dobb's Journal*
Edited by Allen Holub
Item #40-2 $24.95 (book)
Item #49-6 $39.95 (book / disk)
This comprehensive anthology contains the popular "C Chest" columns from *Dr. Dobb's Journal of Software Tools*, along with the lively philosophical and practical discussions they inspired, in addition to other information-packed articles by C experts. The software in the book is also available on disk with full source code. MS-DOS format.

Turbo C: The Art of Advanced Program Design, Optimization, and Debugging
Stephen R. Davis
Item #38-0 $24.95 (book)
Item #45-3 $39.95 (book / disk)
Overflowing with example programs, this book fully describes the techniques necessary to skillfully program, optimize, and debug in

Turbo C. All programs are also available on disk with full source code. MS-DOS format.

A Small C Compiler: Language, Usage, Theory, and Design
James E. Hendrix
Item #88-7 $23.95 (book)
Item #97-6 $38.95 (book / disk)
A full presentation of the design and theory of the Small C compiler (including source code) and programming language. The author has implemented many features in this compiler that make it an excellent example for learning basic compiler theory. Some of these features are: recursive descent parsing, one-pass compilation, and the generation of assembly language. Here is a look into a real compiler with the opportunity for hands-on experience in designing one.

Dr. Dobb's Toolbook of C
Editors of *Dr. Dobb's Journal*
Item #89303-615-3 $29.95
From *Dr. Dobb's Journal of Software Tools* and Brady Communications, this book contains a comprehensive library of valuable C code. *Dr. Dobb's Journal of Software Tools'* most popular articles on C are updated and reprinted here, along with new C programming tools. Also included is a complete C compiler, an assembler, text processing programs, and more!

The Small-C Handbook
James E. Hendrix
Item #8359-7012-4 $17.95 (book)
Item #67-4 $37.90 (book and CP/M disk)
Also from *Dr. Dobb's Journal of Software Tools* and Brady Communications, the handbook is a valuable companion to the Small-C compiler, described below. The book explains the language and the compiler, and contains entire source listings of the compiler and its library of arithmetic and logical routines.

Forth

Dr. Dobb's Toolbook of Forth
Edited by Marlin Ouverson
Item #10-0 $22.95 (book)
Item #57-7 $39.95 (book / disk)

This comprehensive collection of useful Forth programs and tutorials contains expanded versions of *Dr. Dobb's Journal of Software Tools*' best Forth articles and other material, including practical code and in-depth discussions of advanced Forth topics. The screens in the book are also available on disk as ASCII files in the following formats: MS/PC-DOS, Apple II, Macintosh, or CP/M: Osborne or 8" SS/SD.

Dr. Dobb's Toolbook of Forth, Volume II
Editors of *Dr. Dobb's Journal*
Item #41-0 $29.95 (book)
Item #51-8 $45.95 (book/disk)
This complete anthology of Forth programming techniques and developments picks up where the Toolbook of Forth, First Edition left off. Included are the best articles on Forth from *Dr. Dobb's Journal of Software Tools,* along with the latest material from other Forth experts. The screens in the book are available on disk as ASCII files in the following formats: MS-DOS, Macintosh, and CP/M: Osborne or 8" SS/SD.

BASIC

The New BASICs: Programming Techniques and Library Development
Namir Clement Shammas
Item #37-2 $24.95 (book)
Item #43-7 $39.95 (book/disk)
This book will orient the advanced programmer to the syntax and programming features of The New BASICs, including Turbo BASIC 1.0, QuickBASIC 3.0, and True BASIC 2.0. You'll learn the details of implementing subroutines, functions, and libraries to permit more structured coding. Programs and subroutines are available on disk with full source code. MS-DOS format.

QuickBASIC: Programming Techniques and Library Development
Namir Clement Shammas
Item #004-4 $34.95 (book/disk)
Item #003-6 $19.95 (book)
This book provides the reader with the opportunity to learn the details of creating subroutines, functions, and libraries to permit more structured coding.The remainder of the book is dedicated to an in-

depth discussion of building original libraries and functions to fulfill individual programming needs. Programs and subroutines are available on disk with full source code.

Turbo BASIC: Programming Techniques and Library Development
Namir Clement Shammas
Item #016-8 $34.95 (book/disk)
Item #015-X $19.95 (book)
Advanced programmers will be introduced to the flexible Turbo BASIC environment, programming framework, data types, and the use of libraries, functions and subroutines to permit more structured coding. As with the QuickBASIC book, the techniques discussed in this volume are then put to use building a selection of useful libraries. All programs and subroutines are also available on disk with full source code.

HyperTalk

Dr. Dobb's Essential HyperTalk Handbook
Michael Swaine
Item #99-5 $39.95 (book/disk)
Item #99-0 $24.95 (book)
Well-known columnist Michael Swaine provides a complete analyses of HyperTalk in this new book. Complete coverage of topics such as the move from authoring to scripting, concepts and components of the language, programming style considerations, full language exposition and discussion, and more, are presented. Programs available on disk.

Turbo Pascal

The Turbo Pascal Toolbook
Edited by Namir Clement Shammas
Item #25-9 $25.95 (book)
Item #61-5 $45.95 (book/disk)
This book contains routines and sample programs to make your programming easier and more powerful. You'll find an extensive library of low-level routines; external sorting and searching tools; window management; artificial intelligence techniques; mathematical expression parsers, including two routines that convert mathe-

matical expressions into RPN tokens; and a smart statistical regression model finder. More than 800K of source code is available on disk for MS-DOS systems.

MIDI

C Programming for MIDI
Jim Conger
Item #86-0 $22.95 (book)
Item #90-9 $37.95 (book/disk)
For musicians and programmers alike, here is the source that will help you write programs for music applications. The author begins by outlining the features of MIDI (Musical Instrument Digital Interface) and its support of real-time access to musical devices. An introduction to C programming fundamentals as they relate to MIDI is also provided. The author fully demonstrates these concepts with two MIDI applications: a patch librarian and a simple sequencer.

MIDI Programming for the Macintosh
Steve De Furia and Joe Scacciaferro, Ferro Technologies
Item #022-2 $37.95 (book/disk)
Item #021-4 $22.95 (book)
This book equips the musician and programmer alike with the background necessary to program music applications and to take advantage of all the Macintosh and the MIDI interface have to offer. Specific examples are presented and all source code is available on disk.

Business

PC Accounting Solutions
Editors of *PC Accounting* (formerly *Business Software*)
Item #008-7 $37.95 (book/disk)
Item #009-5 $22.95 (book)
This anthology serves as a well-rounded source of expert information for managers who want to implement a PC-based accounting system or to gain better control of their existing system. From choosing and maximizing your accounting systems and software to building better spreadsheets and budgets, this book is an immensely valuable source

that will improve your ability to analyze the information that is critical to the success of your business.

Public-Domain Software and Shareware: Untapped Resources for the PC User, Second Edition
Rusel DeMaria and George R. Fontaine
Item #39-9 $19.95 (book)
Item #47-X $34.95 (book/disk)
Organized into a comprehensive reference, this book introduces the novice and guides the experienced user to a source of often overlooked software—public domain and Shareware. This book will tell you where it is, how to get it, what to look for, and why it's for you. The sample programs and some of the software reviewed is available on disk in MS-DOS format. Includes $15 worth of free access time on CompuServe!

Time and Task Management with dBASE III
Timothy Berry
Item #09-7 $49.95 (manual/MS-DOS disk)
Like an accounting system for time and tasks, this package helps users organize hours, budgets, activities, and resources. Providing both a useful time-management system and a library of dBASE III code and macros, this package has practical as well as educational value. To be used with dBASE III. Source code and documentation is included. MS-DOS disk format.

Sales Management with dBASE III
Timothy Berry
Item #15-1 $49.95 (manual/MS-DOS disk)
Sales management works with dBASE III to provide a powerful information system that will help you to keep track of clients, names, addresses, follow-ups, pending dates, and account data. This system organizes all the day-to-day activities of selling and includes program files, format files, report files, index files, and data bases. Documentation and full source code is included.

Programming Tools and Source Code Libraries

C

Small-Windows: A Library of Windowing Functions for the C Language
James E. Hendrix
Item #35-X $29.95
Small-Windows is a complete windowing library for C. The package includes video functions, menu functions, window functions, and more. The package is available for MS-DOS systems for the following compilers: Microsoft C Version 4.0 and 5.0; Small-C; Turbo C 1.0 and 1.5; and Lattice C 3.1. Documentation and full C source code is included.

Tools

Small Tools: Programs for Text Processing
James E. Hendrix
Item #78-X $29.95 (manual/disk)
This package of text-processing programs written in Small-C is designed to perform specific, modular functions on text files. Source code is included. Small Tools is available in both CP/M and MS/PC-DOS versions and includes complete documentation.

Small Assembler: A Macro Assembler Written in Small C
James E. Hendrix
MS-DOS version: Item #024-9 $29.95 (manual/disk)
CP/M version: Item #77-1 $29.95 (manual/disk)
Here is a full macro assembler which was developed primarily for use with the Small-C compiler. It provides an excellent example for learning the basics of how assembler works. The manual provides an overview of the Small Assembler, documents the command lines that invoke programs, and more. The accompanying disk includes both the executable assembler and full source code.

NR: An Implementation of the UNIX NROFF Word Processor
Allen Holub
Item #33-X $29.95
NR is a text formatter that is written in C and compatible with UNIX's NROFF. *NR* comes configured for any Diablo-compatible printer, as well as Hewlett Packard's ThinkJet and LaserJet. Both the ready-to-use program and full source code are included. For PC compatibles.

Turbo Pascal

Statistical Toolbox for Turbo Pascal
Namir Clement Shammas
Item #22-4 $39.95 (manuals/disks)
Two statistical packages in one! A library disk and reference manual that includes statistical distribution functions, random number generation, basic descriptive statistics, parametric and nonparametric statistical testing, bivariate linear regression, and multiple and polynomial regression. The demonstration disk and manual incorporate these library routines into a fully functioning statistical program. For IBM PCs and compatibles.

Turbo Advantage
Lauer and Wallwitz
Item #26-7 $29.95
A library of more than 200 routines, with source code sample programs and documentation. Routines are organized and documented under the following categories: bit manipulation, file management, MS-DOS support, string operations, arithmetic calculations, data compression, differential equations, Fourier analysis and synthesis, and much more! For MS/PC-DOS systems.

Turbo Advantage: Complex
Lauer and Wallwitz
Item #27-5 $39.95
This library provides the Turbo Pascal code for digital filters, boundary-value solutions, vector and matrix calculations with complex integers and variables, Fourier transforms, and calculations of convolution and correlation functions. Some of the *Turbo Advantage: Complex* routines are most effectively used with Turbo Advantage. Source code and documentation included.

Turbo Advantage: Display
Lauer and Wallwitz
Item #28-3 $39.95
Turbo Advantage: Display includes an easy-to-use form processor and thirty Turbo Pascal procedures and functions to facilitate linking created forms to your program. Full source code and documentation are included. Some of the *Turbo Advantage* routines are necessary to compile *Turbo Advantage: Display.*

Operating Systems

OS/2

The Programmer's Essential OS/2 Handbook
David E. Cortesi
Item #82-8 $24.95 (book)
Item #89-5 $39.95 (book/disk)
Here is a resource no developer can afford to be without! Cortesi succinctly organizes the many features of OS/2 into related topics and illuminates their uses. Detailed indexes and a web of cross referencing provide easy access to all OS/2 topic areas. Equal support for Pascal and C programmers is provided. *The* essential reference for programmers developing in the OS/2 environment.

UNIX

UNIX Programming on the 80286/80386
Alan Deikman
Item #83-6 $24.95 (book)
Item #91-9 $39.95 (book/disk)
A complete professional-level tutorial and reference for programming UNIX and XENIX on 80286/80386-based computers. Succinct coverage of the UNIX program environment, UNIX file system, shells, utilities, and C programming under UNIX are covered. The author also delves into the development of device drivers; some examples of these are video displays, tape cartridges, terminals, and networks.

On Command: Writing a UNIX-Like Shell for MS-DOS
Allen Holub
Item #29-1 $39.95
Learn how to write shells applicable to MS-DOS, as well as to most other programming environments. This book and disk include a full description of a UNIX-like shell, complete C source code, a thorough discussion of low-level DOS interfacing, and significant examples of C programming at the system level. All source code is included on disk.

/util: A UNIX-Like Utility Package for MS-DOS
Allen Holub
Item #12-7 $29.95
This collection of utilities is intended to be accessed through SH but can be used separately. It contains programs and subroutines that, when coupled with SH, create a fully functional UNIX-like environment. The package includes a disk with full C source code and documentation in a UNIX-style manual.

MS-DOS

Taming MS-DOS, Second Edition
Thom Hogan
Item #87-9 $19.95
Item #92-5 $34.95
Described by reviewers as "small in size, large on content," and "fun." The second edition promises to be just as readable and is updated to cover MS-DOS 3.3. Some of the more perplexing elements of MS-DOS are succinctly described here with time-saving tricks to help customize any MS-DOS system. Each trick is easily implemented into your existing tools and for programmers, Hogan includes many complete source code files that provide very useful utilities. All source code is written in BASIC.

Program Interfacing to MS-DOS
William G. Wong
Item #34-8 $29.95
Program Interfacing to MS-DOS will orient any experienced programmer to the MS-DOS environment. The package includes a ten-part manual with sample program files and a detailed description of how to build device drivers, along with the device driver for a memory

disk and a character device driver on disk with macro assembly source code.

Other

Tele Operating System Toolkit
Ken Berry
This task-scheduling algorithm drives the Tele Operating System and is composed of several components. When integrated, they form an independent operating system for any 8086-based machine. Tele has also been designed for compatibility with MS-DOS, UNIX, and the MOSI standard.

SK: THE SYSTEM KERNEL
Item #30-5 $49.95 (manual/disk)
The System Kernel contains an initialization module, general-purpose utility functions, and a real-time task management system. The kernel provides MS-DOS applications with multitasking capabilities. The System Kernel is required by all other components. All source code is included on disk in MS-DOS format.

DS: WINDOW DISPLAY
Item #32-1 $39.95 (manual/disk)
This component contains BIOS level drivers for a memory-mapped display, window management support and communication coordination between the operator and tasks in a multitasking environment. All source code is included on disk in MS-DOS format.

FS: THE FILE SYSTEM
Item #65-8 $39.95 (manual/disk)
The File System supports MS-DOS disk file structures and serial communication channels. All source code is included on disk in MS-DOS format.

XS: THE INDEX SYSTEM
Item #66-6 $39.95 (manual/disk)
The Index System implements a tree-structured free-form database. All source code is included on disk in MS-DOS format.

Chips

Dr. Dobb's Toolbook of 80286/80386 Programming
Edited by Phillip Robinson
Item #42-9 $24.95 (book)
Item #53-4 $39.95 (book/disk)
This toolbook is a comprehensive discussion of the powerful 80X86 family of microprocessors. Editor Phillip Robinson has gathered the best articles from numerous key programming publications to create this valuable resource for all 80X86 programmers. All programs are available on disk with full source code.

Dr. Dobb's Z80 Toolbook
David E. Cortesi
Item #07-0 $25.00 (book)
Item #55-0 $40.00 (book/disk)
This book contains everything users need to write their own Z80 assembly-language programs, including a method of designing programs and coding them in assembly language and a complete, integrated toolkit of subroutines. All the software in the book is available on disk in the following formats: 8" SS/SD, Apple, Osborne, or Kaypro.

Dr. Dobb's Toolbook of 68000 Programming
Edited by Phillip Robinson
Item #13-216649-6 $29.95 (book)
Item #75-5 $49.95 (book/disk)
From *Dr. Dobb's Journal of Software Tools* and Brady Communications, this collection of practical programming tips and tools for the 68000 family contains the best 68000 articles reprinted from *Dr. Dobb's Journal of Software Tools,* along with much new material. The book contains many useful applications and examples. The software in the book is also available on disk in the following formats: MS/PC-DOS, Macintosh, CP/M 8", Osborne, Amiga, and Atari 520ST.

X68000 Cross Assembler
Brian R. Anderson
Item #71-2 $25.00
This manual and disk contain an executable version of the 68000 Cross Assembler discussed in *Dr. Dobb's Toolbook of 68000 Programming,* complete with source code and documentation. The Cross-Assembler requires CP/M 2.2 with 64K or MS-DOS with 128K.

The disk is available in the following formats: MS-DOS, 8" SS/SD, and Osborne.

General Interest

Interfacing to S-100/IEEE 696 Microcomputers
Mark Garetz and Sol Libes
Item #85-2 $24.95
This book helps S-100 bus users expand the utility and power of their systems. It describes the S-100 bus with unmatched precision. Various chapters describe its mechanical and functional design, logical and electrical relationships, bus interconnections, and busing techniques.

Building Local Area Networks
Patrick H. Corrigan
Item #025-7 $39.95 (book/disk)
Item #010-9 $24.95 (disk)
The specifics of building and maintaining PC LANs, including hardware configurations, software development, cabling, selection criteria, installation, and on-going management, are described in a detailed, "how-to" manner with numerous illustrations and sample LAN management forms.

Dr. Dobb's Journal Bound Volume Series

Each volume in this series contains a full year's worth of useful code and fascinating history from *Dr. Dobb's Journal of Software Tools*. Each volume contains every issue of *DDJ* for a given year, reprinted and combined into one comprehensive reference.

Volume 1: 1976	*Item #13-5*	*$30.75*
Volume 2: 1977	*Item #16-X*	*$30.75*
Volume 3: 1978	*Item #17-8*	*$30.75*
Volume 4: 1979	*Item #14-3*	*$30.75*
Volume 5: 1980	*Item #18-6*	*$30.75*
Volume 6: 1981	*Item #19-4*	*$30.75*
Volume 7: 1982	*Item #20-8*	*$35.75*
Volume 8: 1983	*Item #00-3*	*$35.75*
Volume 9: 1984	*Item #08-9*	*$35.75*
Volume 10: 1985	*Item #21-6*	*$35.75*
Volume 11: 1986	*Item #72-0*	*$35.75*
Volume 12: 1987	*Item #84-4*	*$39.95*
Volume 13: 1988	*Item #027-3*	*$39.95*

To order any of these products send your payment, along with $2.95 per item for shipping, to M&T Books, 501 Galveston Drive, Redwood City, California 94063. California residents, please include the appropriate sales tax. Or, call toll-free 800-533-4372 (in California 800-356-2002) Monday through Friday between 8 A.M. and 5 P.M. Pacific Standard Time. When ordering disks, please indicate format.